THE DEMONICS OF BUREAUCRACY

1964 Winner,
Iowa State University Press Annual Award
for the Most Significant New Book
by an Iowa State Faculty Member

THE DEMONICS OF BUREAUCRACY

PROBLEMS OF CHANGE IN A GOVERNMENT AGENCY

HARRY COHEN

THE IOWA STATE UNIVERSITY PRESS, AMES, IOWA, U.S.A.

ABOUT THE AUTHOR

Harry Cohen based this book on his experiences as an employment interviewer in a government employment agency, where he had daily contact with the workings, and the pathologies, of a large bureaucratic structure. After three years as a bureaucrat, he left the agency and went to the University of Illinois, where he received his Ph.D. degree in 1962. While at the University of Illinois, he collaborated with Peter M. Blau in the writing of three sections in Blau's revised edition of *The Dynamics of Bureaucracy*. Prior to his appointment as Assistant Professor of Sociology at Iowa State University, Cohen served in the same capacity at the University of Miami, Coral Gables, Florida. He is a Visiting Assistant Professor for the 1965-66 academic year under a joint appointment with the Institute of Labor and Industrial Relations and the Department of Sociology at the University of Illinois.

© 1965 The Iowa State University Press
All rights reserved. Printed in the U.S.A.
Library of Congress Catalog Card Number: 65-10570

TO MY PARENTS

DINA and SOL COHEN

One may be taught how to pursue a course of questioning, how to map a neighborhood, or how to tabulate and treat statistically the votes cast in an election; but to know how to do these things is not to be assured of meaningful conclusions. Besides these skills, one needs also the ability to enter imaginatively, boldly, and, at the same time, self-critically into that little fraction of the human comedy with which one has become scientifically concerned.

—ROBERT REDFIELD

Preface

IT HAS BEEN SAID that life is really a drama in which a person wishes one story but writes another. My life-drama—or perhaps more specifically in my case, the comedy of errors called my life—led me through a series of totally unpredictable events which, in turn, led to the writing of this book.

I accepted a position as a bureaucrat in a government employment agency in order to earn an adequate living after my graduation from college with a bachelor's degree. Although our belief system indicates that men choose jobs, in my case as perhaps in many others (more often than we would like to admit), the job selected the man. My original intent was far from that of becoming a bureaucrat; hence, wishing one story, I already began writing another. The bureaucracy into which I was hired provided me with the title of "employment interviewer" and I was assigned to an employment agency servicing the clothing industry in a large city—a chance event with important implications for this book. Soon after I began working, my life-story took another unanticipated turn, thrusting my interests in yet another direction when a colleague at another agency informed me that a sociologist

(Peter M. Blau) had once studied an employment agency also servicing the clothing industry in this same city. I read Blau's book, *The Dynamics of Bureaucracy,* and found that it offered many insights into my own observations as a bureaucrat. I took further university training and degrees in the field of sociology, wrote about my own experiences and observations as a government official, compared my findings with Blau's study,* and finally compiled my information into this book.

This, then, is an "inside story," an intensive case-study of some specific pathologies of bureaucracy, written by a former working bureaucrat (three years) turned sociologist, and author.

I wish to thank the many people and organizations that helped me in the preparation of this book. I am grateful to Professors Joseph Gusfield, Clinton L. Folse, Robert W. Janes, Bernard Karsh, and Solomon Levine, all of the University of Illinois, for their advice when this work was in its earliest stages. Professor George M. Beal of Iowa State University made suggestions when the book was in its later stages. I am also indebted to Peter M. Blau who provided information and suggestions. His book, *The Dynamics of Bureaucracy,* his personal communications, and basic ideas have often been referred to and used in my work. I thank Linda Randolph, my student, for the hours saved through her help with tedious proofreading and other clerical tasks.

Top-level government officials in two states and Washington, D.C., provided needed information. A former government colleague sent a report of observations on the subject of certain informal modifications of bureaucratic procedures. Numerous operating-level officials unknowingly provided data and acted as integral parts of this study through their behavior which is recorded and analyzed in this book. Pro-

*See Cohen, "The Demonics of Bureaucracy: A Study of a Government Employment Agency" (unpublished Ph.D. dissertation, University of Illinois, 1962). I also collaborated with Peter M. Blau on the following sections of his revised edition of *The Dynamics of Bureaucracy* (Chicago: University of Chicago Press, 1963): pp. 32-34, 50-55, 95-99.

fessional ethics require strict anonymity, but I must yet acknowledge their contribution, and do so here. I also appreciate the permission granted by a newspaper to reproduce certain articles without crediting the source by name, so that my research locale will remain anonymous.

I must thank my friend, Robert Herrick, formerly of the University of Illinois and now at Westmar College, LeMars, Iowa, for suggesting the title for this work in a few seconds when I had not been able to find a suitable one after months of deliberation. His suggested title, *The Demonics of Bureaucracy,* which plays on the title of Professor Blau's book used extensively throughout my work, also conveys the point of this study, that is, *dynamics* of bureaucracy, but in a pathological direction. Of course, I take full responsibility for the title in answer to those who do not appreciate the play on words involved as I do for the entire study.

I also wish to thank the following sources for permission to quote from copyright material:

The American Sociological Association and Erwin O. Smigel for permission to quote from Smigel's "Public Attitudes Toward 'Chiseling' With Reference to Unemployment Compensation," *American Sociological Review,* 18 (February, 1953).

Brandt and Brandt for the use of material from *Nineteen Eighty-Four* by George Orwell, Harcourt, Brace and Co., Inc. Copyright 1949, by Harcourt, Brace and Co., Inc. Reprinted by permission of Brandt and Brandt.

Constable and Co., Ltd., London, for use of material in Sir William Beveridge's *The Public Service in War and Peace,* 1920.

The Free Press of Glencoe for use of material in Robert Michels' *Political Parties,* 1949; Robert K. Merton's *Social Theory and Social Structure,* 1957; and Emile Durkheim's *Suicide,* 1951.

The Harvard University Press for use of material in Ralph Altman's *Availability for Work,* 1950; and Joseph S. Berliner's *Factory and Manager in the USSR,* 1957.

D. C. Heath and Company for use of material in Carl J. Friedrich's *Constitutional Government and Democracy*. Original copyright by Little, Brown and Company, 1941.

Houghton Mifflin Company for use of material in C. Northcote Parkinson's *Parkinson's Law*, 1957.

Alfred A. Knopf Company for use of material in Kahlil Gibran's *The Prophet*, 1962.

The Macmillan Company for use of material in Herbert A. Simon's *Administrative Behavior*, 1957.

The New American Library of World Literature, Inc., for use of a quotation from the 1961 Signet Classics edition of Nikolai Gogol's *Dead Souls*, translated by Andrew R. MacAndrew.

Oxford University Press, Inc., for use of material in Max Weber's *From Max Weber: Essays in Sociology*, 1958, translated and edited by H. H. Gerth and C. Wright Mills.

Professor Talcott Parsons for use of material in Max Weber's *The Theory of Social and Economic Organization*, translated by A. M. Henderson and Talcott Parsons. Original copyright by the Oxford University Press, 1947.

Prentice-Hall, Inc., for use of material in Bernard H. Baum's *Decentralization of Authority in a Bureaucracy*, 1961; James P. Dixon, Jr., "Meeting Human Needs" from *Goals for Americans* by the American Assembly, 1960, reprinted by permission of Prentice-Hall, Inc., Englewood Cliffs, New Jersey; and Joseph Bensman and Bernard Rosenberg's *Mass, Class, and Bureaucracy: The Evolution of Contemporary Society*, 1963.

The University of Chicago Press for use of material in Peter M. Blau's *The Dynamics of Bureaucracy*, revised edition, 1963; and Robert Redfield's "The Art of Social Science," *American Journal of Sociology*, 54 (November, 1948).

John Wiley and Sons, Inc., for use of material in Melville Dalton's *Men Who Manage*, 1959; and James G. March and Herbert A. Simon's *Organizations*, 1958.

Yale University Labor and Management Center, and Professor Chris Argyris for use of material in Argyris' *Organization of a Bank,* 1954.

Yale University Press for use of material in David Riesman *et al., The Lonely Crowd,* 1961.

HARRY COHEN

Ames, Iowa

Table of Contents

PART ONE

PRELIMINARY CONSIDERATIONS

In modern society it is not possible to escape into the jungle and choose the threat of the lions as a substitute for the annoyances of bureaucracy.

—JAMES P. DIXON, Jr.[*]

---

[*] "Meeting Human Needs," from *Goals for Americans,* by the American Assembly © 1960. Reprinted by permission of Prentice-Hall, Inc., Englewood Cliffs, New Jersey, p. 250.

CHAPTER ONE

An Introduction to Bureaucracy

Prologue: The Development of and the Need for Bureaucracy

IN THE BEGINNING it is said that there was nothing: emptiness, only space, and absolute silence. Then out of the nothingness He created day, night, earth, animals, man, and finally woman. With the creation of Adam and Eve, social relations came into being, but no bureaucracy; at this point, this would have been unnecessary. What a silly thought: to bureaucratize relations between only two people and the Superior Being; creating a large, formal, administrative hierarchy; filling out forms in duplicate, triplicate, quadruplicate, in different colors, with different purposes; writing, codifying, duplicating legalistic rules and storing them in seemingly endless files; with a multitude of desks manned by scribes to record, and specialist-officials to interpret and apply the rules. God said, "Eat not of the forbidden fruit!" Did Adam and Eve need records, files, forms, and the like to remember and administer only one simple command? Face-to-face personal relationships could and did do the job, and not an administrative system known as *bureaucracy*. In fact, two people or a few people likely do not even have the skills, the specialization of occupations necessary, and the population large enough to support bureaucracy, even if by the whim of Eve only, it was desired.

In relationships between only a small number of people, personal knowledge, friendship, and kinship are important for decision-making, aiding the unfortunate, keeping track of obligations, providing services, applying rules and punishments, and the other essentials of day-to-day living. In such small groups, records, rules, and other information could be stored in a most amazing and original IBM-like file system—man's own mind.

Yet there are limits to the mind, and as the population grows, the closer to the limits of the mind the societal tasks approach. The closer to the limits, the more the chance of forgetfulness, the greater the number of arguments between those who remember privileges to be given by neighbors and forget corresponding obligations; whereas their neighbors remember the obligations due, but forget the applicable privileges owed. How many of *us* forget our promises and appointments unless we record them by writing them down? But a busy man in a complex occupation cannot write down, do, and remember everything; he thus becomes dependent on specialists who record, file, and administer. A businessman hires a secretary; a doctor can use a receptionist. The roots of bureaucracy lie here: the administrative specialists proliferate as society does, and as complex organizations such as businesses, hospitals, armies, unions, schools, and governments arise, and become larger and larger. There is a need for bureaucracy to handle the complicated administrative tasks of large societies and organizations.

Originally in many areas, kinship relations were supplemented by the societal system of organization known as feudalism, where a master and several literates kept records, saw that obligations were carried out, and worked through small community groups to maintain social control. But as man multiplied and the population grew, social functions became more complicated and a master with his several literates was no longer sufficient. Urban centers began to develop, and then the problems of control and administration became crucial. There arose the problem of keeping track of the heterogeneous mass of people, their accomplishments, obligations, privileges, and complaints. The larger and the more complex the society, the more the chance for interpersonal and intergroup conflict as people see or want to see only their side of the issues. Some impersonal force is needed to divide and distribute goods, services, and other privileges among the populace, and to prevent and settle disagreements. This impersonal force is available through a system of organization known as bureaucracy.

Survival is also an important issue. If a barn burns, the entire community can call for a barn-raising, all contributing work to help the unfortunate in a small, kinship-oriented society. Does this cooperative spirit exist in large urban areas? In urban areas, people become dependent upon specialized, formal organizations which develop for many purposes; for example, insurance, governing, training of the young, hospital care, and for finding jobs for people who cannot possibly know of all the vacancies, all the employers, and employment market in general in a large city. These organizations in turn need the specialized, salaried, career-oriented, administrative hierarchy dealing "without hatred or passion," serving clients and customers according to the general rules formulated either by vote, legislative, or administrative fiat.[1] This hierarchy is called bureaucracy.

Personalized, non-bureaucratic relationships do remain important, even in an urban society, through family and friendship groups. Nevertheless, for many problems and tasks of an urban society it is so much easier and more efficient to present oneself at the proper organization where a specialist provides the service or looks up the applicable rule and applies it fairly, stores the results of the action, and lets us "get on" with the complex job of life. To be sure,

---

[1] The short quotation comes from Max Weber, *The Theory of Social and Economic Organization,* translated by A. M. Henderson and T. Parsons (New York: Oxford University Press, 1947), p. 340.

the bureaucrat does not always treat all clients fairly. Graft can sometimes smooth the way; likewise, a personal friend in a bureaucracy can often help. But the general principle is clear: bureaucracy is needed to do a special job for complex organizations, for society, and hence for the populace at large.

Could we efficiently operate a large university, or a corporation with branches around the world without bureaucracy? Without the impersonal application of rules and the storing of information and actions taken? What single person could remember the courses into which each of thousands of students enroll, the grades involved, room assignments, payrolls, and the thousands of other bits of information needed to run a modern university? In fact, what *group* of people could do these tasks without the aid of a bureaucratic type of organization that in a rational, routinized, specialized manner arranges and orders affairs in such a way as to overcome the limitations of unspecialized human resources? How could the students, faculty, and the bureaucrats themselves be controlled, accounted for, and evaluated if not for the codified, stored rules and records which live on even after a man's memory; in fact, even after his life fails him? Bureaucracy, which is nothing more than a "system of organization, administration, discipline, and control,"[2] is certainly advantageous; and in fact, essential for our modern-day society.

The essentiality of bureaucracy is not a secret protected by a select few. Bureaucratic forms of administration are used by many organizations, and bureaucracy abounds throughout our society. In fact, the trend is toward large bureaucratic organizations.

According to Peter Blau, in 1820 the U.S. federal government employed a total of 8,000 civil servants. This grew to 250,000 by the early 1900's, and some fifty years later there were ten times that number. When we add the men

---

[2] Joseph Bensman and Bernard Rosenberg, *Mass, Class, and Bureaucracy: The Evolution of Contemporary Society* (Englewood Cliffs: Prentice-Hall, 1963), p. 262.

in military service, we arrive at a figure of 6,000,000, meaning that nearly 10 per cent of the American labor force was employed at that time by the federal government.[3] State and local government employees, and those working in large-scale private concerns increase this total by many millions.

Bureaucracy touches the lives of most members of our modern society. Bensman and Rosenberg tell us that, "Every major occupation in the modern world is organized, hierarchized, incorporated, and bureaucratized. The professions—medicine, law, engineering, dentistry, pedagogy, and the ministry of God—are no exception."[4]

Yet not only are we dependent upon bureaucracies for performance of our occupational tasks—for our employment and hence for our own support and that of our families—but the various organizations upon which we depend for goods and services are likely also bureaucracies. Employment agencies, unions, supermarkets, schools, political parties, etc., are of the type that are often organized in a bureaucratic fashion.[5] The point here is that bureaucracies certainly do provide control, keep records and files, but these are *means* to quite specific goals or ends. One such specific goal, as discussed in the bulk of this book, is finding jobs for the unemployed.

We have seen that bureaucracy does provide certain efficiencies and advantages, cares for certain societal and organizational needs, and provides specific products and services. Let us sharpen our discussion at this point by specifying more clearly what internal advantages bureaucracy has as an *operating entity*. Bensman and Rosenberg have compiled a clear and concise listing of advantages, drawn from the master theoretician of bureaucracy and related fields, Max Weber:

1. *Bureaucracy is efficient.* It is peopled by men and women

---

[3] Peter M. Blau, *Bureaucracy in Modern Society* (New York: Random House, 1956), p. 21.

[4] Bensman and Rosenberg, *op. cit.,* p. 272.

[5] Blau, *Bureaucracy . . ., op. cit.,* p. 21.

who devote full time to their narrow specialties. They have developed a method which, beyond question, is technically superior to administration by amateurs or dabblers. Bureaucrats have the background and the know-how to get things done in the modern world. Theirs is the universe of large-scale organization and centralized control that a money economy has helped to create everywhere.

2. *Bureaucracy is predictable.* Since it proceeds from categorical rules and principles, operating from within a context of tight authoritarian discipline and hierarchical status, top officials have every reason to expect that orders will be dutifully carried out.

3. *Bureaucracy is impersonal.* To administer a modern institution is to be objective, not to be influenced by any primary group sentiment, to be emotionally blank, to subdue all personal vagaries and biases; at best to approximate the impartiality of a judge on the bench, and thus to be fair.

4. *Bureaucracy is fast.* Uniformity of rules makes it possible for the modern administrator to process thousands of cases with general formulae. The speedy disposition of innumerable cases would be impossible if each one had to be considered on its individual merits.

Today administrative decision-making is semiautomatic. (Some of it is totally automatic and can literally be performed by machines.) Once the ground rules have been formulated, it is only necessary to understand which of them cover the case in hand. As bureaucracy grows, its membership swells until there are many specialists, all of whom may be summoned to work on an important problem. They combine their various kinds of expertise and talent. By bureaucratic collaboration, a large volume of business is processed at top speed. [6]

A social instrument with so many advantages and of such importance to our society should be studied, analyzed, and understood. This is the task of this book—to study the case of one bureaucracy in the hope of fruitfully adding to the total body of knowledge on the subject.

---

[6] Bensman and Rosenberg, *op. cit.,* pp. 267-68. Italics in the original. See Weber, *From Max Weber: Essays in Sociology,* translated and edited by H. H. Gerth and C. W. Mills (New York: Oxford University Press, 1958), pp. 214-16, for the original discussion of the technical advantages of bureaucratic administration.

A Paradox

We have seen the rationale for bureaucracy, the importance, advantages, and extent of bureaucratic organization. Yet a striking paradox exists: to call someone a bureaucrat is not to compliment him! This can be stated in stronger terms: not only is it not a compliment to be called a bureaucrat; it is in fact a strong insult! The word "bureaucrat" has become a term of derogation, an odious term, and has become a cuss-word, a *Schimpfwort*.[7] Would *you* be happy if someone came to you and told you that you were "a good bureaucrat," meaning in technical terms only that you administered part of an organization's affairs, dealing fairly, impersonally, and rationally with your clients?

The term *bureaucracy*, originally meaning one thing technically, has colloquially become "an epithet."[8] There is much proof for this feeling, and one of the strongest set of damnations of bureaucracy comes from our literary figures, many of whom cannot write a novel without satirizing or attacking bureaucracy at some point or another.

Balzac in a novel, for example, speaks of the bureaucracy as "a gigantic power manipulated by dwarfs."[9] Gogol, tongue-in-cheek, strikes a blast against the Russian government bureaucracy.[10] The prevalence of this problem has not been pre-empted by novelists and neglected by scholars. Peter Blau echoes Balzac, Gogol, and others when he begins a book on the subject of bureaucracy by stating the common conception of the bureaucrat as stupid (later going on to describe the less commonly understood advantages of bureaucracy and related matters.)[11]

In addition, Northcote Parkinson's witty book on the

---

[7] Robert K. Merton, *Social Theory and Social Structure* (rev. ed., Glencoe: Free Press, 1957), p. 197.

[8] *Ibid.*

[9] Honoré de Balzac, *The Civil Service* (Philadelphia: George Barrie and Son, 1896), p. 21. Cited in Bensman and Rosenberg, *op. cit.*, p. 307.

[10] Nikolai Gogol, *Dead Souls* (New York: Signet, 1961). See, for example, his pp. 159-62 (Originally published in 1842.)

[11] Blau, *Bureaucracy. . . , op. cit*, p. 13.

problems of organization and administration has become the bureaucrat's nemesis. [12] Michels adds to the clamor: "Bureaucracy is the sworn enemy of individual liberty, and of all bold initiative in matters of internal policy."[13] These few examples are sufficient to make the point: bureaucracy is popularly looked down upon as a wart on the nose of society!

How could a technical term fall into such notorious colloquial usage? This book provides possible answers by tracing processes and events through three years in one government bureaucracy. Perhaps self-seeking groups in the bureaucracies try to make their work easier by avoiding the real tasks for which they were hired. Perhaps there are normal chains of events in bureaucracy that lead "good" actions to "bad" results. Perhaps clients (the customers of bureaucracy) press bureaucracy toward bad ends in order to get something they do not legally deserve. These "perhaps" statements are hints of actual findings documented in later chapters.

Let us realize that we really do not appreciate the use of our hands until we lose the use of one. The same is true for the eyes, ears, and other parts of our body which we take for granted—until something goes wrong. We do not shout, "off with the head," when we have a headache, and even most people with intense pain do not want to lose a part of their body. Likewise, we accept bureaucracy without thinking about it, as long as it works well. But if it suffers a malfunction, we shout "away with it," forgetting the much good it provides. Can we really do without bureaucracy? Could we really run our modern society without it? We need bureaucracy. We certainly do not have to put up with its defects without complaining, but we can study the pathologies of the system and try to help it back to health. Medical

---

[12] C. Northcote Parkinson, *Parkinson's Law* (Boston: Houghton Mifflin, 1957).

[13] Robert Michels, *Political Parties* (Glencoe: Free Press, 1949), p. 189. Cited in Hendrik M. Ruitenbeek (ed.), *The Dilemma of Organizational Society* (New York: E. P. Dutton, 1963), pp. 169-70.

doctors study the ill in order to know better how to cure disease, and to prevent illness in the healthy. Should sociologists be less interested in the ill bureaucracies? This book is a study of the pathologies of one specific bureaucratic organization.

By studying *one* patient we cannot learn all we have to learn about *all* patients. There may be special, extenuating circumstances in the one case. In the same way, this study of one government agency is not necessarily representative of all bureaucracies. It therefore cannot tell us all about all bureaucracies, but it can fit one piece into the jigsaw puzzle of a paradox to which others can later add through additional study. We can derive leads and implications from the one case that can then be tested further by application to studies of other bureaucratic organizations.

Let us now turn to some general theories of bureaucracy.

CHAPTER TWO

Theories of Bureaucracy

DATA TEND TO lose relevance if just thrown carelessly here and there. We need theory to help us pigeonhole the facts, thereby providing us with more understanding of the facts gathered and their relationships.[1] In this chapter the aim is to present the theoretical framework into which the rest of the study can be related.

Max Weber

Few works in the study of bureaucracy can proceed without a bow to the master German theoretician, Max Weber. It was he who studied the development of rationalism in modern life and the "push" toward our modern, large-scale industrial order. It is most interesting to note that this man, interested in these areas, also wrote about bureaucracy.[2] In Weber's mind the different areas became closely

---

[1] See Robert Bierstedt, *The Social Order* (rev. ed., New York: McGraw-Hill, 1963), pp. 24-25 for an excellent and concise discussion of this issue.

[2] For some works by and about Max Weber see: Max Weber, *The Protestant Ethic and the Spirit of Capitalism* (New York: Charles Scribner's Sons, 1958); Max Weber, *From Max Weber: Essays in Sociology,* translated and edited by H. H. Gerth and C. W. Mills (New York: Oxford University Press, 1958); Max

related, and they are in reality. Weber strived to identify the characteristics of bureaucracy.[3] He did not emphasize the common negative connotation; rather, it was his aim to indicate exactly what characteristics were present in the "ideal" or "pure" case, realizing of course that not all bureaucracies have this form. He did not mean the characteristics of an "average" bureaucracy; rather, he wished to abstract *the most characteristic* bureaucratic attributes (in the ideal or pure case) of all known organizations.[4]

Weber's characteristics of bureaucracy have been condensed and presented by Blau:

1. "The regular activities required for the purposes of the bureaucratically governed structure are distributed in a fixed way as official duties."

2. "A specified sphere of competence . . . has been marked off as part of a systematic division of labor. . . ."

3. The official "is subject to strict and systematic discipline and control in the conduct of his office."

4. All operations are governed by "a consistent system of abstract rules . . . [and] consist in the application of these rules to particular cases."

5. "The organization of offices follows the principle of hierarchy; that is, each lower office is under the control and supervision of a higher one."

6. Officials are "subject to authority only with respect to their impersonal official obligations."

7. "Candidates [for bureaucratic positions] are selected on the basis of technical qualifications. In the most rational case, this is tested by examinations, or guaranteed by diplomas certifying technical training, or both. They are *appointed,* not elected."

8. Being a bureaucratic official "constitutes a career. There

---

Weber, *The Theory of Social and Economic Organization,* translated by A. M. Henderson and T. Parsons (New York: Oxford University Press, 1947); Reinhard Bendix, *Max Weber: An Intellectual Portrait* (Garden City: Doubleday and Co., 1960).

[3] See James G. March and Herbert A. Simon, *Organizations* (New York: John Wiley and Sons, 1958), p. 36. See their pp. 36-47 for an excellent summary of the various theories of bureaucracy.

[4] Peter M. Blau, *Bureaucracy in Modern Society* (New York: Random House, 1956), p. 34. See his pp. 27-43 for another good summary of the theories of bureaucracy.

is a system of 'promotions' according to seniority or to achievement, or both."[5]

Max Weber felt that bureaucracy provides the same advantages for administration as machine production does for the "line" end of a factory.[6] Machines do not love or hate and hence can proceed efficiently toward their assigned tasks without external biases affecting their operation. A machine in an automobile factory, for example, does not treat a yellow car better than a green one, only because the machine likes the color yellow and despises green. In the same way, the bureaucratic "dehumanization" of administration, the performance of official tasks "without hatred or passion,"[7] is efficient since personal elements are kept away from the situation, avoiding unfair treatment of some in deference to the personal characteristics of others. The young, unmarried, male bureaucrat is expected to treat the shapely, young, alluring female client as well as but not better than the cranky old "hag" who also presents herself at his desk for service during the course of business.

Some Problems

Yet human behavior cannot be as closely regulated as machine production. A pair of shapely female legs sometimes does turn out to have more relevance for the disposition of a case than the actual merits of the case. A Negro may receive inferior treatment at the hands of a bureaucrat solely because of his race. These actions may actually be a conscious attempt and desire on the part of the bureaucrat to be unfair, but sometimes it is not even conscious at all. The young man, for example, may be so "taken in" by the young woman that he does not even think that he is

---

[5] Peter M. Blau, *The Dynamics of Bureaucracy* (rev. ed., Chicago: University of Chicago Press, 1963), pp. 1-2. Characteristic 1 was originally taken from Weber's, *From Max Weber: Essays in Sociology, op. cit.,* p. 196. Others were abstracted by Blau from Weber's, *The Theory of Social and Economic Organization, op. cit.,* pp. 330-34. (Italics in the original.)

[6] Weber, *From Max Weber . . . , op. cit.,* pp. 214-16.

[7] Weber, *The Theory of Social and Economic Organization, op. cit.,* p. 340.

providing special treatment, being overly passionate and hence biased in favor of the client.[8]

The bureaucrat is caught in a precarious balance that is easily upset. He is supposed to operate "without hatred or passion," but too little passion gives us the stereotyped Walter Mitty form of ritualistic bureaucrat who drives clients to despair with his over-emphasis on the impersonal rules. [9] On the other hand, too much passion in the case of one client may provide cries of unfairness by other clients. As Kahlil Gibran aptly states the case in relation to too much and too little passion (referring to life in general and not only to bureaucracy): ". . . reason, ruling alone, is a force confining; and passion, unattended, is a flame that burns to its own destruction."[10]

We also note that many of the other characteristics of bureaucracy stated by Weber, so efficient in the ideal case, turn out to be the opposite in practice. The career orientation makes some bureaucrats more interested in the protection of that career than in dealing with clients. The rules often slow down the work of the organization as they sometimes become more important to the bureaucrats than the actual tasks to be done. Over-emphasis on the rules can lead to the familiar charge of "red-tape." Specialization can lead to ignorance of even related tasks. It can also lead to ritualistic behavior; hence, one reason for the familiar "run-around" so many clients complain about as they are shunted from desk to desk by bureaucrats who feel that the particular case, according to rule, is someone else's responsibility. Bureaucrats have been known to argue over precedent or jurisdiction (to determine which specialty the case falls under and which specialist-bureaucrat is to deal with it), wasting time, irritating the client, sending him here and there, when any one of them could have handled the client, and argued about the

---

[8] See Blau, *Dynamics . . . , op. cit.,* p. 83.

[9] See the discussion by Merton in *Social Theory and Social Structure* (rev. ed., Glencoe: Free Press, 1957), pp. 195-206.

[10] Kahlil Gibran, *The Prophet* (New York: Alfred A. Knopf, 1962), p. 50.

rules relating to jurisdiction for the sake of future cases after the present client had been serviced.

Note what has happened here: Weber has opened the field of study by stating what characteristics bureaucracy ideally has; suddenly, however, we begin to find data from our own experiences or from studies of bureaucracy that show that these characteristics, so efficient in the ideal, actually may lead to inefficiencies too.

Unanticipated Consequences and Informal Relations in Bureaucracy

In actuality there are *unanticipated consequences* when the human organism begins to work within the ideally dehumanized organizational and social characteristics of bureaucracy.

Thus, Merton shows that the organizational attributes of bureaucracy (relating to a consistent system of abstract rules, impersonal application of these rules to particular cases, and the high division of labor in bureaucracy where the bureaucrat becomes a specialist in a specific task) can lead to unanticipated consequences when the bureaucratic specialist becomes so well trained, that he is in fact *over*-trained.[11] Veblen's term, "trained incapacity" applies here. The bureaucrat is so well trained that he becomes incapacitated by this very training. He becomes rigid and can no longer apply the abstract rules to real cases which really require a "bending here and there." All humans and their problems and cases do not fit the same mold. Flexibility is sometimes needed in applying rules to clients. Merton shows that the rules, which are nothing more than a means to an end (that is, getting a job done, servicing a client, etc.), can come to be seen by the bureaucrat as ends in and of themselves. Thus we have a *displacement of goals* whereby "adherence to the rules, originally conceived as a means, be-

---

[11] Merton, *op. cit.*, pp. 195-206.

comes transformed into an end-in-itself."[12] A rule, originally "an instrumental value, becomes a terminal value"[13] for the bureaucrat, and the client roars at the "'horrid hybrid,' bureaucrat"[14] and still suffers. We shall trace some cases of displacement of goals for a particular government agency studied in this book. But to anticipate our findings, the bureaucrat is not always rigid; flexibility in itself can *also* lead to pathological ends.

Gouldner,[15] Selznick,[16] and others studied specific bureaucracies and again show unanticipated consequences deriving from the ideally fast, efficient, impersonal characteristics of bureaucracy so well stated by Weber.

In a similar vein the famed business-executive theorist of administration, Chester I. Barnard, showed the ubiquitous nature of what is called *informal organization.* Informal relationships and unofficial norms arise in all organizations as humans (and bureaucrats are indeed human) make informal arrangements and devise unofficial ways of doing things, even within the specified hierarchy of positions and rules in bureaucracy. This informal organization is necessary for the formal organization. It makes a real "social" and "human" organization of what originally, according to the formal plan, is nothing more than a series of formally related offices (statuses); it helps to humanize a rigid, machine-like, social structure. As Barnard indicates, informal organization acts as a means of communication and cohesion, and it protects the integrity of the individual.[17]

Blau decided to go several steps further, thereby expanding the frontiers of knowledge about the theory of bureaucracy, as well as the empirical study of bureaucracy.

---

[12] *Ibid.*, p. 199.

[13] *Ibid.*

[14] *Ibid.*, p. 197.

[15] Alvin W. Gouldner, *Patterns of Industrial Bureaucracy* (Glencoe: Free Press, 1954).

[16] Philip Selznick, *TVA and the Grass Roots* (Berkeley: University of California Press, 1949).

[17] Chester I. Barnard, *The Functions of the Executive* (Cambridge: Harvard University Press, 1938). See especially his pp. 114-23.

He writes:

> This concept of [informal organization] has greatly influenced recent research in factories and other organizations, but its crucial insight has hardly been exploited. Most discussions on the subject contrast informal relations and practices with the formal blueprint of the organization. This emphasizes the least interesting aspect of the concept of "informal organization," namely, that behavior and relationships often fail to conform exactly to formal prescriptions, which is certainly not a novel discovery. Much more significant is the insight that such activities and interactions are not simply idiosyncratic deviations but form consistent patterns that are new elements of the organization. In other words, Barnard's concept calls attention to the fact that organizations do not statically remain as they had been conceived but always develop into new forms of organization.[18]

Blau then studied two governmental agencies, one of which is of especial interest and importance to the present book, and showed that bureaucrats do change rules. Bureaucracy is, as Blau states, "dynamic." In fact, the title of his book reflects his thesis: *The Dynamics of Bureaucracy.*

This is the point at which we enter this stream of theory, for this book builds upon Blau's work, but takes it one step further. The thesis of this book is that while bureaucracy is dynamic, a tendency in bureaucracy is that one change builds upon another in a series of changes and unanticipated consequences, which become part of the organization, but in such a way that the process leads to pathological ends. So many changes occur that the organizational missions are not efficiently performed. The theory here is not of the dynamics of bureaucracy, but of the *demonics* of bureaucracy, reflecting change, but toward dysfunctional ends.

While this study stands by itself in terms of this theory, it is also directly related to Blau's work: the particular bureaucracy studied here is closely connected to the one Blau studied years earlier. Thus, we have a chance to trace pro-

---

[18] Blau, *Dynamics . . . , op. cit.,* pp. 2-3. Much of the two paragraphs preceding the quotation above is dependent on Blau's statement on this subject on his p. 2.

cesses in bureaucracy over a period of years, showing how far some rules were changed and with what results, as well as to compare findings with those made by Blau, making revisions and explanations of differences when necessary.

CHAPTER THREE

An Introduction to the Study

IN 1949 PETER M. BLAU studied a public employment agency and reported the results of his observations in *The Dynamics of Bureaucracy*, a work now well known in the field of sociology.[1] Some ten years later I performed a study of a related agency. Results are reported here.

The government employment agency studied in my book is part of the same larger bureaucratic organization that Blau analyzed. Both receive their mandate and orders from the same sources, are located in the same city, and serve the clothing industry and clothing workers. I was an employee and therefore mostly participant in the agency studied during the three years from July 1956 to August 1959. Professor Blau performed his research for several months during the first part of 1949, mostly as an observer.

Although scope and methods of both studies are thus not strictly comparable and complete replication cannot be made, there is still similarity enough to trace some of Blau's findings concerning modifications of procedure through the

---

[1] Blau, *The Dynamics of Bureaucracy* (rev. ed., Chicago: University of Chicago Press, 1963). Blau studied two governmental organizations: a state employment agency and a federal enforcement agency. Complete interest in this work is only on the state employment agency.

ten years' time from 1949 to 1959. This adds an historical dimension to both studies.

Blau made his observations during a period of time lasting some three months. He observed certain consequences of changes in procedure and found that some consequences were functional, and others dysfunctional. My findings, however, indicate that the processes of change over a period of time tend to lead to dysfunctional consequences in terms of subversion of the organizational mission.

An analysis will be made of the pathologies of bureaucracy, represented at the study locale by illegitimate practices such as inflation of figures on statistical records of production, useless work performed to "maximize" records, violation by various organizational levels of a law the bureaucracy itself was supposed to help enforce, and a host of other related issues. In addition, the influence of local conditions such as economic trends in the labor market serviced by the agency and pressures by client groups will be discussed. This will show the dependency of this bureaucracy on these more external pressures.

This book, therefore, is aimed in two directions. First, comparisons and contrasts are drawn with Blau's earlier study. Second, the results presented in the following pages can stand alone as a case-study of a specific bureaucracy, showing that bureaucrats deviate from the rules in response to special local conditions and client demands, but with end results contrary to that which might be predicted by popular opinion. Whereas we like to believe that deviation from rigid procedure by bureaucrats is good and that bureaucracy is inefficient because bureaucrats overconform to the rules, the following chapters will show that changes of rules can also lead to inefficiencies. The processes involved are traced in the chapters ahead. These processes will be called the *demonics* of bureaucracy, referring to flexibility and changes of procedures—*dynamics* of bureaucracy, as in the title of Professor Blau's book—but in a direction leading to pathological ends.

Functional Analysis

A method of analysis called *functional analysis* is often used in the fields of sociology and anthropology, and is utilized in this book. This approach focuses on the consequences of observed action. We must ask the question, are the observed consequences functional or dysfunctional? That is, to follow Merton's definition, do they make for the adaptation or adjustment of the particular unit or social system studied?[2] If the answer is in the affirmative, then we call this *functional.* If we have "observed consequences which lessen the adaptation or adjustment of the system,"[3] then we call this *dysfunctional.*

There is the ever-present problem in this scheme of analysis that what is functional for one group is not necessarily functional for another. For this reason it is important to indicate exactly what is meant in this book when these terms are used.

In this study, the major formal goals of the bureaucracy are taken as the base line between functions and dysfunctions. The agency was established to provide a certain set of services (placement service and operation within the unemployment insurance law of the state in which the agency is located). All that disturbs this basic placement (employment and unemployment insurance orientation and thus lessens the adaptation or adjustment of the system, causing the agency to deviate from or to be unable to fulfill its basic goals as set by law, is called dysfunctional. The reverse is called functional in application to the agency in the study. We therefore note that in this book the criteria used for delimiting functions from dysfunctions rest on official organizational goals or missions.

Now various work groups within the bureaucracy might fabricate records to "prove" work that really was not done. This fabrication may be seen as functional if we

---

[2] Robert K. Merton, *Social Theory and Social Structure* (rev. ed., Glencoe: Free Press, 1957), p. 51.
[3] *Ibid.*

take the work group as our unit of analysis because this might help the group in its adjustment. For example, because of the fabrication of figures on records a work group might be kept intact in the face of actual inefficiency. Hence, we can see that the fabrication is functional for the adjustment or adaptation of the work group as a unit. However, in this study we are looking at a larger unit, or in other words a greater whole than only work groups. As a result of fabricated records, upper levels might get a faulty picture of local operations, and might then take action that pushes the *total* organization further away from efficient operation in relation to the job the agency is to perform. If officials can cover lack of work by fabricating records they protect themselves, but clients may not receive the service which they are entitled to receive by law, or at least by dint of their taxpayer status; and it is clear that tax contributions in the ultimate sense support this government agency. If records were treated according to original intent, they would press officials to a heightened service orientation, thereby providing better service to clients. Therefore, the fabrication may be called dysfunctional in relation to achievement of the organizational goals of employment service to clients, and maintenance of the unemployment insurance law. Here we see that from a larger vantage point, which is being taken in this book, we find dysfunctional consequences, which for the immediate work group can be functional in consequences.

This example, which to a degree anticipates some of the results in the following chapters, illustrates the importance of specifying the unit and criteria under which use of the terms *functional* and *dysfunctional* are made.

The matters and definitions discussed above are crucial to an understanding of the analyses in the following chapters. [4]

---

[4] For a complete discussion of functional analysis see Merton, *Ibid.*, pp. 19-84. For emphasis on issues similar to those presented above see his pp. 50-54, and especially Item 4: *Concepts of the unit subserved by the function* on his p. 52.

Methods of Study

As the result of a need for a job and an accidental assignment, I became a government official for three years at the agency discussed in this book. Observations were made as a working participant. This is known as the participant-observation approach, and since the researcher was immersed in his work as a government agent, we have obvious emphasis on the *participant* aspect of the method.

Data adding to and confirming certain observations that were made as a government official have been secured through access to eight reports of a governmental investigating commission, appropriate newspaper articles, reference to inserts in agency manuals of procedure, training manuals, statistical records of agency operations, and occasional written and verbal communication with some agency officials at various levels after participation was terminated.[5] Professor Blau's work certainly also served as a valuable source of information.

---

[5] The officials were not aware of the full purpose and scope of this study. Both operating and upper-level officials were only told (after participation was terminated and only when necessary to secure further data) that a report was being written about bureaucratic procedures. When explaining this, I made no reference to this particular agency, but to bureaucracy in general. Colleagues knew me only as a fellow worker, and in fact, in the beginning even I did not know that this position would lead to a sociological study.

Only one former official was partially aware of the nature of this study, and this was not until two years after I had terminated my employment. This former official then lived more than 2,000 miles from the agency locale, and learned of the focus of a portion of the study only after I had requested and received needed written information on special agency operations. It can be safely assumed, then, that verbal and written communications were made without the effects that might have resulted if the officials knew of my full intent. Blau's research locale, closely related to the one reported on here, also remains anonymous with the exception of a few officials at the locale who are aware of his book and were aware of it even earlier than I. In fact, it was one of these officials who first mentioned in casual conversation that a sociologist (Blau) had studied the agency in 1949. He then provided the title of that work *(The Dynamics of Bureaucracy)*.

The history of how this study began, steps and problems in methodology, advantages and disadvantages of the methods used, and related issues are discussed at length in the appendix for the benefit of the more technically oriented reader.

Terminology

For the sake of clarity, and to retain anonymity of the agencies studied, Blau's research locale in 1949 will hereafter be referred to as Agency B (*Blau's Agency*). The branch studied in 1956-59 will be called Agency C (*Cohen's Agency*).[6] City X and State X will refer to the locales of Agencies B and C.

Agencies B and C were both connected in a bureaucratic hierarchy that extended through the city level, to the state level, and then to the federal level in Washington, D.C. This entire state and federal employment bureaucracy will be known hereafter as the Employment Bureau.[7]

An Introduction to the Agency: The Setting

Agencies B and C are both public, state employment agencies located in a large city, and are specialized in operations. They service two types of clients who are part of the clothing industry in special geographical subdivisions of City X. These clients are job applicants and clothing industry employers. Other branches deal with applicants and employers in other industries. In this way each employment agency in City X is specialized by industry serviced, in order to divide an otherwise overwhelming task into manageable proportions.

---

[6] Blau focuses his attention mainly on one specific portion of the total agency locale, which he calls Department X, although on occasion he extends observations to other departments. (See the discussion of "sections" and "departments" on forthcoming pages of this chapter.) Agency B refers to that *portion* of the total branch that Blau studied. On occasion reference is made to other departments at Blau's branch, and this extension is made clear at such points. When Agency C is discussed, reference is made not only to one portion of the agency, but to the entire operation at that particular location. This again is with the exception of some specific cases where the emphasis is made clear at the time.

[7] Where quotations are hereafter made from agency documents or other sources the terms above will be inserted in place of the real names in order to maintain anonymity of the research locale. Frequently, substitution of the fictitious names will be made directly into the text of quotations without the usual bracket and/or ellipsis designations. This is for the purpose of maintaining readability as well as the necessary anonymity.

One major and formal objective of these agencies is what is known as placement or employment service; that is, finding jobs for applicants and filling openings of employers. The agencies also have an important task connection with the unemployment insurance law, although they are not completely connected with all unemployment insurance matters. The major portion of the unemployment insurance task is handled by other divisions.

Clients who work for a specified period of time in a firm covered by the law, who are unemployed through no fault of their own, and who are ready, willing, and able to work, are allowed to collect government compensation for the period of their unemployment. These benefits continue until the clients are re-employed, refuse a job offer without good cause, or until each individual's quota of unemployment insurance checks allowed in a particular period under the law is exhausted.

All those claiming benefits are sent from the unemployment insurance office after filing a claim, and at regular intervals thereafter to the employment agency. This is to determine whether a client is really ready, willing, and able to work, and also as an attempt to find employment for the unemployed. Those with prior employment in the clothing industry, in a specified geographical area, are required to report to Agency C. Agency B serviced similar clothing industry clients who had employment connections in another area of the city.

This is where both agencies are involved in unemployment insurance matters, for if a benefit client refuses an offer of a suitable job, or indicates similar unwillingness to work, a report must be sent to the unemployment insurance division as a possible cause for disqualification from receiving benefit checks.[8] Thus the second major and formal organizational goal of these public employment agencies is to work within the unemployment insurance law.

---

[8] It must be emphasized that the agencies are not limited to servicing only benefit clients but also service other members of the public.

Most of the Agency C staff are government officials with the title of employment interviewer, and are in daily contact with the public. In general, during the study period, there were about thirty-five interviewers assigned to Agency C, a number that varied depending on the rate of turnover and replacement.

The locale of Blau's study is larger than Agency C. Blau speaks of *departments.* This is one organizational level above the *sections.* Blau's agency was divided into several departments which in turn were divided into sections; whereas Agency C was a small one, on a level similar to *one* department.

Agency C was subdivided into six sub-units, which are hereafter called *sections,* each servicing a different segment of the clothing industry. For example, one section handled workers and employers in the men's clothing industry, another in the dress and blouse industry, etc. Each section was composed of a supervisor, and from three to eight interviewers.

Clothing workers appearing at Agency C for the first time generally went to the information counter. Brief questioning determined to what specialized work section of the office the client was to report for service, based on the individual's previous work experience or special job-finding problems.

Clients then reported as directed to the proper section reception counter. There further brief questioning by the interviewer on duty at the counter determined if the client would be seated for an interview or dismissed with a re-appointment date. Those clients who were interviewed were serviced by employment interviewers and were referred to employment vacancies, as available.

At certain times of the day and at certain seasons of the year, many applicants were either waiting to be seen by the receptionist or waiting for further interviews. Blau's description of Agency B is quite applicable to Agency C too, but with more reference to rush periods when many clients were present:

All morning and most of the afternoon, long rows of men and women seeking employment waited in front of these [reception] counters to be screened by receptionists. Other clients were seated in chairs waiting to be interviewed. Every few minutes, an interviewer called a name, and a client arose and walked to his desk for an interview. Telephone calls from employers frequently interrupted the interviews. One or another official was always leaving his desk, either to search the files or to consult a colleague.

The presence of scores of people in constant movement, the din of voices, and the clamor of telephones bewildered the uninitiated.[9]

Plan of the Book

The purpose of this brief description of the agency and its goals has been to serve as an orientation to several of the important points in the analysis to be made later. The formal tasks of the organization, the type of work performed by the government officials, and the type of clientele, all act as "givens" and mold to a considerable extent the behavior of all parties concerned with the agency. This affects the bureaucracy. The following chapters trace the effects of such conditions on modifications of procedures.

This concludes Part One (the preliminary considerations): an introduction to bureaucracy, a review of the theories of bureaucracy, and an introduction to this study as well as to the actual agency upon which this study is based. Part Two of this book will focus attention on various types of modifications, dealing with quite specific procedures and effects. Part Three is the heart of this study, dealing with an original change in statistical recording procedure that eventually led to a series of informal practices that disrupted not only the specific procedure, but dysfunctionally affected many of the major operations of the agency as well. Part Four shifts emphasis to a further expanded level and discusses discrimination against nonwhite clients, and

---

[9] Blau, *Dynamics. . . , op. cit.,* p. 20.

modifications of anti-discrimination procedure not only at Agency C, but on a state agency-wide basis in relation to upper, as well as lower levels. There is thus a progression in this book from discussion of more specific procedures to more major procedures, and effects on the entire bureaucracy. Part Five ties this entire work together by discussing conclusions and implications.

PART TWO

TYPES OF MODIFICATIONS
OF PROCEDURES

*Given a people composed of a certain number
of individuals arranged in a certain way,
we obtain a definite total of collective ideas
and practices which remain constant so long
as the conditions on which they depend are
themselves the same.*

—EMILE DURKHEIM*

---

* *Suicide* (Glencoe: Free Press, 1951), p. 387.

CHAPTER FOUR

Adjustment of Procedures

SELECTED AGENCY PROCEDURES are analyzed in this chapter with reference to a type of modification known as an *adjustment*. Adjustments, following Blau, involve, ". . . modifications to focus a procedure on its intended objective under existing conditions."[1] Bureaucratic procedure is defined as: ". . . a course of action prescribed by a set

---

[1] Peter M. Blau, *The Dynamics of Bureaucracy* (rev. ed., University of Chicago Press, 1963), p. 24.

If an adjustment focuses a procedure on its *intended objective* under existing conditions, and if movement toward major organizational goals is taken as functional as is done here, then it appears that all adjustments are functional because of focus on intended objectives. Yet in the following pages we shall see that we may have an adjustment, designed to focus the procedure on its intended objective under existing conditions, that in the long run reaches dysfunctional ends. This is because the adjustment might cause *unanticipated consequences* which lead away from organizational goals and create dysfunctions. An adjustment may be made with the *intention* of focusing a procedure on its objective, but may in fact fail to reach this end. In addition, the intended objective of a procedure may be contrary to attainment of the organizational goals. Although the intended objective of a procedure would most often hope to lead to attainment of the organizational goals, we cannot consider them both to always be synonymous. For example, formal procedures may be established to meet personal whims of administrators which lead away from organizational goals. It should also be mentioned that an unanticipated consequence need not neces-

(continued)

of rules designed to achieve a given objective uniformly." [2]

Generic and Local Procedures

At the time of Blau's study in 1949, as well as at the later study date of 1956-59, newly hired interviewers attended centralized training classes where they first received orientation to their jobs and to the organization. They received training devoted to operating procedures and principles of various kinds, such as how to fill out application cards, job order forms, and information about the agency's non-discrimination policy.

Professor Blau's description for 1949 is also applicable to the 1956-59 period:

> The trainee learned that requests for workers, when received from employers over the telephone, must be recorded on a form, the job order. . . . The interviewer was taught the formula: "What? How? Why? What is involved?" as a device for remembering to include in . . . [the] description of the job the tasks the requested worker must perform, how he must perform them, the purpose of these tasks, and the skills and responsibilities involved; . . . training . . . [was] devoted to the use of the four-volume codebook, which contained numerical codes for 29,000 occupations.
>
> . . . Several training lectures were concerned with the procedure of taking applications for jobs. . . . Clients are usually selected for referral to jobs from the file of applications. A series of demonstrations showed how to match the information on the job order with that on the application form in order to select the client best suited for a given vacancy. The applicants selected are called to the office for a referral interview. After the job has been explained in this interview and the client has accepted it, the employer is called to determine whether the position is still

---

sarily reach only dysfunctional ends. See Robert K. Merton, *Social Theory and Social Structure* (rev. ed., Glencoe: Free Press, 1957), p. 51 (footnote).

In addition, it is relevant to specify that there are two types of adjustments: formal and informal. *Formal adjustments* are made by properly constituted authorities in the bureaucratic hierarchy. *Informal* adjustments refer to adjustments made by personnel without the express consent (if required) of upper levels, and are not made in line with accepted bureaucratic procedure.

[2] Blau, *Dynamics* . . ., *op. cit.,* p. 23.

open, and a referral card is written. The last step in the placement process is confirmation that the referred client has been hired, which must be obtained from the employer. . . .

. . . [The Agency] furnish[es] advice on occupational adjustment and training to those who need it. The importance of this counseling service was strongly emphasized by the training staff.[3]

Central training was interspersed with local training. Local supervisors and other personnel provided instruction in the use of certain local forms and procedures that were not applicable to all other agencies.

When the section supervisor explained the work to a new interviewer in Department X, the procedures he described were quite different from those discussed in the training course. Occupational codes were not used. The "job formula" was never mentioned. Application forms were rarely made out. Selection of candidates for jobs was not made from application files but from incoming applicants. Counseling was virtually prohibited. These illustrations suffice to show that basic changes in operating rules had occurred as they were transmitted from agency headquarters down to department and sections.[4]

These findings refer to Agency B studied by Blau in 1949, and also apply to Agency C, but with two exceptions. Unlike the operations Blau observed in 1949, occupational codes *were* used at Agency C, and counseling was *not* "virtually prohibited," but was extremely encouraged.

The case of occupational coding procedure shows that adjustments may be made to meet special local conditions, but they are not always made. The management at Agency B adjusted occupational coding procedure because special conditions of the clothing industry made these codes useless. The management at Agency C did not adjust in the same way even though local conditions were comparable to Agency B. Useless occupational codes were required on various forms. However, the *tendency* toward adjustment to meet special local conditions is evident because Agency C management adjusted *partially* on this point and printed

---

3 *Ibid.*, pp. 22-23.
4 *Ibid.*, p. 23.

booklets which were distributed to interviewers with codes suitable only for the occupations serviced by each agency section. These relatively few special codes were abstracted from the 29,000 in the *Dictionary of Occupational Titles* and this made the task of coding much simpler and faster. What pressures made Agency B management adjust completely and Agency C management adjust partially cannot be determined. The point, however, is that comparable local conditions did not yield the same scope of adjustment, and Agency C officials wasted their time with codes that were required on forms but were rarely used, while Agency B officials were not required to use the occupational codes.

Counseling procedure, and differences on this item between the two agencies will be discussed in the next chapter.

Unanticipated Consequences of an Adjustment

Adjustments do not operate only as single changes. One adjustment can have wide, although unanticipated ramifications when it causes other changes on a chain-reaction basis. A case in point concerns application card procedure and selection of applicants for jobs. According to Blau:

> The clothing industry in this city was characterized by alternating seasons of feverish activity and widespread layoffs, by erratic variations in demand caused by changes in fashions, and by standardization of occupational tasks. Seasonal fluctuations in employment created a large volume of work for this division, requiring speed in operations. Besides, employers demanded workers immediately or not at all, since sudden shifts in demand created pressing needs for workers. Finally, employers who needed unskilled workers not only called the employment agency but also advertised the vacancies by placing signs in the street in front of their shops. Department X could serve its applicants only if it referred a qualified worker before a passer-by responding to the sign had been hired.[5]

There is a difference here between observations at Agency C and those at Agency B which is probably due

---

[5] *Ibid.,* p. 24.

to a changed economic situation and a difference in the skill-level of clients serviced at the two locales. The description applies mostly to *unskilled* occupational groupings at Agency C. At this agency job orders for *skilled* workers often went unfilled for many weeks because the demand for such workers in season exceeded the supply. Continuing from *The Dynamics of Bureaucracy:*

These conditions required adjustments of the selection procedure. Since job openings had to be filled the same day or not at all, there was no time to call to the office clients selected from an application file. Moreover, relatively little information on the qualifications of a worker sufficed for adequate selection in the standardized occupations of the clothing industry. Consequently, workers were selected for referrals directly from the flow of incoming applicants, and the rules governing interviewing were modified in the interest of speed. In most cases a sentence or two describing the applicant's last job and the amount of his experience were sufficient occupational information, and the suitable jobs found in the file could be explained to him in a few words. If he accepted one, a call to the employer revealed whether the vacancy had been filled, and the client was given a referral card with travel directions. The average interview took only ten minutes. The rules governing the selection of candidates from a file of applications became largely irrelevant in this situation, where application forms were made out for only a few occupations in great demand.[6]

This description again applies to Agency C, but with exceptions. At Agency C application cards tended to be made out not only for "a few occupations in great demand" as Blau observed for Agency B, but more often such cards were prepared for clients who were *difficult to service.*

Handicapped clients and the troublesome—for example, those with physical limitations such as heart conditions, arrested TB cases, allergies, travel sickness; those with mental problems, such as the retarded; those who were argumentative; and malingerers—generally had such cards made out for them. This was for the purpose of providing

---

[6] *Ibid.,* pp. 24-25.

a record of dealings with these difficult clients, or providing a record of claimed limitations because of handicap, as a folder for medical reports on work capabilities, or for counseling action taken, or for similar reasons. However, it must be said that Blau's description of applications (". . . application forms were made out for . . . a few occupations in great demand [at Agency B] ") also does apply to Agency C in reference to occupations requiring a high skill-level for which few clients and few vacancies existed. Examples are the occupational classifications of foremen and fore-ladies. However, these groups were well in the minority in relation to the total clientele, and generally application cards tended to be filled out mostly for "difficult" clients.

In addition, job openings were not filled the same day at Agency C, with the exception of unskilled occupations, and in most cases there was certainly "time to call to the office clients selected from an application file." This, how-ever, most often was not done despite a change in con-ditions allowing for time to call clients. This was because of the need for speed in interviewing. Speed was necessary because more clients came to the office at certain times than the staff was able to efficiently service, and this made time-consuming generic application card procedure unsuitable. In turn this meant that there were few cards for selection in the files even if there was time for searching the files.

This matter is also related to another unanticipated consequence at Agency B which Blau discusses:

> These adjustments of the selection procedure, designed to achieve the objectives of the agency under the special conditions in which Department X operated, had unanticipated consequences for these objectives. The original procedure was intended not only for the purpose of finding suitable jobs for clients but also to assure the selection of the *most* qualified applicant among all those available for a job. This requires the simultaneous examination and comparison of all these applicants, which is possible only on the basis of written application forms. The suc-cessive examination of applicants leads to the setting-up of minimum qualifications rather than the use of standards to de-

termine maximum qualifications for a given job. The first client meeting these minimum qualifications was usually selected. Sheer chance—that is, the coincidence of the applicant's appointment and the employer's request—largely determined the client's likelihood of being placed. His abilities beyond the minimum qualifications did not appreciably enhance his chances of getting a better job.[7]

This is repeated at Agency C; furthermore, there is another interesting aspect to this application procedure. In other agencies servicing better educated clients, for example, the clients were asked to fill out application forms prior to being interviewed. But *officials* filled out those few application cards in 1956-59 that were taken at Agency C. By having clients fill out their own applications, speedy operations were not disrupted at the other agencies and they also had an application card for each client. Time was saved, because interviewing officials were able to scan each card with all relevant employment information and could focus their interviewing on these points without having to ask as many questions. However, most clothing workers applying at Agency C had little education. Many could not read or write English, and some could not even speak English. Most were unable to fill out application cards properly.

Type of clientele was thus one more special local condition that required an adjustment in procedure, and officials rather than clients filled out the cards. This meant that in order to save time application cards were not taken for most clients. This was one adjustment. The adjustment, in turn and in part, led to the unanticipated consequence that the first client reporting, rather than the most suitable, was referred to a vacancy.

The processes of change did not halt here: there were still further changes as a result of the first, and these led to inefficiencies of various types. This came about when the original purpose of the application form was inadvertently

---

[7] *Ibid.*, p. 25. Italics in the original.

changed at Agency C because of results of the modifications already mentioned.

Officials at Agency C tended to fill out application forms mainly for the handicapped as well as for other difficult and often troublesome clients, and these cards were rarely scanned for referral to jobs.[8] If they had been, in many cases in reference to the employers' criteria, the *least* suitable worker would have been referred to a job. This would have meant that the agency was not performing its goal of providing a preselection service; that is, of finding suitable applicants for employers.

In reality, this meant that in most cases application cards at Agency C no longer served the purpose of being applications for employment, but rather were used for the purpose of providing *record sheets* of dealings with difficult clients. Counseling action, records of service given, special problems, medical limitations, dates that the client reported to the agency, and similar information were listed on these forms.

Upper hierarchical levels, however, still acted in terms of the original purpose of application cards, even though this had actually been changed locally as an unanticipated consequence of the original adjustment in procedure.

Once every year, a week called National Employ The Physically Handicapped Week (abbreviated to N.E.P.H. Week in agency argot) was proclaimed. Directives by upper-level authorities were issued to local agencies requiring that personnel stress special services to handicapped clients during this week. Special work with employers was also to be performed in the days prior to the N.E.P.H. period to promote the employment of handicapped clients. All agency files were to be scanned, application forms on active file for handicapped clients were to be removed from the files, and notifications were to be sent to these people, asking them to report

---

[8] There were some exceptions. Sometimes a cooperative client much in need of employment had an application card placed on file, and was contacted as soon as a suitable opening was secured.

to the agency for special efforts to help them find jobs.

This procedure treated application cards in terms of their original purpose (as applications for work). But the formal purpose of these forms had already been altered as an unanticipated consequence when these forms were used as records of service and action taken for troublesome clients, rather than as applications for work. The yearly directive, however, was obeyed on operating levels, and handicapped clients were notified to report to the agency. Clients with handicaps of all kinds came.

Jobs were not immediately available for most of these people, even in times of labor demand, in spite of the promotional activities of agency personnel that were supposed to have taken place prior to N.E.P.H. Week. It must be mentioned that much of the promotional activity was also informally modified by operating officials.

Officials who visited employers at their business establishments were told to emphasize N.E.P.H. Week activity, stressing the need for employment of the handicapped and the qualifications of handicapped clients. Officials tended not to do so. This was an informal modification of the directive by the operating officials which came about because officials knew that most employers in the clothing industry already employed people with handicaps of the type that Agency C clients usually had. The shortage of skilled workers, the non-public contact nature of the jobs involved, and the fact that many workers were aged meant that all who could perform the work, regardless of handicap, could and were being hired. *Skill, ability to do the work, and the desire to work,* not only physical condition (with exceptions), were important in the clothing industry. For this reason, officials tended not to promote employment of the handicapped, for such clients who were employable were already being hired. More important, visits to employers were generally completed within minutes and they were generally treated as useless by many officials. Officials rarely discussed matters of importance when they visited employers, and generally did not trouble with the promotional aims of N.E.P.H. Week. This is discussed further in Chapter Seven.

In addition, most of the handicapped clients who were unemployed, and who were notified to report to the agency had special characteristics. Some did not have the requisite skill, while some had personality flaws in addition to physical handicaps which made them difficult to employ. Others were only temporarily unemployed. Some were malingerers who did not want to work, but preferred to collect unemployment compensation.[9] The limitations of some handicapped clients were so great that they could do little work at all, or else they would have already been employed with the great demand for skilled workers.

The application cards of these clients were scanned as ordered by the N.E.P.H. Week directive. Many of these clients were notified to report to the agency and they did, but in rushed conditions of work little service was performed. In most cases no jobs were available for such clients with characteristics as discussed, and they were dismissed after

---

[9] It is sometimes difficult for many people in certain strata of the population in the United States, where status is connected with occupation and earning a living, to believe that some workers actually *prefer* to be unemployed and "chisel" government unemployment compensation. There were quite a few "chiseling" clients reporting to Agency C. One study of malingering clients (although not necessarily covering clients at Agency C) is: Joseph M. Becker, *The Problem of Abuse in Unemployment Benefits, A Study in Limits* (New York: Columbia University Press, 1953).

See also Erwin O. Smigel, "Public Attitudes Toward 'Chiseling' with Reference to Unemployment Compensation," *American Sociological Review,* 18 (February, 1953), pp. 59-67. Smigel in a study of 218 nontransient adults in Bloomington, Indiana (not necessarily the locale of Agencies B and C), finds that while the majority of the sample disapproved of "chiseling" the government of unemployment compensation, there were still differences in attitudes (p. 61). Those who did not disapprove of such "chiseling" which included malingering, had some special characteristics. People with poor jobs, low socioeconomic status, and low occupational levels were more inclined to approve of "chiseling" behavior. This is relevant to Agency C, for most clothing workers serviced by this local agency were of lower occupational levels and low socioeconomic status. "Chiseling" of various types was common at Agency C, although most of these "chiseling" clients did not conceive of their actions in the same way as did officials.

Blau also discusses difficulties officials had at Agency B with some benefit clients who did not want to accept referrals to jobs, and effects of this on the service-oriented employment interviewers. See *Dynamics . . ., op. cit.,* pp. 100-112.

interviews, wasting the time of both clients and staff.

This was dysfunctional on an internal agency level, as well as in relation to organizational goals. On an internal level there was a waste of time and energy expended, as well as a detrimental effect on handicapped clients who wasted their time too. On a broader level the formal organizational goals had not been achieved.

Handicaps that clothing workers tend to suffer are also significant. Travel sickness, stair climbing problems, varicose veins, and similar ailments that clothing workers had were coded as handicaps at the agency, as were heart conditions, emotional impairments, and related disabilities. It appears that upper levels and the public, in focusing special N.E.P.H. Week attention on handicapped clients, conceived of them mainly as the blind, amputees, disabled veterans, and those with related impairments.[10] In addition, it seems clear that the N.E.P.H. directive was focused on handicapped clients who wanted and needed jobs, but could not find employment because of physical disability. In the clothing industry most handicapped as well as other applicants were collecting unemployment insurance benefits. Some of the handicapped claimed that they were only temporarily unemployed, did not want new jobs, but preferred to collect unemployment benefits while waiting for recall by the former employer. More were malingerers who used alleged physical disabilities as an excuse to avoid work. N.E.P.H. directives meant that many of these handicapped people were also notified to report to the agency. Dysfunctions of this entire matter have been discussed. However, it should be mentioned that this served the *latent*

---

[10] A publication by the federal level of the bureaucracy illustrates steps taken to help handicapped clients. Both of the two pictures in one section of the publication show wheelchair applicants. However, the writer as a government official never saw one client in a wheelchair at Agency C in three years. This is not implying that the federal publication is misrepresenting, for it covers all agencies in all states, many of which are unlike Agency C in clientele. In addition, the magazine illustrations aim at emphasizing a point made in the text. However, it is this common conception of a handicapped client that is referred to here.

function of making these unwilling benefit clients report at an early date to the agency for possible referral to a job and job test.[11] This, although unintended, served unemployment insurance objectives. However, in many cases where no jobs were available meeting the client's legitimate limitations, a job test could not be made, and this situation was dysfunctional. This is because it wasted the time of client and staff but did not attain N.E.P.H. objectives, nor did it meet the unemployment insurance, *or* placement goals.

Sometimes there were jobs available for a particular handicapped client, but the client was dismissed with little attempt at service, even after being ordered to appear at the agency for special help. This was because many handicapped clothing workers did not want an immediate job, and the interviewer only dismissed them to meet their desires and to avoid conflict. This illustrates that contrary to the stereotype of the rigid bureaucrat in our society, some officials did modify rules to meet special desires of some clients. However, in this case there is deviation from the organizational goals as a result.

Some of the handicapped limited themselves to such an extent that they were really almost completely outside the labor market. For example, some of the handicapped clothing workers were older women collecting unemployment benefits who claimed that they could not climb stairs and could not travel to work because of high blood pressure, or heart problems, or varicose veins, or other ailments. Under these limitations it was necessary to find a clothing employer within walking distance from such a client's home, and on lower floors or with elevator facilities. If the client lived in a neighborhood in which there were few clothing plants meeting the stair climbing limitations, then this client was almost completely outside the labor market. When such

---

11 Whereas manifest functions refer "to those objective consequences for a specified unit (person, subgroup, social or cultural system) which contribute to its adjustment or adaptation and were so intended . . . [latent functions refer] to unintended and unrecognized consequences of the same order." (Merton, *op. cit.,* p. 63.)

clients were called to the agency as part of N.E.P.H. Week, officials soon became entirely frustrated and exasperated with them because of their numerous limitations, and often merely sent them home without attempting the prolonged or intensive service desired in the generic N.E.P.H. procedure.

In summary, upper bureaucratic levels wished to provide a special service for handicapped clients. In the ideal case, agency officials were to perform promotional work stressing the capabilities of these people. Vacancies for the handicapped were to be secured, and they were to be notified to report to the agency through their application cards on file. In the ideal they were to be referred to jobs specially solicited for them through the promotional activity. The entire N.E.P.H. preparation was for the functional end of providing some special service for these unfortunate clients who might have been neglected in the normal rush of business by both employers and agency personnel.

Local conditions in the agency studied, however, were such that these ideal ends often could not be reached. This was because modifications caused by special local needs yielded unanticipated consequences, and a change in the ends of application form procedure. Applications were being made out most often for clients who were troublesome and difficult to service, and were in most cases really record sheets, rather than applications for work. Many of the handicapped did not need or want new jobs! They were not *really* applying for work.

Lower levels were working with one set of adjusted procedures and within the unrecognized effects of several unanticipated consequences resulting from these adjustments. Higher levels were dealing with the formal goals of application card procedure in reference to all agencies, and not merely the clothing industries agency. [12] This imbalance caused by lack of knowledge of higher levels of actual

---

[12] The effect of N.E.P.H. Week at other agencies is not known. This discussion must be limited only to Agency C, although it is possible that there were also problems at other locales somewhat similar to Agency C.

results of modifications and local conditions at lower levels in a specific local agency, caused dysfunctional consequences where functional ends were the original aim of the entire N.E.P.H. Week procedure. In addition, N.E.P.H. Week had been devised to help unfortunate handicapped clients who needed and wanted jobs. The special type of clientele connected with the clothing industry and the seasonal nature of the industry itself (where even many handicapped clients collected benefits and were only temporarily unemployed), did not meet the ideal aim of the procedure.

Local conditions where employers already employed handicapped clients, and a displacement of goals of employer visits (to be discussed in Chapter Seven) made for further problems on the promotional end and led to informal adjustment on the local level. This again caused deviation from desired results of N.E.P.H. activity.

Conclusions

We have seen, through analysis of two cases, that generic procedures were certainly changed to meet local conditions. Blau writes of Agency B:

> . . . progressive specification of procedures could be noted as one moved down the organizational hierarchy to the point of actual contact with clients. The conditions under which such contacts took place, notably the characteristics of the industry served, gave rise to *adjustments* of procedures in the interest of operating efficiency. [13]

Adjustments of procedures prevailed at Blau's research locale as well as at Agency C. Blau's findings of adjustments at Agency B and the present replication, i.e., findings of adjustments at a related organization years after Blau's observations, lend weight to Blau's thesis, succinctly contained in his title, *The Dynamics of Bureaucracy*. These data show that bureaucratic operations are not completely rigid and un-

---

[13] Blau, *Dynamics* . . ., *op. cit.*, p. 24. Italics in the original.

yielding as is so popularly thought, but rather bureaucratic operations are flexible in some respects.

The present findings, however, show that not all adjustments that were needed were made at Agency C. The procedure requiring use of occupational codes, even under a procedure formally adjusted from the generic (the special booklets), serves as an example. This also points to the conclusion that an adjustment in and of itself is not necessarily functional in total. An adjustment may be functional where it meets local needs, but an adjustment may not meet *all* local needs pertaining to that situation. The special booklet with abstracted occupational codes prepared at Agency C really was an adjustment to meet local conditions, but it was only a partial adjustment since codes were most often useless under the special local conditions of the clothing industry. Agency C officials still had to use codes, while Agency B officials did not use these codes.

Another important point is that flexibility and adjustments, functional because local needs are thereby met which enhance attainment of major organizational objectives, can eventually lead to dysfunctional results because of further changes occurring as a result of the initial adjustment (unanticipated consequences). A bureaucracy is a complicated, dynamic social system. One change can lead to others, which lead to still yet others with consequences far removed from the aims of the original change.

Interest in this chapter was on only one type of modification: the adjustment of procedures. The next chapter presents data on two other types of modifications.

CHAPTER FIVE

Redefinition and Amplification

THE LAST CHAPTER dealt with adjustment of procedures. Selected agency procedures are analyzed in the present chapter with reference to two other types of modifications known as redefinition and amplification. *Redefinition,* "deliberately sacrifices the original objective of a procedure in order to achieve another organizational objective more effectively."[1] *Amplification* broadens an original procedure, and is a special type of adjustment.[2]

Counseling of Clients

According to Blau, counseling service was strongly emphasized by the central training staff in 1949.[3] However, at the operating level at Agency B at the same date, there was a redefinition of this procedure and "counseling was virtually prohibited."[4] Blau writes:

---

[1] Peter M. Blau, *The Dynamics of Bureaucracy* (rev. ed., Chicago: University of Chicago Press, 1963), p. 26.

[2] *Ibid.,* pp. 26-27.

[3] *Ibid.,* pp. 22-23.

[4] *Ibid.,* p. 23.

The dispensing of occupational advice was relegated to a minor role in Department X. This was not intended to improve counseling service by adjusting it to prevailing conditions; on the contrary, it almost eliminated this service. Finding jobs for applicants and finding workers for employers were considered the only "real" responsibilities of the department, because the administration evaluated its operations largely on the basis of the number of placements made. This emphasis, in turn, resulted from the fact that the legislature based its appropriations for the agency primarily on the number of placements. Counseling procedure was consequently modified in terms of this dominant objective of maximizing placements. The supervisor's permission for counseling a client was required, and it was rarely granted, leaving more time for speedy placement service.[5]

It is interesting to note that this redefinition was not repeated at Agency C studied years later. Contrary to Blau's findings, counselings were not "virtually prohibited" by supervisors at the local level but were strongly encouraged. Superiors at sectional conferences frequently stressed the need for counselings as did central training staff, and they deplored the small number actually performed for credit when compared to the statistical goal. Permission was certainly not needed for performance of counselings; in fact, it would have been redundant to ask superiors for such permission. Officials had been told time and again that they should perform many counselings. Emphasis on counseling at Agency C is also shown by the fact that all personnel were taught how to perform all but special types of counseling. At Agency B only some few special interviewers in each department were trained to counsel. Other interviewers were only given training on how to recognize counseling need in order that transfer could then be made to the special counselor for this service.[6]

Such a wide difference in findings can help us to understand processes in bureaucracy, because we can look for changed conditions over a period of time which might have

---

[5] *Ibid.*, pp. 25-26. Footnote eliminated from the original.
[6] *Ibid.*, p. 23, footnote 6.

caused the different forms of behavior in the two cases. A single case-study allows us to hypothesize only about what could have been *if* conditions were different. Here we can actually look at the effect that changed local and operating conditions had on this counseling procedure. For this reason, counseling procedure is analyzed at length at this point.

The factors of time and budgetary procedure affected treatment of counselings at both Agencies B and C. While time, personnel and jobs for applicants were scarce at Agency B in 1949,[7] they were not as scarce in 1956-59 at Agency C. In addition, in 1949 the government based its appropriations primarily on the number of placements made, leading to a local level redefinition of counseling procedure in the interest of making more placements.[8] However, in 1956 the agency even on the local level emphasized counseling when it was made one of the several "pay-items," in addition to placement activity, in the new total Employment Bureau budgetary appropriation system that had been established.[9]

In Blau's case, to add to his findings on a hypothetical basis, merely because permission was rarely granted for counseling did not mean that interviewers could not counsel in actuality. They could do so without asking permission,

---

[7] *Ibid.*, pp. 30 and 58. In addition, there is evidence of a "substantial surplus of labor" in City X at the same period. (From a federal study of people reporting to state agencies.)

[8] Placement service refers to employment service. A placement is an agency term for a hire of a client who had been referred by the agency.

See Blau's footnote 7 on p. 26 *(op. cit.)* for a statement concerning the scarce time, and managerial decision to rationally allocate this time mainly on placement activity, offering less counseling service.

[9] There were four "pay-items" in the budget (allocated in terms of work-minutes per unit). These pay-items were: placements, counselings, testing, and new applications. Some other activities received budgetary allotments on a percentage basis of placement time, and others on a percentage basis of all four items mentioned. New applications were also stressed as a pay-item, despite the discussion in the last chapter about few applications made out at the clothing industry agencies. There were short and long form applications at Agency C. "Short" application figures could, and *were* easily inflated to meet the stress at the same time that the "long" applications discussed earlier were de-emphasized to meet local conditions. This will be discussed in Chapter Seven.

by giving advice, and *without reporting it.*[10] It is a most interesting situation that when Agency C encouraged counseling years later, and unlike Agency B in 1949, no permission was required, interviewers were reluctant to counsel formally for statistical credit. They often counseled without reporting it, despite pressures from superiors to the contrary![11]

There were several reasons for this. First, local conditions of work at times made the performance of counseling difficult. Some officials felt obliged to work rapidly under certain rushed conditions when numerous clients waited for interviews.[12] A few words of advice to clients sufficed and normal interviews were over, as Blau also observed, in about ten minutes.[13] This is the problem of scarcity of time which occurred at certain seasons of the year and at certain hours of the day at Agency C, although it does not appear that the problem was as severe at Agency C as at Agency B. At Agency B, a formal redefinition was made by managerial officials to limit the performance of counselings. At Agency C managerial and supervisory officials were doing the opposite by formally demanding many counselings, but operating level interviewers made an informal redefinition and were reluctant to provide as many as superiors desired. This met the local constraint of scarce time in rushed conditions. However, time was not the only, nor the major condition

---

[10] This covers a *possibility.* There is no proof at hand for this statement.

[11] It would be useful to compare the number of counselings reported at Agency B during the period of redefinition with the number reported at Agency C when counselings were encouraged (but staff did not report as many as they performed). Unfortunately, data available do not allow such comparisons. First, the agency publication listing records of operations shifted from departmental reporting at Agency B to total agency figures at the time that Blau was making his observations. Thus figures for Blau's Department X cannot be separated from the total agency counts of counselings credited. There are also difficulties in comparability since Agency C and Department X at Agency B were assigned a different number of staff members who were trained to counsel, and serviced clients with different skill levels.

[12] There are exceptions. At times officials restricted output severely by reducing their work speed even under rushed conditions. This will be discussed in Chapters Six and Seven.

[13] Blau, *Dynamics. . ., op. cit.,* p. 25.

causing the informal modification at Agency C, for time was not always scarce, and staff in fact often counseled by giving clients professional advice but did not always report these counselings for credit.

A second and more important reason than time scarcity concerned the writing of counselings. Supervisors were made aware of the importance of this matter and rigidly demanded full compliance with procedures relating to form and content of counseling reports. They required that each counseling card, with a write-up of the problem, facts of the case, counseling plan and action taken, attached to an application form, be placed on their desks for review prior to filing.

According to formal procedure, a counseling could not be called such unless a report was written, and this was despite any professional advice that may have been given to clients. In other words, even though an official was in fact giving a client advice, which anyone else would call "counseling," the agency did not call this a counseling, and credit could not be recorded on official records. A counseling for credit, according to agency procedure, meant that the interviewer had to fill out an application card for that client and in addition, a full counseling report had to be written in tedious longhand. At times supervisors were known to return these cards when they were thought to be of insufficient quality. In short, there was extra work connected with counseling for credit, and an increased visibility of interviewers' work to their superiors. In a normal interview, officials did their work without knowledge of anyone else of exactly what was said and done (unless the supervisor was sitting in on the interview on an occasional "audit"). However, in a counseling interview, all forms listing information received and action taken had to be filled out and sent to the supervisor prior to filing. The supervisor now knew what action was taken in the interview, and had forms in his grasp which could be, and often were, reviewed for accuracy and completeness. This visibility also decreased the willingness of officials to counsel for credit. In fact, some officials at times found the increased visibility and its results so distasteful, that even when a counseling for credit was performed they occasionally tried to file the report and application form without following the procedure of clearing this with the supervisor first.

A third reason for the reluctance of officials to counsel for credit concerned the reduced level of need for counseling in the formal manner under the special local conditions at Agency C, and its lack of importance as viewed by the majority of interviewers on regular assignments. This occurred because in the clothing industry jobs were fairly standardized and there was little advice that could be given for intra-industry occupational shifts. Most clients were on temporary layoff only, and many were middle-aged or older women, a good proportion of whom were only secondary wage earners. These clients needed little counseling of the major type that other clients might have required. Many had limited education, and quite a few did not understand English well which made communication of counseling or other information sometimes difficult. On the average, these were not the kind of clients who would need counseling of definite and overriding importance, such as, for example, men who are primary wage earners, or returning war veterans. Clothing industry clients could still be given advice on where to secure extra training, on the advantages of taking the agency aptitude test, on unemployment insurance law obligations, on how to look for a job, or other similar matters. But while there were certainly exceptions, these generally were not the type of problems that were striking. Therefore, officials were willing to give and often did give advice to clothing workers, but often saw no reason to call these counselings, nor did officials see cause to prepare a lengthy report on these matters that they thought were of minor importance. This is especially so when the writing of this report was so irksome to officials, as has been discussed. Superiors, however, did not see the issue this way because counselings were a "pay-item" in the budgetary appropriation system.

It is interesting to note that those few interviewers on special Agency C assignments generally counseled frequently in the formal manner, for this was an integral part of their work, and there was often a frequent and definite need for counselings. Officials servicing handicapped workers who needed special help (other handicapped clients were serviced by the regular interviewers), the official assigned to service older workers in need of special help, the special counselor for younger clients (e.g., high school graduates) did counsel more frequently. However, even for these officials, strong managerial and supervisory pressures added to the exigencies caused by the nature of work, leading these officials to report more counselings than they would have otherwise done.

According to a former Agency C colleague who had at one time been assigned to the Special Services section after 1956 (dealing with clients with characteristics mentioned above):

> The statistics pressure . . . was tremendous—especially in that Spec.[ial] Services Unit—counselings were the BIG THING and almost every applicant became a counseling situation.[14]

Thus counselings in the formal manner were *not only* performed because of the special characteristics of the clientele, but also because of supervisory pressures which demanded a high record of counselings reported on the statistical records. However, had it not been for the special characteristics of the clientele, superordinate pressure, present in all sections, still would not have yielded the high number of counselings desired. The special clientele serviced made supervisory pressure stronger for this section than for others and more effective as well, for the end of having more counselings reported. Supervisory pressures on interviewers servicing usual clients could often be met with the statement that few clients with problems needing counseling

---

[14] From a letter (dated June 24, 1961) to the author written in response to some questions relating to agency matters. This letter is quoted extensively in Chapter Seven. The official had been hired at the same date as the author, and terminated her employment at the same date to leave for another state. Her observations thus cover the same period of time as that of the author. The capitalization in the quotation above is in the original.

were being interviewed. This rebuttal could not work in the Special Services section, for many clients were presumed to have special problems, or else they would not have been reporting there.

Most officials did counsel frequently, but did so un-officially without reporting it as an official counseling.[15] Officially they only reported one, two, or perhaps three counselings per month.[16] This minimum number, generally much less than counselings actually performed, was reported

---

[15] Evidence for this assertion, other than that of the writer's own actions in participation and observations of others is that supervisors frequently brought this matter up in conferences, stressing the need for reporting all counselings performed. This stress, however, was on the fact that *statistical records of pro-duction* were not being maximized on this activity, rather than stress on service factors (i.e., helping a client). In addition, a training official, while lecturing on counseling procedure, said he thought that too rigid supervisory demands concerning "write-up" provisions caused some officials to counsel without re-porting it.

[16] Access to records of production (years January 1956 through December 1959) for Agency C shows a high in this period of 145 counselings reported in the month of May 1956 and a low in this period of 42 in December 1957. There were approximately 35 interviewers assigned to Agency C. This means that at the point of highest number of counselings reported for credit, interviewers re-ported an average of about four each that month. At the lowest point each inter-viewer reported an average of about one each for the month. These figures corroborate the observations above, for the number of counselings reported per interviewer is low considering the number of clients interviewed in total (e.g., more than 8,700 were interviewed in May 1956 which means that somewhat less than one and three quarters per cent were counseled for credit at that time).

The figures listed are only broad approximations, for the number of inter-viewers assigned to the agency varied from time to time, and the number at work (e.g., absences because of sick leave, or vacations) also varied. In addition, some few interviewers, because of their special assignments, had many counselings per month and were expected to report many because of the nature of the clientele that they serviced. Some few interviewers consistently turned in many counselings to impress superiors, whereas some few were able to withstand supervisory pressure and reported none at all. Most, in order to relieve supervisory pressure, reported perhaps one or two per month, although they were much more free with their advice to clients.

Reference to the author's own records of operations also shows a small number of counselings reported for credit. In the 31-month period of participation for which data are available, he had never reported more than two counselings per month. There were ten months in which no counselings were reported at all. In a 31-month period only 25 total counselings were reported and this is of thousands of clients serviced, and despite supervisory desire for many counselings.

mainly in order to decrease supervisory pressures. Interviewers who reported no counselings were frequently reminded of their lack by supervisors, and were urged to correct this.[17] Yet supervisors had no strict control over the *total* number of counseling interviews subordinates performed—although sufficient prodding made many, but not all, report a minimum—since this depended on extraneous factors, e.g., the chance appearance at an interviewer's desk of a client who needed counseling. For this reason, some interviewers found this a convenient method of restriction of output reported and some highly disgruntled interviewers, wishing to "punish" the agency or supervisor, restricted counseling for credit to a degree more extreme than that already mentioned. This served to reduce the statistical credit accumulated on sectional production records for this operation, and supervisors then had difficulty meeting sectional goals.

Often pressure from supervisors became very strong toward the end of the statistical period when it was evident that sectional production goals were not being met. At these times the minimum one or two counselings would be performed and reported for credit by some officials only because

---

[17] Supervisory pressures have been mentioned several times. These pressures often were no more than repeated proddings and reminders to staff members that they had not performed a sufficient number of counselings (or other interviewer operations), were not filling out forms as required, etc. Constant prodding was disliked by most interviewers, and hence this was a pressure on officials to meet supervisory demands, although this pressure did not always yield the ends desired by the superior.

There was generally an implicit threat that repeated failure to respond to pressures and to correct operations according to supervisory desires might affect the interviewer's periodical personnel rating. This implicit threat sometimes was carried out. For example, the author as an official once received a personnel rating lower than average, and when he indicated displeasure at this evaluation the supervisor referred to statistical records of operations and in part justified the evaluation by pointing out, among other things, that the author had performed too few counselings in the rating period.

There were also cases known where repeated failure to abide by supervisory desires resulted in charges being brought against the offending official for dismissal. However, this generally was rare, and was often the result of a long series of disagreements and bad feeling between superior and subordinate.

supervisors were demanding them. The need for counseling was stretched by some officials to meet this strong "last-minute" demand and clients were then "counseled" when they might not really have needed it. Sometimes the interview progressed in a normal manner without any real counseling, but the interviewer stretched points here and there, and substituted mere advice on very minor matters for counseling activity. A stereotyped report was then written. This type of counseling was clearly dysfunctional because it wasted time, detracted from speedy placement activity, and did not help reach generic placement, unemployment insurance, or counseling goals. The service goals of this procedure were displaced and counseling was merely performed for the statistical credit involved.[18]

In certain cases, counseling without reporting it was dysfunctional too, and not only because proper governmental budgetary appropriations could not be given for this service rendered, but also because other officials interviewing the same client at a later date were not aware that the client had been counseled and did not know what action resulted from this special service. Counseling might have been repeated unnecessarily, and officials in later interviews could not base their action on the special service provided earlier, for there was no record of such counseling.

Training officials, supervisors, and managers repeatedly mentioned in conferences and staff meetings that they knew counselings were being performed without being reported for credit. However, most attributed this lack of reporting to the belief that the officials were so used to dispensing advice, that they did so without realizing that they were counseling and therefore were not reporting it as such. Some managerial and training officials were of the opinion that more training on *recognizing* the actual performance of counseling was necessary. Despite training which was given to newly hired

---

[18] It should be emphasized that not all counselings were of this unnecessary type. Occasionally a real counseling was provided a client, a report was written, and it was reported for credit.

interviewers and all the periodical exhortations by managers and supervisors, counselings reported in 1956-59 remained at approximately the same low level of quantity. Some agency sections repeatedly fell below their statistical goals.

Initiation of detailed statistical records of interviewer performance at the agency had certain special consequences, as Blau discusses. This will be extensively traced in the next chapters. Blau notes that these records served to increase production at Agency B.[19] Agency B statistical records of interviewer production did not require a listing of the number of counselings performed. However, Agency C records included this activity in 1956-59. The inclusion of counselings on statistical records made counseling activity (in terms of number performed) by each interviewer visible to superiors. Yet the case of counselings at Agency C is an illustration of a changed emphasis to be recorded on statistical records that did not increase recorded production substantially because the pressures of visibility of what occurred during a counseling interview and the pressures of forms, time, and the other matters were generally stronger than that of the records and the demands of supervisors.

Thus a changed emphasis on an upper level (a modification in the budgetary allotment system which served to include counseling service), and a lower level managerial decision to allocate time for counseling, did not fully reach the ends anticipated by management when the lower level operating officials informally modified the procedure once again as the result of various constraints.

Occupational Demand Sheet Procedures

Reception counter activity served the purpose of screening clients. Those clients for whom no service was thought possible because no jobs were available were to be sent away. Unemployment benefit clients were to receive reap-

---

[19] Blau, *Dynamics . . ., op. cit.,* p. 39. Blau's interest on his page is on *placement* production.

pointment dates, i.e., a date to return to the agency if still unemployed.

Agency B receptionists were clerical employees.[20] At Agency C the receptionists were not clerical employees on a lower hierarchical level, but were interviewing officials who alternated on a rotating basis between regular interviewing duties and reception activity. In most cases interviewers spent one week at the reception counter, and then the next several weeks performing regular interviewing duties until the turn came up again for reception work.

At Agency B, the clerks manning the reception counter did not alternate between interviewing tasks and counter. For this reason their knowledge of employment conditions with which interviewers dealt on a daily basis was somewhat limited. Discretion, in turn, was limited for these clerks and they were given a list of occupations (called occupational demand sheets in agency argot) for which job openings were currently available. Those people with skill in occupations on this list, as well as other special categories of clients, were to be seated for further interviewing. Clients whose occupations were not on the list were to be sent home, each with a reappointment date.[21]

At Agency C in 1956 there was no such list of occupations to limit discretion of officials. Interviewers had such a list "in their minds," and dismissed or seated clients according to two formal criteria: first, their knowledge of job conditions and demand for that client's occupation, and second, the number of clients that the section could service at any one period. The latter was determined by the number of interviewers at work that day, speed of interviewing, and client load.

In 1959 a newly promoted manager was assigned to Agency C to replace one who left. This manager had previously worked at a department of Agency B where

---

[20] *Ibid.,* p. 28, footnote 9.
[21] *Ibid.,* p. 28.

occupational demand sheets were in use at reception counters.[22] Taking notice of the large area of discretion that Agency C interviewers had while on reception duty, and anxious to improve the relatively sagging statistical counts and records of this local agency, the new manager required that occupational listings be prepared and used at reception counters. An amplification of reception procedure at Agency C was thus made to avoid too liberal use of discretion on the part of reception interviewers, and to make certain that clients who were in demand occupations were not being dismissed with reappointment dates.

The manager, however, acted without taking into account special conditions at his new assignment at Agency C. He did not take into consideration the fact that interviewers already knew through daily operations which occupations were in demand and which were not, *without* reference to a list. This was unlike Agency B where clerks manned the reception counter. He also neglected in his amplification to note the criterion of amount of work a particular section could handle in very rushed periods. This local agency to which the manager had been newly assigned was a small one. When hordes of clients appeared at one time, many had to be dismissed, even though their occupations were in demand. This was because three to eight Agency C interviewing officials per section were limited in the number of clients they could possibly service at any one period. On the other hand, in periods of slack activity, clients were frequently seated for interviews even if no jobs appeared to be open.[23] At such times officials could take much care in interviewing. A skilled interviewer was frequently capable of calling selected employers, based on his personal knowl-

---

[22] It is not known whether this newly promoted official was at Agency B *in 1949*. Professor Blau in a personal communication to the writer says that this man was not assigned *to the department he studied during his observation period*. It is known, however, that he had worked at an Agency B department sometime prior to his assignment to Agency C.

[23] This did not always occur and there were frequent periods of restriction of output among interviewers. This will be discussed.

edge of the industry. Through personal contacts with employers or other agency officials, he often was able to refer a client to a job vacancy for which the agency had previously never been notified.

For these reasons occupational demand sheets were not advantageous at Agency C except for control of one condition: restriction of output. By controlling the flow of clients, interviewers acting as receptionists could ease the burden of work for their co-workers. The informal norm at Agency C was to limit severely the number of clients to be serviced in late afternoon hours, while colleagues checked results of job referrals made during the day, completed clerical tasks, and then socialized with one another. Discretion allowed on the part of the receptionist, and informal pressures on the part of the interviewers on the receptionist, constrained him to use this discretion broadly. This was not so much in terms of occupations in demand, but rather to limit the number of clients seated for interviews to that which could adequately be serviced by staff, and at certain hours to aid in restriction of output.[24]

The new manager had ordered the use of occupational demand sheets. These occupational demand sheets were prepared according to managerial directive and were placed on every reception counter, but then most interviewing officials informally modified the managerial amplification, and did not refer to this listing! It was merely kept on a corner of the reception counter, frequently fell out of date and was not used. On occasion the manager visited each reception counter to determine whether or not his occupational demand sheets were being prepared as he had required. The sheets were there and he was satisfied that the amplified procedure was being maintained. However, it was not really followed, through lack of use by most officials for the months while the author was in

---

[24] The reception interviewer also used this discretion to dismiss some benefit clients who preferred not to search for work, in violation of the unemployment insurance law. This will be discussed in the next section.

participation.[25]

This case illustrates a formal amplification of procedure by a new manager, but instead of having the desired functional effects, it was informally modified once again by operating officials. This really served to maintain the status quo.

Reappointment Date Procedure

Blau discussed the reappointment date (also known as "due date") procedure that he observed at Agency B in 1949. Reappointment procedure was defined in general terms on the *administrative* level:

"The renewal practice . . . is designed to bring workers into the office when needed. . . . Because of the highly seasonal nature of the [clothing] industry . . . dates assigned may vary from one week to four months."[26]

There were more specific rules on the *departmental* level. On this level it was specified that some clients were to receive a 30-day due date, and others were to receive 60 days, or different dates depending on occupation and other special factors.[27]

On the *supervisory* level it was explained that:

. . . many factors had to be taken into account in determining the due date for a client, such as his occupation, his eagerness to work, his qualifications, present and prospective labor-market conditions, etc. "There are many different rules about

---

[25] There were some few officials, conformists in their operations at the agency, who were observed to use this demand sheet. In addition, participation was halted in 1959 shortly after this procedure was amplified, and therefore long-term effects cannot be fully determined. An official in *1961,* however, said that personnel still do not use the demand sheet in spite of its preparation for two years. This official said that when a reception official occasionally wants to bring himself up to date on certain vacancies that may have been received without his knowledge during the course of the day, he only turns to one of his interviewing colleagues and asks if vacancies are available. The demand sheet is of little use in such immediate cases, for it is generally out of date, even shortly after being prepared.

[26] Blau, *Dynamics . . ., op. cit.,* p. 28. Blau has taken this from a document f the division. Parenthetical note and omissions are his.

[27] *Ibid.*

what date to give them." This constituted an implicit recognition of the need for exercising discretion in the determination of re-appointment dates and thus permitted earlier due dates than the one or two months demanded by the general rule.

All five receptionists interpreted this procedure liberally. They exercised discretion, frequently giving earlier due dates than specified, and occasionally seated a client for an interview who should have been sent home.[28]

Blau discussed reasons for such modifications by the receptionists:

The clerks modified the due-date procedure to make their work experience more satisfactory. Having to refuse clients a badly needed service created conflicts for receptionists, who were identified with the service philosophy of the agency and who had experienced the aggression of some clients whom they had sent home. To tell clients, in addition, not to return for two months would have placed the receptionist under severe pressure. By giving earlier due dates than required, receptionists escaped such conflicts and improved their relationships with applicants, that is, the public relations of the agency. Furthermore, by exercising some discretion when giving due dates, they transformed a routine, mechanical duty into an interesting social experience. This was partly due to the feeling of power derived from being able to "sneak somebody through [to be interviewed] that really shouldn't get through," and thus help him get a job, or from determining whether a client might return within a few days or must wait for many weeks.[29]

A comparison of Blau's findings for Agency B and the Agency C findings shows that there is one great change on the informal level by interviewers assigned to the reception counter. Agency B receptionists gave some clients earlier reappointment dates than required, and "sneaked in" some clients for interviews who should have been sent home. However, a most interesting reversal occurred at Agency C where receptionists were supposed, in general, to give from one- to three-week due dates (depending on occupation) but modified informally and tended to give *longer* dates.

28 *Ibid.*, pp. 28-29. Footnote omitted.
29 *Ibid.*, p. 29. Footnote omitted. Parenthetical addition is Blau's.

Officials also engaged in the practice of "sneaking out" some clients for whom jobs could have been found, but who nevertheless were sent home without service. This striking reversal of informally modified procedure by receptionists came about as a result of several factors.

According to Blau's description, clients at Agency B, with some exceptions, desired employment. The department he observed handled unskilled clients, and the labor market was such that in 1949 there seemed to be a glut of these clients for the few jobs available. According to Blau, the department head:

> . . . explained in her directive that the scarcity of job openings made more frequent interviewing of clients useless and that the scarcity of personnel made it impossible. [30]

Formal procedure at Agency B then required longer dates and dismissals of many clients. This was changed by operating level officials who sometimes gave shorter dates than required and "sneaked clients in." In contrast, sections at Agency C handled clients in both skilled and unskilled categories with most clients in the skilled occupational categories. In this agency there was a scarcity of skilled clothing workers, although there were still more clients than jobs available in some of the unskilled occupational categories. Thus there were many vacancies available for skilled workers. Yet many of the skilled workers reporting to the agency were unemployment insurance benefit clients who expected to return to their former employers in a short period of time, and so in general could not fill many of the permanent job openings available. These clients did not want to be interviewed for jobs, and desired to be "sneaked out" with longer reappointment dates. Agency C officials in response also redefined procedure, as did their colleagues at Agency B, but not in the same direction.

The Agency C practice is a reversal of actions Blau observed because of different job market conditions and

---

[30] *Ibid.,* p. 30.

different *client desires* in the two branches. It is important to indicate that when Agency C officials gave longer dates and "sneaked out," they, as did Agency B officials, secured good relations with the clients through modifying procedures to meet the desires of clients. This also served the personal needs of interviewers by avoiding the troublesome conflict with clients which often occurred when client desires were blocked by the official rules. However, while Agency B officials secured good relations with their clients by "sneaking in" and giving shorter reappointment dates, they nevertheless defeated the original purpose of the due date procedure which aimed at limiting the flow of applicants.[31] Similarly, Agency C officials secured good relations with benefit-collecting clients who preferred not to find other employment, by giving longer dates and "sneaking out." Nevertheless, the placement service goal was being neglected, as was the unemployment insurance task of "testing" unemployed clients by a job offer, and reporting client refusals to accept referral to the job to the Unemployment Compensation Office for possible disqualification from receiving benefit checks.[32]

---

[31] *Ibid.,* p. 30.

[32] It is important to indicate that the discussion here is on the level of gross activity. It should not be thought that Agency C receptionists always allowed client desires to influence official action. There were many clients who preferred to be "sneaked out." Many of these *were* "sneaked out," but many also were seated for interviews because of supervisory demands, some allegiance of officials to the bureaucratic goals, as well as the personal feelings of officials against clients who would rather collect benefit checks than work. In addition, Blau makes reference to the difficulty some officials at Agency B had with clients who did not want to work. (See *Ibid.,* pp. 100-112.) However, Blau's description of the situation at the time is that many clients were demanding work, and Agency B was not able to meet this demand in all cases because of local conditions in the clothing industry. At Agency C there certainly were clients who wanted jobs, but the situation was reversed, and the gross situation was that most preferred to be dismissed with longer reappointment dates and frequently complained if seated for an interview, or if asked to return to the agency at an early date.

In addition, it occasionally occurred that a client at Agency C was "sneaked in" because he was much in need of help and desired it, even though the reception official knew that there were no jobs available in the files meeting that client's skill. (A highly motivated and skilled interviewer was often able to find a vacancy

(continued)

Superordinate Amplification To Counteract Too Liberal Interpretation of Due Date and Dismissal Procedure

At Agency B, Blau found that:

Superordinates in two different positions responded to these modifications [concerning due dates and dismissal of clients] in opposite ways. The supervisor made allowances for them by acknowledging that so many factors had to be taken into account when determining due dates that no simple rule could be followed. The department head, on the other hand, not only established a clear-cut procedure but also amplified it in an attempt to discourage deviation. She explained in her directive that the scarcity of job openings made more frequent interviewing of clients useless and that the scarcity of personnel made it impossible. In another department—perhaps indicating a later stage of organizational development—the department head insisted on such precise criteria for deciding due dates that clerical discretion was eliminated.[33]

At Agency C ten years later, a manager previously at the agency Blau observed was newly assigned as head of the local office. This man also amplified in an attempt to counteract the effects of too liberal deviation from established procedure. Use of discretion at the reception counter was limited. Reappointment (due) dates were specified for each occupational classification, and in almost all cases the date formally provided was substantially less in time than that given by use of the interviewer's sole discretion. A list of required due dates was prepared for the reference use of officials.

In this amplification the office manager did not himself specify the new reappointment dates to be assigned, but delegated this responsibility to supervisors who were to decide on the new dates in conference with the operating officials. The dates were to vary according to occupational classification, and conferences were to be held periodically

---

for a client even if no job vacancies originally appeared to be available. This was achieved through use of contacts at other agencies, special knowledge of the clothing industry, and related special skills.) The more usual situation at Agency C, however, was that of "sneaking out."

[33] *Ibid.,* p. 30.

to bring the formalized due dates up to date with local market conditions.

The manager made it clear, however, that he expected such conferences to decide *stricter,* meaning shorter due dates for almost all occupational categories. This did occur even though the interviewers themselves, headed and guided by the supervisor, were determining the dates. In other words, the interviewers of each section as a group were deciding on reappointment dates which were shorter than those that they were giving on the basis of their own discretion. [34] Interviewers complained often and bitterly about this loss of discretion and on the new dates decided, and this was so despite the conference method. These numerous complaints point to the importance of discretion in this matter to the interviewing officials. [35]

It is interesting to note that both in 1949 at Agency B and in 1959 at Agency C, similar amplifications were made to meet the same local need. In both agencies this was caused by informal modifications by interviewers and receptionists to meet client demands. However, in Blau's case at Agency B, the amplification stressed the need for the required *longer* due dates and limited "sneaking in," whereas at Agency C in 1959 the amplification stressed the required shorter due

---

[34] This discretion had been somewhat limited before amplification too, because superiors had required shorter due dates for applicants whose skills were more in demand. However, within this limitation, the interviewers still had much leeway (and some did not follow the superior's order). This occasionally caused difficulty when some clients serviced by one official received short due dates, and co-workers at the same plant serviced by chance by another official received the desired longer due dates. Complaints often resulted under these conditions. In such cases flexibility, and use of discretion caused client complaints. This is the reverse of what the popular connotation of the term "bureaucrat" might lead us to believe. It should, however, be mentioned that the official giving the shorter renewal date was likely to have been following procedure more rigidly than his colleague giving the longer renewal date. But it was often the *discrepancy* between dates received by client co-workers that caused the one receiving the shorter date to complain.

[35] The occupational demand sheet procedure discussed earlier was also designed to limit use of discretion by interviewers, and in fact both amplifications were made within a short time interval of one another by the same newly promoted manager.

dates and limited "sneaking out." This case illustrates the strain for managerial amplification to refocus informally modified procedures back to original objectives. It is especially interesting because it illustrates the similar processes involved through replication of similar managerial action taken at two different agencies ten years apart in time, but occurring as a result of similar, yet opposite conditions.

Conclusions

Redefinitions and amplifications have been traced in the two agencies. There were both similarities and differences between Blau's findings and those of the present writer on the subject of counseling. Study and analysis of these similarities and differences lead to the conclusion that both *external and internal pressures* (local conditions) *affect operations of an organization and create the strain for formal managerial changes.* Market conditions leading to many clients reporting for service, more internal factors such as a scarcity of personnel (hence scarce time) and the budgetary allotment system, as well as the major placement goal of the agency led to formal managerial redefinition at Agency B of counseling procedure in the interest of maximizing placements. But a change in market conditions where jobs for skilled workers were plentiful, time less scarce, and a changed budgetary procedure which paid for counseling activity, led to formal managerial emphasis at Agency C on counselings; the reverse of what had occurred years earlier at a related agency performing the same tasks. Yet this is not all, for the organization was affected not only by local conditions, but also by feelings of personnel. Agency C managerial and supervisory officials formally emphasized counselings, but operating level staff members de-emphasized the reporting of counselings as a result of the various reasons discussed. *Managerial actions and desires do not always lead to attainment of the formal ends,* because *lower level operating personnel informally modify* to meet their own conceptions of work, perceptions of importance, etc.

Reception procedure, formally changed by a new manager at Agency C through requiring use of an occupational demand sheet, was once again informally modified by receptionists. This also lends evidence to the conclusion presented immediately above.

The reappointment date procedure is another illustration of formal and informal modifications of procedure that were brought about by changes in local conditions, and this too follows the conclusions discussed. The wide discrepancy between Blau's finding of "sneaking in," and the later finding showing "sneaking out," is well accounted for by *different local conditions at different points in time.* Local conditions in the form of market conditions and client desires affected the actions of the operating-level bureaucrats who informally modified to meet this constraint; the informal modifications in both cases leading to *managerial amplification* to counteract them. "Sneaking in" at Agency B and "sneaking out" at Agency C also show responsiveness to client desires. This points to flexibility, which belies the stereotype of the operating-level bureaucrat as rigid.

A frequent complaint is that bureaucrats are insensitive to client desires and needs. In both Blau's and the present study this view was found to be incorrect, at least in the cases presented. However, flexible response to demands of clients and informal changes to meet these demands caused officials to deviate dysfunctionally from formal organizational objectives. Good relations were maintained at Agency C in cases where clients were dismissed without service if they so desired, but the unemployment insurance law was being dysfunctionally neglected, as were employers' needs for skilled and scarce workers.[36] This points to the sensitive balance within which this bureaucracy worked. Redefinition which yielded public relations improvement neglected major organizational placement and unemployment insurance goals. Emphasis on organizational goals—for example seating un-

---

[36] It must be emphasized that in many cases good relations were not always maintained with clients because of other constraints, such as pressures of statistical records. This will be discussed in Part Three.

employed clients for interviews to result in referral to jobs when they did not want to work, or giving short reappointment dates at Agency C—led to poor public relations. The bureaucrat here is "damned if he does and damned if he doesn't." Is it any wonder that the word, "bureaucrat" has become a cuss-word?

This chapter and the last pointed to the processes involved in both formal and informal modifications of various types. The next series of chapters will show how statistical records of production were also modified and how this led to extremely dysfunctional consequences.

PART THREE

SOME EFFECTS OF STATISTICAL RECORDING PROCEDURES

> *But actually, he thought as he readjusted the Ministry of Plenty's figures, it was not even forgery. It was merely the substitution of one piece of nonsense for another. Most of the material that you were dealing with had no connection with anything in the real world, not even the kind of connection that is contained in a direct lie. Statistics were just as much a fantasy in their original version as in their rectified version. A great deal of the time you were expected to make them up out of your head.*
>
> —GEORGE ORWELL*

---

* *Nineteen Eighty-Four* (New York: Harcourt, Brace and Co., Inc., 1949), pp. 41-42. Reprinted by permission of Brandt and Brandt.

CHAPTER SIX

Statistical Records

THIS CHAPTER is the first of several dealing with the agency statistical recording procedure and effects.

Early Records

Blau noted that statistical recording procedure in 1948 required only that interviewers report the number of client interviews completed during work operations. These early records are rudimentary in comparison to the more complex records that were later required.

These records led to functional consequences because they pressed officials to work faster, since the number of interviews completed was now visible to superiors who could evaluate their work. According to Blau:

> The supervisor wanted to know the number of interviews completed by each subordinate only in order to take corrective action in case any of them worked too slowly. The fact that the very counting of interviews had induced them to work faster facilitated operations by making such corrective steps superfluous. The use of statistical records not only provided superiors with

information that enabled them to rectify poor performance but often obviated the need for doing so.[1]

These rudimentary records also led to dysfunctional consequences:

Until the beginning of 1948 the number of interviews held per month was the only operation that was statistically counted for each interviewer in Department X. (Although detailed statistical reports were kept in the agency, they were presented only for departments as a whole, not for individuals.) As long as jobs were plentiful during the war, this rudimentary record seemed to suffice. However, when jobs became scarce after the war and time and effort were required to find one for a client, this count of interviews had a detrimental effect on operations. . . .

Except for the information obtained by direct observation, the number of interviews completed by a subordinate was the only evidence the supervisor had at that time for evaluating him. The interviewer's interest in a good rating demanded that he maximize the number of interviews and therefore prohibited spending much time on locating jobs for clients. This rudimentary statistical record interfered with the agency's objective of finding jobs for clients in a period of job scarcity.[2]

The statistical reporting emphasis on the number of interviews completed, caused officials to dysfunctionally neglect important agency goals. "There existed an organizational need for a different evaluation system."[3]

Detailed Statistical Records

A new department head was assigned to Agency B in March 1948. Two months after she had been assigned, she had instituted new performance records. These records were more detailed than the rudimentary records discussed above,

---

[1]Peter M. Blau, *The Dynamics of Bureaucracy* (rev. ed., Chicago: University of Chicago Press, 1963), p. 38. Blau's observations at Agency B took place in 1949. However, he acquired information relating to the previous year, 1948, as well.
[2] *Ibid.*
[3] *Ibid.*

and were issued monthly for the use of all interviewing officials.[4] Agency B interviewers now had to record:

1. The number of interviews held.
2. The number of clients referred to a job.
3. The number of placements . . . made [credited when a referred client was hired by the employer].
4. The proportion of interviews resulting in referrals.
5. The proportion of referrals resulting in placements.
6. The proportion of interviews resulting in placements.
7. The number of notifications sent to the insurance office.
8. The number of application forms made out.[5]

Detailed records were still in use years later at Agency C, but these had been somewhat expanded and changed. Agency C interviewers in 1956 had to report:

1. The number of interviews held.
2. The number of clients referred to jobs.
3. The number of placements (hires) made.
4. The number of notifications of possible disqualifying conditions sent to the unemployment insurance office.
5. The number of application forms made out.

Up to this point, these are the same operations that were recorded by Agency B interviewers in 1949. However, the proportions listed by Blau were not formally required on Agency C records, although supervisory and interviewing officials also considered such proportions. While the proportions were not listed on the records or computed on paper, many officials still were inclined to "compute in their minds" approximately what the proportion was for some of the activities above. This computation was not exact, nor in numbers, but rather in the gross terms of, for example, "*too few* referrals considering the number of interviews conducted." This will be further discussed in Chapter Seven.

Agency C interviewers in 1956 recorded other activities that were not required at Agency B in 1949. These are, to continue with the listing:

---

[4] *Ibid.*, pp. 38-39.
[5] *Ibid.*, p. 39.

6. The number of clients "called-in" to the office for service by use of application cards on file.
7. The number of counseling interviews performed.
8. Telephone solicitations made on the behalf of clients.
9. The number of job vacancies (job orders) received.
10. The number of visits to employers that were made.
11. The number of telephone calls made to employers for promotional purposes.
12. The number of interviews conducted that were "not elsewhere classified."

In addition, interviewers with special assignments had further activities to report. For example, the interviewers providing aptitude tests had to record the number of clients tested.

Thus we see that activities reported on Agency C detailed statistical records in 1956 were well expanded from those required at Agency B in 1949. However, not all of these reported interviewer activities at Agency C received emphasis. For example, the number of "call-ins" made was not emphasized, and officials were inclined to neglect use of application files for calling in applicants to the office for jobs (because of special local conditions).[6] This was despite inclusion on the records. In other words, records had expanded from the time of 1949, but some of the expansion was of recorded activities that were unimportant in local operations and were treated as such by superiors and subordinates. Hence, despite the fact that these activities were listed on records, staff did not emphasize them. This is unlike the functional aspect of the detailed records as abstracted from Blau here and discussed more fully later: "By altering the performance record . . . higher officials can induce lower echelons to change their practices immediately."[7] But under the direction of the new manager in 1959, Agency C detailed records were further modified and the number of activities to be reported was reduced. Vacancies received, telephone solicitations, and clients "called-in" were no longer

---

[6] See page 37 and the discussion on other pages of Chapter Four.
[7] Blau, *Dynamics* . . ., *op. cit.*, p. 43.

to be reported by each interviewer on the detailed production records, although the other nine activities listed above were still required.

The initiation of detailed statistical production (performance) records had functional consequences as observed at Agency B in 1949. First, they led to increased productivity.[8] Blau presents data in proof of this statement, but the Agency C study finds evidence contrary to this. Full discussion of this point is made in the next chapter. Second, statistical records helped facilitate hierarchical control over operating officials. According to Blau:

> Procedures governing operations were often modified when interpreted by lower hierarchical levels. . . . If the department head had relied on rules that showed how qualified clients must be selected for referral, for example, these might have been modified by supervisors, and again by interviewers. The use of the proportion of referred clients who were hired as one element in the evaluation of subordinates enforced careful selection more effectively than rules could, because it identified the interest of interviewers with being selective in their referrals.[9]

Third, these records enabled superiors to institute changes in operations quickly and effectively. New procedures are not always opposed, but sometimes they are, and usually a period of adaptation is required before they become fully effective. By altering the performance record or the relative emphasis on various factors, higher officials can induce lower echelons to change their practices immediately. The introduction of extensive statistical records in Department X illustrates this. . . .[10]

As we have seen, this latter function of statistical records is not fully repeated in the matter of counseling activity for Agency C. Mention has already been made of the fact that there were also some activities that were recorded in quantity on records but were not emphasized by superiors or interviewers. This meant that in these

---

[8]*Ibid.,* pp. 39-43.

[9]*Ibid.,* p. 42. Dysfunctional aspects of the proportion of interviewed clients who were referred to jobs, and of the referred clients who were hired, will be discussed for Agency C in Chapter Seven.

[10]*Ibid.,* p. 43.

cases, contrary to Blau's point, officials were not induced to change their practices in performance of these activities.

In addition, emphasis on the records often did induce lower echelons to change some practices immediately at Agency C, but in a dysfunctional direction! Instead of improving service factors, there was sometimes fabrication made, or cutting corners to "improve" records.

To continue with Blau's discussion:

> Fourth, use of performance records improved the relations between supervisors and interviewers. The supervisor's responsibility for operations required him to criticize subordinates whose performance was inadequate, as a means of improving it. This task was greatly disliked, since such criticism was often resented, and resentful subordinates were less co-operative. Performance records either relieved the supervisors of this duty or reduced the resentment it created. Sometimes they were substituted for verbal criticism. . . . Even if a supervisor actually talked to an interviewer about the ways of improving his performance, the existence of statistical data transformed the nature of these discussions. Instead of telling the interviewer that *he* considered his performance inadequate, the supervisor tried to help him improve his record. Finally, the onus for giving a low rating was partly removed from the supervisor because he could transfer responsibility to the record of the official. Since these records reduced the chances for the development of conflict and antagonism, they made possible a more cordial and co-operative relationship between subordinates and their supervisor. [11]

This was not repeated at Agency C. Some practices of supervisors (see the next section and others) caused some ill feeling between supervisors and subordinates. Overemphasis of supervisors on "statistics" rather than on the service the statistics were designed to measure, also caused dysfunctions.

Blau also did not find that these detailed statistical performance records were completely functional but found some dysfunctional consequences too. He presented a case where a supervisor disregarded the high production records of a subordinate when rating him. The performance records

---

[11] *Ibid.* Italics in the original.

of this interviewer had at one time been outstanding, but after the low rating of his superior, his productivity fell, remaining at a low level even after a new supervisor had been assigned. This official had been expecting a rating based on his good performance as indicated on the detailed records of production. When the previous supervisor disregarded the records in the personnel rating of his subordinate, he antagonized an interviewer, and also destroyed the effectiveness of the detailed statistical records as incentives for work. This was not only in relation to the immediate supervisor's action, but also carried over into relationships of this official with another superior to whom he had been assigned at a later date.[12]   Similar inefficient administration in relation to use of records as a basis for personnel ratings also was repeated in cases at Agency C.

Competition as a Dysfunctional Consequence of Detailed Statistical Records

Another dysfunctional consequence resulting from the use, or perhaps we should say *misuse,* of detailed records that Blau reported derived from the resulting overpreoccupation with productivity, which led to competition. At Agency B this was found to be ". . . the most serious dysfunction of statistical reports," because interpersonal relationships between interviewers were affected.[13] Competition did occur at Agency C too, but was certainly not as prevalent as at Blau's agency, nor as serious.

The stress toward maximization of placement figures on records led to dysfunctional competition in the form of monopolization and hiding of job orders and created antagonisms between Agency B interviewers.[14] If a job order

---

[12] *Ibid.,* pp. 44-45.

[13] *Ibid.,* p. 46.

[14] *Ibid.,* pp. 46-47, and pp. 57-81. It should be mentioned that some cooperative practices *did* develop in one section at Agency B, unlike the observations Blau made for another section which was the highly competitive one. The

(continued)

is hidden by the official receiving it from an employer, then only he can fill the opening for placement credit, rather than allowing co-workers a chance. This means that suitable clients may leave the agency without a job referral even though a vacancy exists, because of a chance appearance at an interviewer's desk who does not have such an opening, rather than at the desk of the person hiding it. According to formal procedure, the order was to have been placed in a common file, open to the use of all officials.

Such competition was not as frequent an occurrence at Agency C as it was at the B locale, although different kinds of competition did occur. The difference seems to have come about as a result, among other things, of several changed conditions in time, and the different skill-levels of clients serviced in the two agencies. In 1949, according to Blau, there were many more clients available for jobs than there were vacancies. Jobs were difficult to find, but the statistical records emphasized placement productivity. In such a situation some officials felt the need for monopolization of those few job orders that were available. This was to obtain the statistical referral and placement credit involved, which was difficult to attain because of local market conditions. At the C locale, monopolization of orders for most occupational categories was unnecessary, for it was the skilled client and not the job that was in demand.

Agency C officials rarely monopolized orders for skilled clients because this would have been a useless practice for the end of raising production figures. In fact, they sometimes did the opposite by helping their colleagues find openings for clients. However, competition for scarce job orders for *unskilled clients* was not completely unknown at Agency C. Local conditions affect bureaucratic behavior. At Agency B there was a demand for jobs, and at Agency C a demand for skilled clients. This was reflected in the generally different

difference was due, according to Blau, to structural differences between Agency B sections. Cooperative norms had developed in one section and this made competitive practices ineffective there. See his pp. 63-74.

actions of the officials at the two study locales.

Another reason for the difference in the two agencies is that the Agency B department Blau studied serviced mainly unskilled clients while Agency C served mostly skilled clients. In times of job scarcity, positions requiring little skill and training are generally more difficult to obtain than are vacancies for skilled workers. As mentioned, if monopolization occurred at all at Agency C, it was likely to be for unskilled job vacancies, which were still rather scarce in relation to client demand.[15]

Competition for Clients

There was great competition in a section at Blau's locale for job orders, but this was not completely so at Agency C, as has been discussed. However, there was a de-

---

[15] The total Agency B locale in 1956-59, ten years after Blau's study, was *still* known by officials for a greater degree of competitive practices than at Agency C at the same date, even though skilled clients were now in demand at *both* branches. There may be some pervasive structural differences at both agencies accounting for this continued difference in amount of competition engaged in by staff. Agency B officials during the years of 1950-60, for example, worked under a special quantitative evaluation system where different operations as reported on individual statistical records received various point scores (and weights) according to quantity. The desire to make many points, which reflects an official's value to upper levels, might lead staff toward a high level of competition.

Yet, according to the Agency B management:

"It [the point scoring system] was an evaluation devise [sic] to measure quantitative achievement. It was never considered as a device to induce staff to maximize production.

" . . . [this] individual quantitative achievement was introduced in this office [Agency B] in 1950 and was used in one section for a period of two years. In 1952 its use was extended throughout the entire office. [It was discontinued in 1961.]" (From a letter to the author by the bureau commissioner, top state-level official of the bureaucracy. The information above was sent to the commissioner's office by the Agency B management in response to questions about various Agency B operations.)

According to the Agency B management, the scoring scheme was *not meant* to be a device to maximize production, but this seems to have occurred despite managerial intent. Perhaps this led in part to the continued high level of competition at Agency B. Agency C did not operate under such a point system, and operations were merely recorded in quantity on the daily performance records.

gree of competition for what can be called "easier" *clients* at Agency C.[16] This was in response to the demand for skilled clients (as well as the desire for increased job satisfaction), rather than demand for job openings for skilled workers.[17]

Officials generally were supposed to interview clients in the order of their arrival, but sometimes delayed or speeded work, as necessary, in order to interview an "easier" client, thereby avoiding a recognized "difficult" case. Sometimes work was delayed in an entire section while officials busied themselves with "papers" and stretched interviews, trying to avoid a recognized difficult case, until one unfortunate interviewer could no longer stretch his work and had to interview the client.

Clients complained at delays, and also when some officials went a step further, calling "easy" clients outside the order of time at which they arrived, and hence ahead

---

[16] There are no quantitative data that can be presented in proof, but it appears from careful matching of the author's experiences as a participant with Blau's report, that Agency C competition for clients was still not as great as that described for job orders at an Agency B section.

[17] Blau's data offer no extensive information on whether or not officials at Agency B competed for clients as well as for job orders. However, some inferences can be made from his work. For example, one Agency B respondent explained: "I always *try* to see non-benefit applicants. *Most people* [interviewers] *prefer* them . . . because they want to work." (Blau, *op. cit.,* p. 91. Italics added.) As shall be seen above, Agency C interviewers also tried to interview nonbenefit applicants which sometimes led to competition for these more satisfying contacts, and easier interviews. Perhaps such competition also occurred at Agency B.

Blau also did make the observation that extreme competition for *job orders* occurred at the department he studied. However: "It did not occur in other departments, in which interviewers also competed for making the best records, but not for job openings, since each handled a different occupational category, and there were no common pools of job orders." (*Ibid.,* p. 60.) There were, in other words, differences in the degree and kind of competition between different departments at Agency B. (Perhaps one kind of competition at departments other than the one studied by Blau was that of competition for clients.) Different conditions at Agencies B and C, as has been seen, can also account for the differential degree and type of competition observed at the two locales.

Blau has written (in a personal communication to the author) that there were other forms of competition at his locale, in addition to the monopolization of job orders: ". . . there was some competition by trying to avoid difficult clients as well as in various other ways . . . ." (Letter dated October 3, 1961.)

of other waiting workers. This meant that colleagues had to interview the more difficult cases that were left. Interpersonal relationships between bureaucrats were affected when officials became annoyed at one another for these competitive practices.

This competition for clients was related not only to the desire to increase production listed on statistical records, but also for increased job satisfaction. Difficult clients were often argumentative, and caused other frustrating difficulties which made dealing with them a harrowing experience.

Emphasis on Quantity and Supervisory Reception Sifting Policy

Supervisors were trying to maintain good sectional statistical records, referring to high-level production credited by their staff. This was because each supervisor was rated in good part by his own superior, the manager, on productivity of all interviewers combined in his section.

Superiors often forced reception officials to "put more through," meaning to seat more clients of all kinds for interviews. This demand, aimed at increasing productivity, was sometimes made even if few employment vacancies were available for specific client groups.

When many clients were waiting for service, the supervisor often relieved the official at the reception counter; the reception official now performing interviewing tasks and reducing the backlog of clients. The supervisor, temporarily acting as receptionist, tended to seat even more clients for interviews without reference to service that could be given, in an attempt to maximize statistical production figures. The number of interviews, and not reception counter service, counted on statistical production records.

Visibility (to the manager) of sectional production on statistical records and production goals set for his section, caused the supervisor to want many clients seated for interviews, often without complete reference to the organizational placement and unemployment insurance goals. To be sure, some workers for whom service was possible were seated. However, the goals of the reception sifting procedure to limit the flow of clients to those who could be serviced in the time available was being neglected where others were seated without regard to service factors, but only in the hope of maximization of production figures.

At the extreme, sometimes so many people waited that all seats in the waiting area were filled and some clients had to stand until called for an interview. With a large backlog of clients, the superior appealed for help to the manager, asking him to send interviewers on loan from other sections. These officials could help reduce the backlog. When this was done, the supervisor had more interviewers and therefore more production for the records of his section.

In this way interviewers were taken from their sections where they might have better been able to provide needed services, to handle another section's clients, many of whom should have been dismissed according to procedure at the reception counter with reappointment dates. A supervisor was thus able to maximize his own records at the expense of the other sectional superior's records.

Other superiors also "stuffed their boxes," which in agency argot meant seating more clients than could be efficiently interviewed. If many clients were waiting in other sections, these superiors also could demand help from the manager, asking for temporary loans of interviewers. At the least, a large number of waiting people served as justification for section supervisors *not* to lend interviewers to other sections. Superiors were frequently observed jockeying for position at rush periods by seating more clients than necessary, and then attempting to take interviewers from other sections on loan, while the other supervisors tended to point to the fact that they too had many applicants waiting and could not provide help. Supervisors and managers walked from one section reception counter to another at these times, "weighing" in their hands the number of client booklets in each intake box (which referred to the number waiting for interviews). This was done without reference to quality of service that could be given, but rather to quantity, i.e., the total *number* waiting. Managers then tried to allocate staff accordingly.

This supervisory action was dysfunctional because it wasted the time of clients and staff for the sake of supervisory competition, a far cry from the original aims of statistical production records. This practice also removed officials from the service of those who might have really needed help. However, functional ends were gained when one segment of the clothing industry was on layoff, overloading one section with work, while other segments were still at full employment, and few clients were reporting. In such situations it occurred that in one section interviewers worked frantically to keep up with the rush, while other interviewers in other sections had little if anything to do. Where loans were made under these conditions, functional results followed. The dysfunctional results occurred when the supervisor "stuffed the box," merely to be able to request extra interviewers and improve his sectional statistics at the expense of the co-superior's statistical totals. When many supervisors engaged in this activity at the same time, and conditions were rushed, many clients waited lengthy periods for interviews, for no reason except to maximize agency statistical records.

Reaction of Interviewing Officials to Supervisory "Box Stuffing"

Interviewing officials were not oblivious to this supervisory action. When supervisors seated too many clients, officials modified their interviewing activity in response. "Stuffing the box" caused a great backlog of people waiting for interviews and this put pressure on officials to work faster. Deliberate slowdowns resulted when it became evident that the faster one worked, the more people there were waiting for service because of the supervisor's reception sifting policy.

Various dilatory tactics were employed. Clients were engaged in personal conversation. An official searched the files of all sections, stopping to consult with colleagues, even though he knew no jobs were available for the particular client. Some engaged in personal telephone calls, pretending they were speaking to employers or conducting official business. Many other delaying tactics were engaged in and the backlog grew, while clients fidgeted and milled about, waiting impatiently to be called for interviews.

Clients complained sharply when they realized that no service could be performed for them but they were still required to wait for long periods of time for interviews. These complaints caused some interviewers who were already angry at the supervisor for his reception sifting behavior to react accordingly with hostility or annoyance. Brusque treatment of the clients sometimes followed, especially when officials were pressured in rush periods, for this tended to fray tempers over and above supervisory or client actions. This was one element making for antagonisms between applicants and staff. This antagonism added to client hostility caused by the desire of some to be "sneaked out," which had been thwarted by the supervisor's reception behavior.

Many complaints were also directed at the receptionist (the supervisor in this situation), and thus he too was subjected to hostility.[18]

---

[18]This description above focuses on supervisory action when the superior filled in for interviewers at the reception counter. There were some officials who tried to impress superiors or who were strict conformists to procedures, fearing unlike the majority of their colleagues to informally deviate from supervisory requests. These nonsupervisory officials frequently engaged in practices similar to that described above and with the same results.

Sometimes the supervisor's presence near the reception counter caused even flexible reception interviewers to seat more clients than necessary in order to meet supervisory demands. In such cases colleagues tried to dispense with some of these "excess" clients by interviewing them rapidly in succession with no attempt at service. Poor statistical referral records which then resulted were often manipulated, as will be discussed in the next chapter.

Restrictive practices occurred when this rapid "interviewing" still did not serve to reduce the client load because the superior still hovered near the reception counter and the reception official was forced to seat more clients. This restric-

The superior could not effectively speed his sub-ordinates' work because interviews naturally varied in length of time, depending on problems of the client. The supervisor knew he had seated difficult people for inter-views, and as a result there was nothing he could do except "sweat out" the numerous barbed assaults.

The supervisor had one additional worry when the time of day approached noon, for if the backlog of applicants could not be serviced completely before the lunch period for staff, he would be left with a group of complaining people who would not be serviced until his staff returned from lunch one hour later. If he requested his staff to remain during the lunch hour to service those waiting, the sub-ordinates would still require a full lunch-time period, and he would be left with insufficient personnel to handle the one o'clock rush. These worries, if he could not secure enough extra help, obliged the superior to dismiss more without service, and hence the staff "fixed" the supervisor for his activities, at the same time reducing the amount of work they had to do.

At such a point it tended to occur that all clients re-porting were dismissed, because there were too many already waiting. Applicants who could have been serviced because they had skills that employers desired were also dismissed haphazardly, only because others had earlier been hap-hazardly seated for interviews. Sometimes there were still

---

tion also troubled the supervisor, for clients complained about waiting too long, and it was his duty to maintain proper operations and calm the ire of more agitated clients.

When nonsupervisory officials seated too many without the superior's presence, restrictive practices also tended to follow. When too many clients were waiting, the supervisor often relieved the official at the reception counter, so the official could interview; this in turn meaning that he had to interview some of the very same difficult clients he had seated while he was the receptionist. Since this was unpleasant, there was always a constraint for the reception official to try to avoid "stuffing the box." This led some receptionists to dismiss more clients, and to such an extent, that restrictive interviewer practices (to be discussed on other pages) were furthered. Other receptionists, however, were less affected by col-league pressures, and still "stuffed the box" to meet the superior's demand.

too many waiting in spite of the supervisor's dismissals, and the hour was very close to the lunch period. At such times the officials tended to interview these clients very quickly and carelessly only to be finished in time for lunch. In this situation clients had been kept waiting only to be rushed through interviews which turned out to be worthless.

Reception sifting procedure was being redefined in order to maximize production figures. Had the formal reception sifting procedure been followed, service would have been increased, public relations more completely maintained, and records could have been legitimately maximized. These informal changes caused deviation from service goals, and eventual restriction of output by staff, sometimes sacrificing the maximization of figures on records originally desired through the informal supervisory redefinition.

Conclusions

In this chapter we have traced the origin of statistical records at Agencies B and C, and have seen the transformation of statistical records toward dysfunctional ends. The "dynamics of bureaucracy" became "demonics of bureaucracy" and were adversely affecting client service, whereas the original change intended improved service to clients through better agency operations. There was "too much of a good thing" here; that is, supervisors and interviewers were interested in production, but became so highly interested in it that they forgot the original aims of the procedure. "Stuffing the box" is an example. There was a displacement of goals where "an instrumental value becomes a terminal value."[19] Statistical records, figures and recording procedure, instrumental to attainment of service-oriented goals, became terminal values; ends in and of themselves. Yet these are only hints of the final results of modifications of statistical recording procedure. The following chapters

---

[19]Robert K. Merton, *Social Theory and Social Structure* (rev. ed., Glencoe: Free Press, 1957), p. 199.

trace numerous other dysfunctional consequences, which are so extreme in nature that they actually match quotations from George Orwell's fictional *Nineteen Eighty-Four.* Statistics did turn out to be ". . . just as much a fantasy in their original version as in their rectified version," and, "a great deal of the time . . . [interviewers] *were* expected to make them up out of . . . [their] head[s]."[20]

---

[20]George Orwell, *Nineteen Eighty-Four* (New York: Harcourt, Brace and Co., Inc., 1949), pp. 41-42. Reprinted by permission of Brandt and Brandt. Italics added.

CHAPTER SEVEN

Activities Reported on Detailed
Statistical Records of Production

> *As the best mill in the world will not extract*
> *wheat flour from alfalfa, so pages of admin-*
> *istrative statistics will not provide reliable*
> *information from loose or invalid data. Valid*
> *data on . . . [statistical forms] are absolutely*
> *essential if these data are to be useful in*
> *planning, directing, controlling, and eval-*
> *uating local office operations or for release*
> *to the public.**

THE LAST CHAPTER traced the history and some effects
of agency statistical records. This chapter focuses more in-
tensively on detailed statistical counts by analyzing effects
of this procedure on some of the *activities* reported. We
shall see how emphasis on production quantity in various

---

* From a Federal-level Employment Bureau Handbook on Statistical Reporting.

operations reported on the statistical records led to a whole series of informal practices that not only distorted the records, but also adversely affected the actual operations performed.

Crediting of Placements at Agency C

One of the major organizational goals of an employment agency is to provide for the *placement* of applicants in jobs. Superiors considered placement figures recorded in quantity on the detailed statistical records as an important indicator of an interviewer's value as a staff member, and this reflected a major organizational goal. Emphasis on maximization of placement figures was relayed to subordinates who were anxious if their placement records were too low. This emphasis and visibility of work on records led to an informal practice called "broken needle" placements.

Clients claiming skill as machine operators were referred to clothing firms and tended to receive a job trial, perhaps of ten or fifteen minutes at the employer's establishment as a test of ability. An inexperienced worker could be expected not to do well on the job test, and as a result likely either spoiled the test garment, broke the needle of the machine, or in other ways showed lack of sufficient skill.

Interviewers generally checked results of agency referrals through telephone calls to employers, where each client referred was identified, and the interviewer asked whether or not a hire resulted. If the client was hired and had worked, the official took placement credit and this was recorded on statistical forms according to established formal procedure.

When a client was not hired, the importance of a good placement record pressured some interviewers to probe, questioning further instead of accepting an employer report of "no hire."

"Did the applicant work *at all*?"

If the applicant was not hired, but was merely given a job test, the employer tended to reply that the client did not work, because a job test of a few minutes was not "work," nor a hire in the usual sense of the words. However, this was still insufficient for some interviewers who wanted to maximize their placement records.

"Did you *try* her at all?" was the query that tended to follow.

If the employer gave the client a job test, he answered in the affirmative, but tended to say, "I tried her for a few minutes, but she was unsuitable." He might add, "She broke the needle," or, "She ruined the [test] garment."

The interviewer thanked the employer, promised an attempt to find another applicant for him, and terminated the telephone conversation.

Credit was then taken for a placement, which formally meant that the applicant was hired! The interviewer placed a notation on the job order referral form, to the effect that the client had worked for a short time but was not especially suitable. Placement credit was thus recorded when the client had only been provided with a *job trial lasting several minutes*. This was called a "broken needle" placement.

The term "broken needle" derives from the taking of placement credit when the client did no more than break the needle of the machine in a job test. Breaking the needle because of insufficient skill was only one of many reasons for lack of hire, but the term, "broken needle," was adopted into informal agency argot, and it meant *any* placement credit taken for *any* extremely short job trial.

An exact count of the number of "broken needle" placements credited is not available. However, participant-observation leads to the conclusion that the crediting of "broken needle" placements was widespread. Additional evidence comes from the fact that a special term was created in agency argot to refer to this practice; the concept in this case implying the action. Some interviewers used this practice much more often than others, but most interviewers were known to only occasionally credit such "place-ments," the action of all interviewers in this regard taken together making the practice widespread.

The job order appeared to be "filled" when a "broken needle" placement was credited, but the employer, unless he had hired someone else from another source, still desired another worker. In reality a vacancy remained even though a "hire" was credited, and thus the interviewer was led to modify once again in order to solve this discrepancy. He reopened the job order, crediting the agency with receipt of *another* vacancy, which was also listed on statistical records, and in this way vacancy figures as well as placement figures were inflated.

Budgetary appropriations, the number of interviewers assigned to the agency, and other matters were to be desig-nated in good part by upper-level officials according to agency placement records. Statistical records, which ideally could have given an accurate picture of agency activities to upper echelons, led to "broken needle" crediting when place-ment quantity was emphasized by superiors.

The Blau Findings: Improved Placement Operations: Application to Agency C

Blau found that the introduction of detailed records at Agency B in 1948 had unintended consequences (e.g., competitive practices). The present findings replicate Blau's on this general level, for Agency C records in 1956-59 also had unintended consequences in the form of a whole host of illegitimate, informal practices by personnel. [1]

Blau, however, also presents data to show that, "The introduction of these [detailed statistical] records improved placement operations [at Agency B] considerably."[2] This, if

---

[1] Some such practices have already been discussed. Other informal practices will be traced further.

[2] Peter M. Blau, *The Dynamics of Bureaucracy* (rev. ed., Chicago: University of Chicago Press, 1963), p. 39.

TABLE 1

PLACEMENT RESULTS PRIOR TO AND AFTER THE
INTRODUCTION OF DETAILED PERFORMANCE
RECORDS AT DEPARTMENT X STUDIED BY BLAU [3]

	Job Openings (No.)	Placements (No.)	Jobs Filled (Per Cent)
2 months without records (January and February, 1948)	3,944	2,159	55
2 months with records (March and April, 1948)	3,425	2,286	67

it refers to *actual* operations, and not to statistical *figures* only, shows a functional consequence of the new records. Professor Blau's data leading to his conclusion are presented in Table 1.

Blau's findings agree with the Agency C study results on the general level of unintended consequences, but on an empirical level Blau's interpretation that the detailed records improved placement operations considerably cannot fully be applied to Agency C. Based on observations made at Agency C, there were good reasons why placement and other figures *could have appeared higher in numbers* even though they were not so in *real* employment service to

---

[3] *Ibid.* The writer has also referred to Agency B 1948 records of operations, and data found do not completely match the figures listed by Blau above. While Blau lists 3,944 openings in the period without records, the figure found by this writer reads 3,780. Blau's placement figure for the period without records is 2,159 whereas the writer finds 2,149. The revised figure for placements in the period with records reads 2,277 but Blau's reads 2,286. This means that whereas Blau's original data indicate a 55 per cent figure in jobs filled, the data found by the present author show 57 per cent for the period without the records. Blau finds a 67 per cent jobs-filled figure for the period after the initiation of detailed records, whereas the revised figures yield 66 per cent. Therefore, while Blau finds a 12 per cent difference in jobs filled between the two periods significant at the .01 level *(Ibid.,* p. 40, footnote five), the present writer finds a 9 per cent difference. This is also significant at the .01 level.

clients and employers. This refers to observed Agency C interviewer practices which included cutting corners in placement activity, inflation of figures, informally reduced standards of definition of the term, "placement" (e.g., "broken needle" placements), and emphasis on "former employer" placements where clients were only "referred" back to their *own* jobs until roughly 50 per cent of placements and openings credited were of this latter type (to be discussed fully in Chapter Nine).

The implication is not that Blau's analysis based on the data he collected is invalid, although there are some problems in interpretation which we shall soon see. His observations were made at an earlier date and this present study covers 1956-59 in a related, but yet different local agency. Therefore, differences in observations may be a result of a changed time and place. The issue is that we cannot place faith in *Agency C* records to prove increased "real" production because of many inflations; one which has been discussed, and others which are yet to be discussed.

Blau made a similar observation, even at Agency B, for he noted that a recurring interviewer comment in relation to the records in 1949 was, "Figures can't lie, but liars can figure."[4]

It is significant that evidence of falsification appeared even shortly after the initiation of detailed records. From Blau's observations:

Interviewers had reacted to the introduction of performance records with hostility and continued to dislike them vehemently. . . . The main reason for their antagonism against quantitative criteria of performance was often voiced by interviewers in forceful language:
"The worst thing about these records is that they create

---

[4] *Ibid.,* p. 45. An interviewer at Agency C made a similar comment to the author in 1956: "This [the job of interviewer] is a numbers game." He was referring to the importance placed on, and the manipulation of numbers on statistical records.

competition between interviewers to an extent that is—disgusting. . . . They lead to competition and to outright falsification. I don't say that all do that, but it happens. . . ."[5]

An interesting addition to this 1949 statement by an Agency B interviewer is that in 1959 an official in City X (at an agency other than B or C) was charged with fabricating some placement records completely. It was substantiated that this official recorded hires when in actuality she was not responsible for them. This is discussed further in Chapter Ten.

There are questions that must be asked in reference to Blau's figures: How much of the Agency B increase in production was due to inflations and falsification (including possible practices similar to Agency C "broken needle" placements)? How much of the increase was due to a real increase in terms of service-oriented formal objectives, i.e., finding real jobs for unemployed people? These questions cannot be fully answered in reference to data available.

There are also problems connected with use of agency records. Employment service in general, and the clothing industries agencies in particular, are highly dependent in operations on economic and seasonal factors. This is a confounding variable in analysis of agency records of operations, especially when one wants to compare operations in one period with another in relation to determining various "efficiency counts." For example, Blau noted an increase in placement production after the initiation of detailed records at his Department X when "jobs filled" is taken as the criterion. However, the periodical listing agency records of operations in 1948 noted the following:

Despite seasonal curtailment of activity in the manufacture of women's clothing, placements in the apparel industry rose from 8,149 in February to 9,280 in March. . . . With some exceptions, *all other industries registered gains in placements*

---

[5] *Ibid.,* pp. 46-47.

during the month. [6]

In other words, there were gains in placements on an industry-wide basis in March, which evidently reflected more general economic or seasonal trends for the apparel, as well as for other industries, rather than only increased placement operations at Blau's Department X. If this is so, and if his figures cover such a period of rising placements on an industry-wide basis, then the effects of the change to detailed statis‛ical records cannot be completely separated from more general economic and seasonal trends. [7] But on the other hand, it cannot be determined how much less the rise would have been (even in a period of rising employment) if Agency B interviewers had been working *without* the detailed records; that is, if they were not pressured to maximize production.

Blau also purposely used "jobs-filled" percentages instead of only placements in absolute numbers in order to hold seasonal factors constant. [8] The number of openings received ideally would be thought to reflect seasonal and economic factors, and *determining the percentage of job openings filled should take this factor into account.* Yet job orders received can decrease because of *heavy seasonal activity* (meaning that most positions are filled to handle full production), but employers can be more desperate in the desire to secure needed workers for those few openings that they might not have yet been able to fill. Hence placements can be easier to make, accounting for an increased

---

[6] From a March 1948 governmental publication listing agency records of operations. Italics are added.

[7] This is so unless all agencies in State X changed to detailed records at the same time as Blau's Department X, which might really be the causal factor of an industry-wide rise of placements, instead of economic and seasonal factors only. This however, does not seem likely, although the possibility cannot be completely dismissed without further information on this point, which is difficult to obtain.

It should also be mentioned that this discussion above, indicating that placements were on the rise, and Blau's data, are based on *1948* figures. The reader is cautioned not to confuse this with the date that Blau was actually in observation, which was *1949*.

[8] See Blau, *Dynamics. . ., op. cit.,* p. 39.

placement total at the same time that there is a decreased number of openings received, and without effects of detailed records.

This discussion can be extended with further points in favor of Blau's conclusion, as well as against. However, much of this would approach triviality, for Agency B records do show an increase when "jobs filled" is used as an index, and this could be due, if even partially, to the records. In addition, Blau himself realized the possibility of falsification of figures when he quoted from the interviewer at Agency B.

Suffice it to say then, that Blau seems to have a point. However, Blau's conclusion of increased placement production cannot be applied to Agency C records in terms of real service-oriented increases in 1956-59 without some caution as well as skepticism (because of observed illegitimate practices). Skepticism, it should be indicated, is known as a healthy sign in scientific endeavors.

Quality of Placements: An Amplification at Agency C

The discussion thus far has been on the subject of quantity of placements recorded on the records. Blau made the observation that statistical records at Agency B:

> . . . may be criticized . . . for disregarding the quality of placements made; workers can be sent to and hired for jobs that are more or less suitable for them. It should be noted that the neglect of this factor was due not to the technical limitations of quantification (without denying that such limitations exist) but to a policy decision. It would be simple, and not very expensive, to measure some aspect of placement quality, for example, by ascertaining over the telephone whether clients still hold their jobs after three months and whether they have received any wage raise. The reason that this was not done was an explicit or implicit administrative decision that the cost of obtaining this information outweighed the contribution it would make to operations.[9]

---

[9] *Ibid.*, p. 42, footnote 7.

Agency procedure had been amplified to meet the void Blau discusses. At Agency C, supervisors were required by procedure to check a sample of filled job orders by telephoning employers several months after a hire was recorded to determine if the employee was still at work; and hence to determine quality of placements. This amplification in the ideal would have taken notice of "broken needle" placements which are certainly of a different level of quality than long term hires lasting several months. However, some supervisors modified informally in this case, which served to negate the amplification. Interviewers consistently crediting poor quality placements were not distinguished for corrective action.

Some supervisors, instead of randomly choosing orders themselves for checking, asked selected interviewers to choose several filled order forms from the files. The interviewers, of course, could be expected to choose those that they thought were of good quality and to eliminate the obviously poorer quality hires. [10] This biased sample was checked and recordings were made in the superiors' books.

There were some supervisors who were not observed to have informally modified the procedure this way.[11] However, in all cases, it was never observed in three years of participation, that a supervisor once brought poor quality of placements (measured by length of hire, or suitability of job for client) to an interviewer's attention for correction of interviewing and referral techniques.

The supervisor was led to emphasize quantity of placements, because these were recorded on production records and were visible to managers and other upper-level officials.

---

[10] One supervisor was observed by the author choosing orders himself, but selecting them in a biased manner, e.g., first eliminating placements that appeared to be of low quality. In defense of this superior's actions, it could be that he was eliminating these obviously poor hires first, so that he would not have to waste his time checking when poor quality was visible even before the telephone call to the employer.

[11] This is not to say that this practice was never engaged in by these supervisors, but only that the author never saw or heard of such action by them.

Quality of placements as determined by the supervisory checking was recorded on the superior's books but not on the visible production records. Thus a low quantity of placements led to corrective action by the supervisor, but poor quality did not receive his attention. Checking procedure was thus overtly followed, but little importance was attached to it in actual supervisory operations.

It was also easy for the superior and subordinates to place blame for poor quality of hires on clients instead of on staff, and there was an element of truth here. This was because the clothing industry suffered many layoffs, and in addition many clothing workers were females who were secondary wage earners with major interest outside the work field. Both industry and clientele made for sporadic employment. Thus where placements did not last long, it could easily, and in quite a few cases validly be blamed on the special characteristics of the clients and industry rather than on the officials. This may be a reason other than agency emphasis on quantity of placements for lesser importance attached to this supervisory checking procedure.

Auditing

Quality was not overlooked on the formal level, for there was another officially designated method of checking it at Agency C. This was called the *auditing procedure* where supervisors were required to periodically sit in on interviews of their staff members, and to fill out a rating form for the various phases of operations that they observed.[12]

In the ideal, this procedure aimed at the functional end of supervisory control over interviewing methods, quality, and related matters, but in actuality these ends were not

---

[12] This rating form is not the same as the *personnel rating*. The personnel rating covered all aspects of the interviewer's work, was a *total* rating, and a copy was given to the interviewer at the end of every rating period. The audit form was for the supervisor's own use, generally was not seen by the interviewer, but was more like a "worksheet" for note taking.

attained. There were several reasons for this. First, officials did not perform their work in the manner that they always did when the superior audited, and indeed, the mere presence of a superior nearby even without an audit caused some officials to modify their usual working behavior closer to the formally required procedures. Therefore, many informal changes could not be determined through the audit. Second, this procedure had a deleterious effect on the officials' sense of professional pride since the majority had college degrees, and felt qualified to perform the work without the checking, but still periodically had to undergo observation. Third, the presence of the superior at the interview often affected either the client or the official, and frequently both. In the attempt to be careful, and because of nervousness, officials sometimes erred where they would not have done so in actual operations. When some clients saw the civil servant being observed by an authority and under pressure, they too sometimes began to press toward matters and requests that they normally would not have made, which made interviewing more difficult. Fourth, certain informal modifications, necessary and functional for efficient work under local conditions, could not be made in the supervisor's presence, causing problems for the official at the very time he wanted to make a good showing. Finally, some supervisors were overly cautious and some made many criticisms which most officials felt were trifling. Although some officials argued points with their superiors, others accepted all criticism but neglected and conveniently "forgot" all remarks when the auditing was completed.

The audit uncovered immediate lack of knowledge of certain procedures, but still generally did not improve quality. This is because some informal modifications were necessary under special local conditions on the operating level, and these were resumed after the audit, as were the informal methods of work that pressed toward poor quality. In addition, the frequent supervisory demands for high quantity reported on statistical records served to override remarks made on the matter of quality (in this case referring to interviewing techniques). It should be mentioned that the audit itself also pressed toward quantity, for supervisors expected interviewers to work rapidly, interviewing and placing as many clients as possible. Auditing records were kept in the supervisor's desk, and did not receive the more public attention that records of production quantity received. We see that the pressures toward quantity again served to override the formally prescribed attempts at quality control.

An Overview: The Role of the Budgetary Process and Personnel Ratings in Pressures Toward Maximization of Placement Quantity

According to the 1959 report of a governmental investigating commission:

> The central factor determining the size of the Employment Bureau's budgetary allocation, within the overall Congressional appropriation, are the accomplishments in four "pay item" activities in the prior year or two: new applications, testing, counselling and job placements.[13]

It is clear that the number of placements made by the Employment Bureau is the single most important factor (of the factors subject to its control) in determining the size of its budget. There is no evidence of an inordinate stress on making placements; this would be frowned upon by the Bureau of Employment. But the high quantitative level sought in times of crisis comes to be regarded as an expected level in normal times.[14]

The "crisis" factor derives from the history of the bureaucracy. This shows the importance of time and historical factors in molding bureaucratic operations.

---

[13] From a governmental report not cited in full in order to preserve anonymity of the research locale. There are eight separate reports to the series from which data have been taken. All are cited as from the same total report, without listing the individual titles which would be meaningless to the reader since he lacks the full source and citation for reference.

[14] *Ibid.*

During the greatest part of its existence the public employment system in the United States has functioned not in "normal" times but in times of crisis: war, on the one hand; depression and recession on the other. Under both circumstances, it is important to match as many applicants with jobs as possible. In times of war and a tight labor market, the employer is delighted to get workers. In times of a loose labor market, the worker is eager to obtain a job. Thus for the largest part of its history the public employment system has been under great pressure to place people, over and above the inherent tendency of any placement service to do so.[15]

The budgetary process, historical factors; indeed, a major organizational goal of the agency, all have bearing on stress toward maximization of placement figures. In turn, the personnel evaluation system also stresses placements:

Officially, Employment Bureau personnel evaluation is based in large measure upon quality of performance. No one is ever fired only because he has fallen down in making placements. But the annual and interim, as well as the unofficial, ratings cannot disregard the number of placements an interviewer makes, since these are regarded as the ultimate goal of an employment service.

There is evidence of an unwritten, unspoken "quota" of placements to be made which is the backbone of the Employment Bureau.[16]

This quota is pegged unofficially to the placement figures considered necessary in times of crisis. Thus agency officials feel obliged to maintain critical level placement totals even when local conditions no longer lead to such activity.

The investigating commission reports:

. . . it is apparent that both the budget procedure and the personnel evaluation system used by the Employment Bureau create pressures on many of its professional employees to make placements.[17]

---

[15] *Ibid.*

[16] *Ibid.* This quotation ends with reference to effects of this quota on temptations of interviewers to discriminate in referral of applicants. The discrimination issue is extensively discussed in Chapter Ten.

[17] *Ibid.*

The commission also notes:

Many State [X] Employment Bureau interviewers and senior interviewers [supervisors] report feeling pressure toward quantity of placements to a degree which may cause them to neglect other aspects of the job. . . .[18]

A major organizational goal of the agency was to make placements. The budgetary procedure, personnel ratings and statistical records were all related and reflected this emphasis. However, unofficial quotas and the managerial desire to maintain high placement totals, even when local conditions made this impossible, pressured officials who in turn modified reporting procedure, emphasized easy placements, and cut corners to the detriment of the generic organizational placement, as well as other goals.[19] This is tied to the officials' desires to avoid trouble and to achieve job satisfaction. "Sneaking out" clients, for example, might lead to a reduced placement total. However, the interviewer could emphasize easier and sometimes needless placements to maintain his "figures," at the same time that he avoided conflict with difficult clients and engaged in "sneaking out." [20] There are indications here that placement figures in quantity became more important than service to clients.

Control Over Staff: Constraints Making Officials Desire High Records of Production

Interviewers were pressured to maintain a high quantity of production reported on the records, and supervisors were pressed from above to show a good total sectional record of production. Mere production stress, or in other words,

---

[18] *Ibid.*

[19] Pressures for maximization of placement quantity caused some officials in some City X agencies to neglect the agency anti-discrimination policy. This is discussed in Chapter Ten.

[20] "Former employer" placements provide an example of emphasis on needless placements at Agency C. See Chapter Nine.

demands from above for high levels of production credited, is one thing. However, *that which made officials comply* with the pressure by emphasizing easier placements, crediting "broken needle" placements and engaging in the various kinds of practices to be mentioned in the following pages, must be specified. The question is, what control did upper levels have over lower on the basis of statistical records that made staff want to comply with demands for high levels of production credited?

It must be emphasized that promotion chances, for the most part, objectively did not rest on provision of high quantity reported on the records; nor did for the most part continuance of employment, as was indicated in a quotation already presented from the governmental report.

Promotions were made by written examination, open to all officials who had been in the employ of the agency for a specified period of time. Those passing above a certain grade on the written examination took an oral examination, and those passing this successfully had their names placed on a list. Hiring officials were required to choose one name from the top three on the list (in terms of grade) for hire. An exceptional personnel rating, often, but not always based on "high" production credited on records over a period of time, received some extra points on the promotion examination, but these were very few. Chances of promotion thus played only a small part, if any, in the control upper levels had over lower, which constrained officials to comply with production stress to the point of crediting "broken needle" placements, or engaging in the other practices yet to be discussed.

This is corroborated by the report of a governmental investigation which used an interview sample from Agency C and six other City X agencies:

Both interviewers and senior interviewers [supervisors] appear to believe that the main factor in promotion to the senior interviewer level is the results of the civil service promotional examination. "You must be a good exam-taker," one said. Annual [personnel] ratings are felt to carry little weight. [21]

There was, however, a minority view stated:

> One person, however, after pointing out that annual [personnel]. ratings contribute only a few points to the promotional rankings, emphasized that "half a point can mean a great deal."[22]

Continuance of employment was governed by civil service regulations which indicated that an official could be fired only under specified conditions which became more rigid after the first year of employment was successfully passed. On very rare occasions an official was "brought up on charges" for dismissal, but this was most often a result of repeated disagreements with one or several superiors. Quantity of production credited had little to do with such proceedings unless coupled with other issues as the cause of the problem. According to a governmental report:

> . . . the City X area placement director stated that, to the best of his knowledge, over the past eleven years no one has been separated from the Employment Bureau because of his quantity of production.[23]

Thus the desire for continuance of employment for the most part did not act as the major objective constraint on officials causing them to desire high levels of quantity recorded on statistical reports. It was, however, subjectively felt by officials that extremely poor records, over a long period of time might cause difficulty, but this was not a strong feeling. It was rather a type of anxiety about repeatedly submitted lower records of production in relation to possible future results in terms of continuance of employment. The governmental report substantiates this observation:

> As with other aspects, there is reported variation in the treatment accorded the employee who fails to meet his goal. One

---

[21] Governmental report, *op. cit.*
[22] *Ibid.*
[23] *Ibid.*

interviewer spoke of being "called on the carpet," and another of being "prodded." A number of others said that nothing happens. There is also a middle ground between outright threat and apparent nonchalance. . . .

But even among those who indicated that little apparent importance is attached by supervisors to missing the goal, some appeared a bit uneasy. Said one, "Nothing happens if you don't make the estimate [the goal or unofficial quota]." Then he added, "I don't *think* there's any penalty, but this is pure speculation."

One effective control that superordinates did have was that an official was generally dissatisfied with lower personnel ratings because this showed him that superiors considered him to be less than satisfactory, and the entire matter became a blow to professional pride. Since personnel ratings often were based to a good extent on quantity of production, this was a control leading to "broken needle" activity and other manipulations in the desire to easily impress upon the superior compliance with production stress, and to show a high level of production credited. According to the governmental investigation:

There seems no question . . . that the majority of employees actively cooperate in trying to keep placement levels high. And with this aim as a paramount one, other things may slip. One employee said, "People want to get good ratings, so they will try and make placements any way they can."

Control also existed in the matter of freedom and independence in work. Poor records caused repeated annoyances, suggestions, and requests for improvement of records from the superior. The manager occasionally called interviewers with repeated low monthly production records to his office for a private conference where the individual was "dressed down." The individual came under more frequent observation by the supervisor, and was continually reminded that his work, as measured by statistical records,

24 *Ibid.*
25 *Ibid.*

was below par. This was troublesome and was resented by officials; hence a desire to provide, for the most part, what the superior requested in relation to production.

Despite an office-wide desire at Agency C to improve records on most operations, there was still a visible differentiation between production levels credited by different interviewers. This was a result of different skill levels of interviewers, different levels of motivation, different levels of work speed, as well as differential use of manipulation of figures on records. There was, however, a limit to the manipulation of figures. For example, an inefficient official with a low referral record was limited in the number of "broken needle" placements credited since each placement had to be preceded by a referral to a job, and even under the best of legitimate circumstances not all interviews yielded referrals.

Those officials who repeatedly had poorer records were frequently transferred from section to section. This was because each supervisor tried to "unload" these people to other sections (for supervisors were also in competition with one another for high sectional records). The desire to avoid frequent transfers, especially to less popular supervisors, was one other control causing officials to desire high production levels credited on their records.

These were the controls of upper levels over lower, generally causing operating officials to actually react to the managerial production stress, rather than merely neglect it.

At this point attention will turn to discussion of various activities other than placements reported on statistical records, and manipulations engaged in by officials to meet upper-level production stress.

---

[26] Recall that officials often did manage to restrict the number of counselings reported despite superordinate desire for high quantity. This was because of the special nature of counseling activity.

Proportion of Referrals

An important index in statistical records concerned the proportion of referrals of clients to jobs. This was "the proportion of interviews resulting in referrals."[27] There was no set figure given by Agency C superiors as to what they considered a good or poor proportion because this depended on exigencies of the clothing industry. What was "good" at a certain level of seasonal activity was not so at others.

Interviewers disliked maintaining a proportion that seemed too low to them, i.e., too few referrals to jobs in relation to the number of people interviewed, because this was visible to superiors. They therefore informally checked their proportions against those of other section interviewers as a reference group. Officials at Agency C did not generally directly ask colleagues how many referrals they had. The method was usually more indirect. For example, an official might complain to a colleague by saying, "I can't seem to make a referral today," and then "gauged" this colleague's response, determining in this way whether or not he was the only one with a poor referral index. If all section interviewers indicated a poor proportion of referrals, this could well be due to local market conditions and individuals could not be blamed.[28]

---

[27] Blau, *Dynamics. . .*, *op. cit.*, p. 39. According to Blau's data this proportion was actually on the records at Agency B. This was not listed on the records at Agency C, although both the number of interviews completed and referrals made were so listed. Therefore, a glance at the record sheet could give a quick approximation. Mental calculation of the proportion showed the official if he was too low. This calculation was not in percentages, but rather in terms of, "enough," "too little," and related statements.

[28] Blau made a similar observation for Agency B, but focused on the supervisory level. According to Blau: ". . . superiors in the state agency emphasized that statistical records were not used to 'compare interviewers with each other, but only with standards.' However, fluctuations in the conditions of the labor market made it impossible to establish absolute standards of performance. As one superior explained, 'In each month, we look at the production, and the average becomes the standard.' Consequently, interviewers were indirectly compared, and direct comparisons were, in fact, also made." *(Ibid.,* pp. 57-58.)

An official also was able to gauge through his own activity. An official who had been able to refer none, or even only two or three clients of a large number interviewed, did not have to gauge his activity against that of colleagues, for this was felt to be *too* low, regardless of seasonal factors.

Sometimes some interviewers were referring many clients during the course of a work day and others were not. Those with low proportions wished to improve their records, which should have been functional, for here the records were serving as a control device, ideally leading to improved client referral service. Actually, dysfunctional consequences were observed because of the methods that were used to improve proportions. Let us trace the processes involved.

Receptionists provided interviewers with a *statistical slip* for each client interviewed, and attached this slip of paper to the client's identification card prior to putting this into the "intake box." When an official completed an interview he took another client's booklet or card from the intake box with the statistical slip, and called this client by name, bringing her to his desk. At the end of each interview, the interviewer marked the proper box on the statistical slip to indicate, for example, whether a referral or "no referral" resulted, whether application forms were filled out, or counselings were performed. Each official added the slips he accumulated at the end of the day, and sorted them according to activity, tabulated each activity in total, and placed these figures on the daily production record sheets. These slips thus served as a tally of the daily activities that had to be reported on production records. If this tally method had not been used, the interviewer would not have been able to remember exactly what quantity of each activity he had performed during the day.

The interviewer also used statistical slips as an informal indicator of his daily progress. Thumbing through them several times a day, and occasionally informally checking colleagues' progress showed the official where he needed improvement.

It was possible to improve records in several ways. First, the official could be more careful and precise in his interviewing, trying his utmost to refer a client to a job. This was functional, because in this case a noticeably poor record led to much more care in further interviewing which aided in the attainment of placement and unemployment insurance objectives.

Second, the official sometimes complained to the reception interviewer of his poor referral index. If there were sufficient complaints, the reception interviewer felt obliged to improve his selection procedure at the sifting counter. This was functional where it led him to use more care, seating more clients for whom jobs were plentiful. However, very often it led him to dismiss many clients without service, giving his colleagues less work, and seating only the easiest, such as "former employer" clients (see Chapter Nine) who were referred to their *own* jobs. This deviated from service-oriented goals.

The interviewer sometimes solved his problem in a third manner. Since the statistical slips were counted at the end of the working day, a decrease in the number of slips indicating "no referrals" served to reduce the proportion of "no referrals" to total interviews. Some interviewers frequently destroyed some "no referral" slips during the course of the day. This brought the number of interviews down, the "no referral" total down, and brought the proportion into a better balance, but at the same time this allowed the official to continue his work without improvement. This, of course, was dysfunctional, for energy was expended in maintaining records which in actuality did not serve as the control device intended. This also gave upper levels a faulty record of actual local operations, and there were dysfunctional results on a broader level to the extent that such records were used by upper levels for policy decisions.

Fourth, a poor index of referrals to total interviews

also led some officials to send applicants haphazardly to jobs for which they were not qualified in order to improve the statistical figures. This improved referral records but was dysfunctional, for if the client referred did not have the qualities that the employer obviously desired, the interviewer's, client's and employer's time was needlessly wasted. The most suitable client was not being referred and the agency was not providing a preselection service.

Fifth, a poor proportion sometimes led the official to emphasize "referring" workers back to their own jobs after a temporary layoff (called "former employer referrals" in agency argot). These applicants were easier to refer, and helped improve low referral records, but at the cost of decreased service to clients who had no jobs at all.

Recording of Application Form Activity

Application form procedure has been discussed in an earlier chapter where it was indicated that adjustments were made from the generic, and that few lengthy application forms were filed at Agency C. It will be seen at this point that *further* adjustments of application forms were made at Agency C.

It was difficult to secure information from clothing workers because of their limited education and language problems. Once having received these data it was functional to make a permanent record so the same information (e.g., occupation, length of experience, name of prior employer) would not again have to be ascertained with difficulty and a waste of time at the next client visit. A record of referral activity for each client was also useful in order to help in referral at the client's next appearance at the agency. However, the need for speed in operations still prevented the preparation of a full and lengthy application form for each client. Some method had to be devised to meet the conflicting needs for speed as well as for a permanent record of information.

A formal adjustment was made in response and a *short* application form was devised.[29] This was a card of small size, which fit into the benefit client's identification booklet, and a yet smaller size card for nonbenefit clients. This also served as an identification card. Spaces were provided on these cards for the client's name and address, experience, occupational title, and several other similar items. This was a functional adjustment because it allowed the speed in operations required by clothing industry conditions, but at the same time it eliminated the need for asking the same clients the same questions on each visit. Clients carried these cards with them, and brought them to the agency each time they came.

Detailed statistical records required reporting of the number of application forms filled out. Spaces were provided on records both for the number of long (generic) and short (adjusted) application forms prepared. It should be recalled, however, that few *long form* applications were filled out at Agency C.

If an interviewer was having a bad day, i.e., seeing few clients or referring few, he tended to add tallies for short applications on statistical slips without having done this work. There was no control over these "illegal" additions because it was not feasible to check alleged work performed with the actual number of short applications made out, since these cards were not filed at the agency, but were in the possession of the clients.

It was also required that a small red check mark be placed on the card as soon as it was filled out to indicate that the official did not forget to record statistical credit for his work. Sometimes officials forgot to make the

---

[29] Application forms reflected many adjustments to meet local exigencies. At Agencies B and C application forms were not filled out for all clients. This was one adjustment. In addition, the lengthy applications that *were* occasionally filled out required less information than those used at other agencies servicing some commercial, professional and other related fields. This also met the local needs of the clothing industry serviced. The adjustment discussed above is yet another one of a single procedure.

check mark, but most often they did not forget to take credit, because this was recorded at the slightest provocation, and at times even fabricated. On a later date when the client returned to the agency, another official interviewing the same client and noticing the absence of the red check notation, put the mark on the card himself and took credit for having filled out the application when he really did not. This inflation caused by crediting some applications twice was encouraged by supervisors because it increased sectional production records.

Field Visits to Employers

Promotional visits called "field visits" in agency argot were made to employers and were recorded on Agency C production records. Each official was to call upon five employers per afternoon, each official generally, but not always, performing visits one afternoon each week.[30] Officials were not required to return to the office after completion of the five visits, but went directly home from the fifth and last employer's establishment.

The number of field visits made was important on records in total for the entire section because supervisors were pressed by the manager to have their subordinates perform many visits. However, field visits were not an important part of the individual interviewer's records, and this was because interviewers performed this activity only when required to do so by superiors. In other words, the number of visits made were under the control of the supervisor and not the interviewer. An afternoon was generally set aside for each interviewer, but visits could not be made according to agency procedure without the superior's prior request (or demand) for a series of visits. This was needed to control the field visit-afternoon absence of officials from

---

[30] Some officials did not visit because of physical handicaps which made calls on employers difficult for them to perform.

the office. Whether visits were to be allowed depended in the ideal on the *need* for employer contacts, number of staff members at work at the office, client load that day (to determine if an official could be spared for a full afternoon), and on similar conditions.

This item was under the control of supervisors, and the manager urged them to increase the number of sectional field visits performed. This served to override other poor showings which were not under the control of the agency (e.g., fluctuations in agency placement production because of seasonal activity in the clothing industry).

According to formal procedure, officials were not allowed to perform this operation unless they had a prior *purpose* for each visit, which had to be written into the employer's record file. The agency procedure requiring that a purpose be stated was designed to limit field visits, which removed officials from interviewing activity for an entire afternoon, to situations where personal contact was needed for special employer services. However, in actuality supervisory demands caused by the desire to raise figures on records forced officials to visit even when there was no need for it, i.e., no purpose. This caused a dilemma, *but interviewers met this conflict between the formal procedure requiring a definite purpose, and the supervisory demand for visits when they were not needed, by fabricating purposes!*

It is interesting to note that the fabricated purposes generally were written into the employers' record files on the morning *after* the visits were completed, and this practice was accepted by superiors. Superiors requested that officials see employers, but rarely if ever asked officials what purpose they had in mind for each visit before it was made. The supervisory desire for field visits came before the need as determined by a legitimate purpose.

Sometimes the fabricated purpose appeared insufficient to have allowed an official to visit. Prior purposes for visits performed, as listed in the employer's record file, might have all been the same; for example, "seasonal visit," or "to get orders." Such repeated purposes over a long period of time really showed the lack of need for further visits for the same reasons, and supervisors thus preferred different purposes for subsequent visits. Supervisors then brought the insufficient "purpose" to the interviewer's attention, telling him that future purposes should have relevance to employer needs. The official only "made up" a "better" purpose for subsequent visits.

The interviewer was not prohibited from visiting if he had no purpose in mind, and was indeed still forced to see employers even if he did not want to go. Nor did the official make his field visit behavior meet the "purposes" listed once he was forced to call on employers. Field visit behavior was similar in almost all cases, regardless of the purpose "made up."

In this way a rule which limited field visits only to conditions where there was a special need for them, was informally redefined by supervisors in the interest of increasing the number of employer field visits, and officials were obliged to fabricate purposes even though their field visit behavior remained the same. Supervisors were aware of this and at times even said to recalcitrant officials who did not want to perform visits, "I'm sure you can *think up* a good purpose." Superiors were interested in field visit figures on records, and not in service to employers.

So many visits were being made that occasionally some agency sections had gone through and visited their suitable employers on file, and many officials were forced to revisit employers at a time interval of approximately every three months. When officials had not been to a firm for a long time, employers tended to welcome them, the employer perhaps being friendly, or wanting to talk about special hiring problems. However, when personal calls were made too frequently, many employers seemed to realize that the officials were coming to no avail, and many then did not treat the government representative cordially.

This made some government workers quite unwilling to visit, and created antagonisms between superior and subordinate when the former was obliged to force the latter to call on employers.

An Agency C interviewer writes in a personal letter to the author: "Morale was never lower. Constant changes in procedures, field visits . . . are continually being made."[31]

This statement points to a connection in this official's mind, at the least, between his evaluation of poor morale and pressures toward continuous field visits.[32] The effect of supervisory overemphasis on field visits on total morale cannot be determined. However, it was observed that demands for frequent field visits caused much grumbling among some individual staff members required to perform this operation.

There were other problems too. It will be recalled that Agency C had many more job orders on file for skilled clients than could be filled. In season, employers repeatedly pleaded with agency officials to send them workers, for the absence of several operatives at strategic points on the production line served to tie up an entire plant, and garments could not be produced in time for seasonal sales. When an official appeared once every several months asking for vacancies, or "promoting" the agency, some employers were annoyed and complained to the visitor, for they might have been calling the agency for the longest time without service! Instead of a cordial welcome, the government representative was sometimes subjected to hostility.

---

[31] The letter is dated November 25, 1959, and was unsolicited.

[32] There is another reason for the evaluation of low morale made by the official at the date he wrote the letter. Most staff members suffered (in the author's evaluation) from low morale and this was continuous throughout the period of participation. However, at the date of this letter, a new manager had been amplifying many procedures, and pressured for increased figures on the statistical records. This caused resentment among staff members. (See Chapter Five for two such amplifications.) This is the relevance of the official's statement of "constant changes in procedures."

This was troublesome, for the official could only explain that there was a shortage of skilled operatives, which the employer also knew; but the employer only vented his frustrations on the official who was coming frequently as a representative of a government employment agency which was providing little help. On occasion, an employer put blame on the bureaucrats for allowing workers to collect unemployment checks during the busy season instead of sending them to his firm to work, and this only complicated the issue.

Furthermore, employers in the clothing industry were working people, most frequently filling in on the production line themselves. Employers tended to halt their own work when the government representative came to visit after a long absence, but after frequent contacts with no improved referral service, busy employers frequently did not stop their work during the visits. Officials were forced to converse by shouting over the clamor of machines while employers continued to work, and other clothing workers toiled at full speed nearby. This situation was not a pleasant one for the visitor.

Interviewers informally modified field visit procedure to meet these problems. Superiors were requiring that they call on employers, but too frequent visits were of little use. Under these conditions officials visited employers, asked a few stereotyped questions and left *within a few minutes!* Generally an interviewer finished his entire afternoon of field work, including travel and consultations with employers, in less than an hour. Very often the required five employers were seen within thirty minutes or less, if the official had been able to select employers' establishments that were in the same vicinity. Officials made a definite attempt to arrange their calls this way, and were frequently successful, sometimes selecting firms within a radius of several city blocks. At times the official was not able to arrange his work this way, and this required much walking, often in slum neighborhoods, and much travel by train or bus. This is another reason why officials tended to dislike field visiting, over and above the items discussed thus far.

Interviewers were not required to return to the agency after completing their visits. Since they often completed their tasks in a short time, they went home with many work hours to spare.[33] Upon return to the office the next morning officials fabricated a purpose, and prepared a stereotyped report for each visit.

Supervisory officials appeared to be aware of this "short visit" practice, and it is certain that at least two were definitely aware of this work behavior for they were known to have engaged in it themselves.[34]

---

[33] There is much evidence for this modification, during participation and after. Some sources and examples follow: *First,* the author himself frequently completed his full afternoon of visiting tasks within thirty minutes. *Second,* other interviewers boasted to colleagues upon return to the office the next morning of how fast they were able to complete their visits. *Third,* the author as participant, once searching for an employer's establishment on an upper floor of a building during an afternoon of field visiting, unexpectedly met a colleague preparing to call on another employer at the very same address. The author and colleague called on other employers together, both finishing in a very short time. *Fourth,* in the summer of 1960, the author, at that time no longer employed at the agency, was walking from a local library when he unexpectedly met a former colleague, sitting on the porch of her home. This was early in the afternoon. This official said that she was home from work so early because she had been visiting employers. *Fifth,* in July 1961, the author was conversing on the telephone with a former colleague. The conversation shifted to "the sport of kings." The official then said that he had been accustomed to completing his employer visits in a short period of time and went thereupon (in season) to a nearby race-track, spending the rest of the afternoon there. This official said that since the date he had been assigned to another division, he did not perform field visits and was not able to attend the horse races as had been his previous practice. *Sixth,* several times three officials in different sections who were also performing field visits on the same afternoon made special meeting arrangements in the heat of the summer. They completed government tasks within a short time, met at a predetermined place, and went together to a nearby swimming area. Since the author was one of these officials, he had a chance to either fully observe or infer the practice of rushing visits by other officials.

[34] The author and one of these men visited some employers as part of the author's training as a government official. These visits were rapidly completed by the supervisor, who advised the author to tell managerial officials, if asked, that we had finished visiting close to the end of the work day, although this

(continued)

It is obvious that much more time than a few minutes was needed if a field visit interview was to be held for real consultations, advice, and public relations value. Employers were not sorry to see officials leave so hurriedly for they were generally busy with their own work and therefore did not complain about this practice. Furthermore, if an employer wanted to talk and took the initiative, the official generally (but not always) remained longer than the usual few minutes.

Sometimes, but not often, a lengthy visit was held. When this occurred, it was likely because there was a real purpose (i.e., there were special matters to discuss) and the employer was cordial as well as taking the initiative himself in bringing certain problems to light. It is significant to note that even in lengthy visits, a good portion of the time was often spent discussing nonagency matters. This in itself was not dysfunctional, for these friendly conversations provided a personal relationship between official and employer, and further dealings with him from the agency by phone were greatly facilitated.

There were times when some few highly disgruntled officials complained to employers about the inefficiency and problems of their own government organization! This ad-

---

was not so in reality. The author was never asked. In this case, local training by one supervisor focused on the informal modification of field visit operations, instead of on the formal way. (These visits were performed for the purpose of acquainting the author with the occupations in the clothing industry through a firsthand observation of work performed in several plants. The visits were not made for the purpose of training on how to visit employers. It is known, however, that this supervisor completed his own employer visits on other occasions in a rapid manner, and in fact once even called one of his interviewers at the office on the telephone very early one day and said that he had at the time completed his visits.)

There was also an unverified story circulating at Agency C that an official at another branch not only made up purposes but fabricated the entire visit, for he merely went home, never visiting employers although he reported such "contacts" on return to the office. According to the grapevine, he was fired when this informal modification was determined by supervisory officials. If this is true, then fabrication of purposes was expected by supervisors and short visits were allowed without reprisal, but not *complete* fabrication which was punished by dismissal.

versely affected employer conceptions of the agency when the visit was formally aimed at the opposite.

According to their own admission, those few who preferred visiting employers did so because it gave them a chance to leave the office and arrive home early, but in spite of this personal advantage, these officials were in the minority. Many found field visits distasteful and tried to find every excuse possible to avoid them. However, once forced to visit they generally aimed at finishing early in order to complete personal errands or to arrive home early.

Strains with employers resulting from too frequent and unnecessary visits, the forced fabrication of purposes, and the realization by the officials that field work was most often useless (as well as the possibility and definite personal advantage of completing work at an early hour), often carried over even into other visits where employers were friendly and where the call could have been of use. For example, the officials who had decided to complete some personal errands after visiting, or to meet other officials, were in a hurry and often rushed their calls even where the employer was cordial and was willing to talk. In addition, the frequent need to fabricate purposes led many officials to overlook situations where there could have been a legitimate purpose to the visit. These officials merely wrote the first purpose that entered their minds into the records, doing this after they had already finished the visits and had returned the next morning to the office. Many did not even review the employer's file before the visit for *possible* points of purposeful discussion! The fact that past experience showed officials that most visits were only for statistical figures on records made them treat almost all such calls this way, even if on occasion there was a real purpose, which could have been easily determined if the officials had only studied the matter with some interest. [35]

---

[35] According to one interviewer in 1961, the field visits were, "a farce." The writer had been conversing with another official on the telephone two years after the termination of participation (1961). The short visits to employers, and sub-

(continued)

In summary, field visits in many cases were performed for "statistics" rather than for service to employers. Once again the dysfunctional effects of emphasis on quantity on records is evident.

Testing Clients at Agency C

An aptitude testing program was organized to help meet the scarcity of skilled workers in the clothing industry. Employers were notified of this service and orders for trainees were originally secured. Clients meeting certain qualifications, who were anxious to move from the unskilled job category to skilled, were to be counseled, given an appointment for the test morning, and then were to be given a special test to determine possible aptitude for skilled work on the sewing machine. Those showing aptitude were to be referred to an employer who had a job opening as a trainee machine operator, the employer providing the training.

This was functional in the ideal, for it provided a service to unskilled clients, enabling them to move to a better position if they had the aptitude. This also ideally met employers' needs caused by the scarcity of skilled workers. The development of the testing program thus showed a flexible responsiveness of the agency to local worker and employer needs. Some officials were trained to administer these tests, and one morning per week was set aside for this service.

sequent attendance at the horse races, discussed in an earlier footnote, was brought to light in this conversation. The official referred back to the time period when he had engaged in this practice. "Visits were made only as a race to see how fast we [interviewers] could get through." Officials tended to see this operation as a useless task.

Interviewers were known to take time on the morning of the day they were to visit, looking through employers' files and "preparing" for the visits. Preparation was mainly made by the official for two reasons: first to check travel instructions and to choose employers in the same geographical vicinity, to be sure that he would not suffer the inconvenience of protracted travel and of getting lost; second, the official "prepared" to waste time, *appearing* busy so he could remain out of operations instead of interviewing.

In time the testing program began to have less success than expected. Many employers found that the training period was a long and tedious one, and took up much of their time. Also, after employer time and money spent in training, some trainees, after becoming sufficiently skilled, resigned their positions to accept work elsewhere. One reason for this situation was that applicants were willing to travel long distances to work, and to accept other disadvantages if they were being trained for a better position. Once gaining skill, these workers found that they were in extreme demand, could find jobs closer to home, and at better pay. Therefore, they resigned.

Another problem was that many employers did not understand what the program intended. The seasonal nature of the industry also decreased the effectiveness of the trainee program established.

A former official at Agency C, who had worked in the Special Services section (which serviced many of these test-selected applicants) writes to the author:

. . . we were not dealing with bright people in the field of employers. We were trying to discuss a good program for the . . . [clothing industry] with men who could really not comprehend what we were saying.[36] They wanted . . . [sewing machine operators]—but they were not really able or willing to train the . . . [test-selected applicants] we were trying to sell them. They thought that by "test-selected" we meant these girls had been tested on sewing machines and could actually run the machines. They did not realize these girls had not touched a machine and would not even be able to control the machines for a while. They had very little patience with the girls—we couldn't really always blame them, however, because it was a

---

[36] Many clothing workers were of foreign background and had some difficulty with the English language. Others were poorly educated. Quite a few clothing industry employers also matched this description. They knew the garment production business, but often were of a type that does not meet the popular conception of "employer" in the United States. Many of these men themselves worked alongside employees on machines in shirt sleeves. Many were foreign born, and many had limited education. This made official dealings with some clothing employers as difficult as with some clothing industry applicants. It is this situation to which the former official comments in her letter above.

vicious circle. They wanted the girls in the busy season when they needed operators, and yet they could not afford to spend time to teach these beginners. And they could not afford to tie up a machine with a learner. Then when it was slow season, they did not want a beginner because they did not want to pay . . . [the minimum wage] for nothing. [Many of the clothing industry employers operated on a very narrow profit margin.] [37]

In addition, some employers began to use the agency testing program in a way that was not intended, causing a disservice to agency applicants. Again, from the respondent who had worked in this special testing program:

> . . . several times we were really sucked into a trap. We would get info. [*sic*] that a brand new shop was to open . . . . We were asked for as many as 50 or 100 . . . [test-selected applicant-trainees] and we lined the girls up for the prospective employer. He seemed to be hiring the girls we referred but somehow they never started work. Either the factory still was not opened or the boss decided he did not want real beginners (he figured if he said he'd take trainees we'd fall all over ourselves to also get him experienced . . . [sewing machine operators. It will be recalled that such skilled workers were in extreme demand and in short supply.] and also, if he called them trainees he could pay less for the work.) The . . . [test-selected applicants] were just strung along and so were we. [38]

Testing was a budgetary "pay-item" and the number of clients tested was to be recorded on agency statistical records when Agency C began its program. [39] A dysfunc-

---

[37] From a letter of a former Agency C official who had been in participation during the same time period as the author. The letter was written in response to a request in 1961 for information on the testing program.

[38] *Ibid.*

[39] The agency kept records of the total number of clients tested, and this figure was important to the manager because it reflected his department's emphasis on this new and important activity (important ideally in service as well as in budgetary terms). All officials were able to channel clients to the test by arranging an appointment. But not all officials serviced tested clients. *Special* interviewers were assigned to handle these clients once tested, and referrals and placements of these applicants were reported on the 1956 records. Thus it is evident that statistical recording emphasis on this activity was not so much in

tional use of agency statistical records was that once having achieved a certain production record, or once having set a goal (an "unwritten quota"), managerial officials felt obliged to continue that high record and often would not allow the agency to formally meet new local conditions. Managerial officials demanded the same high level of referrals to these tests even though the new service was not proving as successful as was originally intended.

Some officials began to neglect this program when they realized that fewer legitimate trainee vacancies were being received, and scheduled fewer appointments for the tests. Some interviewers continued to refer clients to the test in response to the managerial demand, but referrals were at such a low level that sometimes there were not enough people scheduled to justify (according to the formal procedure) providing an official for the scheduled test administration. When this occurred, the assistant manager and several supervisors sometimes scanned the lines of clients in front of reception counters on test mornings, searching for a "likely candidate" for testing.

A stereotype had developed at the agency about the kind of client that was a "likely candidate." Since they were looking for an unskilled applicant and many of the unskilled clients were young, Negro, and female, the assistant manager and some supervisors tended to point out such a client from among those standing in line and broadly hinted to the receptionist that this client be seated for an interview leading to a test appointment. Such haphazard selection neglected agency policy on the need for competent, professional selection on the basis of interviewing to determine the applicant's interests, abilities, desires, and needs.

These clients were literally yanked from the reception counter line, and an appointment was made for the test to be held that morning, after some "sales talk" to

---

relation to each individual interviewer's records (with the exception of the special interviewers), but was more important in relation to the total agency as a whole, and as a department.

convince the bewildered client of the benefits of this test. Some few nonsupervisory officials, either wishing to impress superiors, or under supervisory pressure, also tried to find candidates from among those that they were interviewing. The former agency official also writes of this in her letter:

> When . . . [test morning] came around, if there were not enough girls scheduled for the test, we dragged in lots of people who never should have been tested. They had neither the interest, nor the qualifications (really) and they were not always counseled properly first, so they did not have the motivation to do well, either.[40]

It will be recalled that this "selection" was engaged in on the morning of the test when it appeared that too few candidates had been scheduled. The selected client now waited several hours until the test was given, spent time in the testing room, waited through the lunch hour until the scores were established, and interviewers returned from lunch, and was interviewed once again after waiting in turn. Often clients who had been haphazardly chosen were either dismissed without referral to a job after having spent many hours at the agency, or sometimes were sent to unskilled openings for which they had come in the first place.

> . . . it was not always fair to the girls because they were sometimes built up for a let down (when they did not qualify or when we did not have a suitable job for them whether or not they qualified). . . .[41]

The former official writing this evaluation also notes that sometimes one client had to be mishandled for the benefit of another. This was because of a procedure that had not been adjusted to local conditions.

> . . . on the other hand, we did need a group of at least three girls in order to test perhaps one who was really interested and qualified and motivated. If we had not dragged in the others, perhaps we were not giving a good possibility a fair chance to show what she could do.[42]

---

40 Former official's letter, *op. cit.*
41 *Ibid.*
42 *Ibid.*

Procedure could have been formally modified, allowing only one applicant to be tested at one time, instead of having to mishandle two others for the benefit of one. It would have been more efficient had an official provided the test to one applicant than to have recorded three tests on statistical forms, wasting the time of the other two applicants. The procedure of having at least three take the test was designed to avoid the inefficiency of having one test administrator take up his time with only one client, when he could handle many more at the very same time. Managerial decision was that three was the minimum that would make it worthwhile to take the official's time in test administration. However, the goal of this procedure was left far behind when management pressured officials to select at least three clients, and three were chosen without regard to service factors. Two clients had to be "dragged in" to allow the official to administer the test to one motivated and qualified client. This meant that the official still was giving the test to *only one* client where the special service could be useful.[43]

These matters were dysfunctional, because the agency continued the testing program as it had originally been conceived for the sake of maintaining a high number of tests reported on statistical records, even after conditions became such that this testing was of decreased use to applicants and employers. Instead of halting the testing program temporarily, reducing its frequency, changing procedure to meet local conditions, or attempting a solution to employer complaints and problems, the agency continued its original program. Officials were tied up in work, and clients wasted their time.

The former official who had worked closely in this program corroborates and summarizes the author's own observations:

---

[43] This probably did not occur at every testing session. There were probably times when all clients were qualified and motivated, and perhaps times when none was.

My feeling about the aptitude testing at . . . [Agency C] is this: it was a good idea but it was not conducted correctly. I was not in on the program when it started, but from my experience with it . . . it was more for statistics than for real service, although it could have been a very valuable service if used correctly. . . .

. . . .

My general comment on the whole program at . . . [Agency C] is that the management was so much more interested in statistics and F.E.'s [the former employer policy where clients were referred back to their own jobs] than in anything else, that it was really a wonder we did anything with the testing at all. [44]

"Statistics" on records once again became more important than service to clients!

Restriction of Output

Interviewers tried to maximize placement and other production records and were pressured to do so. However, there was an informal norm at Agency C which had reference to what interviewers felt was a fair day's work. Increases over this standard first brought boasts. (An example of an interviewer boast is, "I saw *twenty* people today," meaning that the official had interviewed twenty clients which was somewhat above the norm of sixteen to eighteen generally and very broadly considered to be a "fair day's work.") However, when the informal norm was over-reached much further because of heavy seasonal activity, or reception sifting policy, then grumbling occurred.

When the norm was not reached, interviewers often tried to increase their daily production by extra work, and this was functional. Sometimes increases were attempted by dysfunctional means, which have been discussed.

Restriction of output generally followed when officials interviewed many more clients than they usually did, and many more were still waiting for service.[45] This was in

---

[44] Former official's letter, *op. cit.*

[45] Restriction of output because of the supervisor's reception sifting policy has already been discussed on pages 85-88.

spite of the fact that quantity of interviews and other production was reported on statistical records.

Slowdowns resulted while officials stretched interviews, made personal telephone calls, printed all records even though they generally wrote in longhand, pretended they were busy with paper-work, left their desks on unnecessary errands, took rest periods that ran over the time allotted, consulted unnecessarily with colleagues, listened to a busy tone on the telephone for a lengthy period instead of turning to other work while waiting, and engaged in other related practices. This put pressure on the receptionist to seat fewer clients, for a backlog of complaining clients was constantly growing.

Sometimes officials "interviewed" clients without even attempting to find employment for them, which also occurred when too many clients were waiting and too many had been interviewed according to the informal norm. Clients in such situations were kept waiting for no reason, and time of all parties concerned was wasted.

Even in busy seasons, interviewers could be found staring out the window or socializing with colleagues at late afternoon hours (and often at other times too). This was possible because receptionists frequently dismissed almost all clients without service at hours later in the day. In addition, reappointment times were given for earlier hours which kept most clients away from the agency at other times.

Formal reappointment procedure for the client's return date required that officials assign a definite return hour according to a specific plan. The formal procedure was that officials were to assign the same time for benefit clients as listed by the unemployment insurance division on the client's compensation card, unless this conflicted substantially with the job search effort (e.g., unskilled clients could better be able to find employment if reporting at a very early hour, for these vacancies were rapidly filled and few existed at later hours). The formal procedure intended to apportion the flow of clients, but many officials assigned early morning and early afternoon hours, even for clients who should have formally been assigned other times; meaning that conditions tended to be rushed at certain hours, but quiet at others. To an extent this was functional, for officials were able to use quiet hours to catch up with the work neglected during rush hours (checking results of referrals, writing reports, writing uncompleted orders, and performing related tasks). However, it very often occurred that this work was completed in a short time and the government employees then socialized with one another.

The official work day was from 8:30 A.M. to 12:15 P.M. and from 1:00 to 5:00 P.M., but in one section, as an example of more extreme restriction of output, officials inter-viewed and did other work from about 8:45 to 11:30, and from 1:00 to about 2:15. This practice was generally re-peated on a daily basis. [46]

It can thus be seen that detailed statistical records did not always press for increased production. There were officials who were unwilling to increase their production over a certain point, and this adversely affected client services.

In the discussion of employer field visits it was men-

---

[46] These hours are approximations and varied somewhat day by day depending on client load and other considerations. In other words, officials did not have complete control over client load, and had to adjust their restrictive practices accordingly.

Examples of restrictive practices are numerous. The author appeared at the agency section discussed above on a follow-up visit in June 1960, after partici-pation had terminated. The time was 2:30 P.M. and interviewers were performing little work. The receptionist seated a client for an interview and a colleague im-mediately called her to his desk, for no one else was waiting. He dismissed her without service in several minutes, and then continued to socialize with the other staff members. In another case observed that same afternoon, the author was standing next to the reception counter, conversing with an interviewer. A client came to the counter, and the interviewer said he would, "get rid of her." He dismissed the client immediately without even attempting service, and continued to talk to the author. This had been a frequent occurrence as observed and prac-ticed by the author when an employee at Agency C. The phrase, "get rid of her," referred to dismissing clients without an attempt at service (before another official might decide to seat the client for service), in order to aid in restrictive practices.

tioned that certain strains and the uselessness of most of the work caused officials to neglect situations where real service could have been given to employers. The same occurred at Agency C in reference to restriction of production. So much work at Agency C was performed for "statistics" rather than for service, so much work was useless in the manner performed, there were so many strains between officials and clients who were malingerers, or who did not understand their obligations under the law, that officials desired only to maintain the "proper" figures on the statistical records, and to do no more. On occasion applicants who really wanted and needed help were dismissed at later hours, because the officials had already made their "quota," and many were too tired, too annoyed, and too hostile to clients in general to perform the necessary service. Pressures of statistical records and conflict with clients flowed over into relations with clients who could have been serviced properly if the officials had only been responsive.[47]

Conclusions

Statistical records, designed for functional ends, formally reflected emphasis on production and performance of major agency activities. Emphasis on quantity as recorded on records certainly did induce Agency C interviewers to change practices; but they did so frequently in a dysfunctional direction.

We have seen that there were many informal modifications of procedures by staff members in the interest of maximizing figures on statistical records. Figures were placed on records, but these were sometimes inflated and fabricated. Statistical records reflected a "shadow-world" of

---

[47] Officials varied in their responsiveness to clients. There were some interviewers who would take time at any hour of the day to help a client, and there were some who would rarely go out of their way to help a client at any time. These are extreme types. The discussion above emphasizes not the extremes, but the usual behavior of most officials.

bureaucratic operations, for the records were based on inaccurate figures, and did not give upper levels the exact data ideally necessary for use in budgetary appropriations, in assessing "efficiency," or in control of interviewers' work toward better achievement of the service goals of the organization. To the extent that inflated records were used by upper levels to justify budgetary and policy action, dysfunctional consequences may have resulted, for upper level decisions were based on incorrect information. In addition, officials needlessly expended much time and energy on filling out and totaling detailed records, which in actuality were not accurate, thereby having only limited use in relation to attainment of organizational goals. A related dysfunction is that the great desire to maintain "good" records in turn not only distorted the records, but even adversely affected the services the records were designed to measure, control and improve, when clients were mistreated or neglected in the desire for maximization of records with the least possible work.

Statistical reporting procedure, designed to lead to better placement service, detracted from this end in the long run, when the statistical records became more important in quantity than the actual placement service to clients and employers. Here we have a displacement cf goals of statistical recording procedure.

Thus far the case of statistical records at Agency C shows us that a procedure does not statically remain on the level of operation as when first instituted, or as originally and formally intended. Change upon change, and managerial and supervisory emphases, as well as operating level reactions to the procedure itself, reactions to supervisory emphases, and response to local operating conditions, lead the procedure from its intended form.

Statistical recording procedure had to be carried on within the rigidly specified formal framework. Officials were required to fill out daily records. However, they still modified to meet superordinate emphases and local conditions, by informally modifying within the formal framework; they filled out records on a daily basis, but provided inflated figures. This applied at Agency C not only on the interviewers' level, but on supervisory levels too, for supervisors themselves pressed toward matters which they knew were only inflating the records in terms of numbers. Supervisors thus forgot their control function and they pressed their subordinates for more "figures" on records.

Restriction of output has also been traced in this chapter. The records emphasized productivity, but within this emphasis, officials still restricted output and often to an extreme degree. When unofficial quotas were met, interviewers desired to do no more. This restriction of output is especially interesting because it is here performed by white-collar workers. This practice has been most often studied in relation to blue-collar factory workers.[48]

It has been necessary to separate all matters discussed in this chapter for analytical purposes although in reality all operated in connection with one another. Changes in one procedure yielded strain for changes in others, and dysfunctions of each item discussed served to reinforce the dysfunctional series of modifications. For example, *actual changes in production caused supervisory demands for manipulation of time records* in order to bring the "time" credited into line with production credited. We shall now turn to a discussion of time records.

---

[48] The literature on restriction of output by blue-collar workers is extensive. Examples are: F. J. Roethlisberger and William J. Dickson, *Management and the Worker* (Cambridge: Harvard University Press, 1956), Donald Roy, "Quota Restriction and Goldbricking in a Machine Shop," *American Journal of Sociology*, 57 (March 1952), pp. 427-42. W. F. Whyte also discusses such restriction in *Money and Motivation* (New York: Harper and Brothers, 1955).

CHAPTER EIGHT

Time Distribution Records

Former Soviet citizens like to relate the anec-
dote of the director who interviewed a number
of chief accountants for a job. "How much
is two and two?" was his crucial question.
"How much do you need, Comrade Director?"
replied one candidate, and he got the job.
— JOSEPH S. BERLINER [1]

---

[1]This quotation, which illustrates well matters to be described in this chapter, shows that the problem of manipulation of figures on records as discussed in Part Three of this book is not unique to Agency C or even to American bureaucracy. The Soviet industrial enterprise, for example, is known for much fabrication of production records of various kinds and on various levels. See Joseph S. Berliner, *Factory and Manager in the USSR* (Cambridge: Harvard University Press, 1957). The quotation above is from his p. 240. Also see David Granick, *Management of the Industrial Firm in the USSR* (New York: Columbia University Press, 1954).

Ridgway also discusses general dysfunctional effects of various kinds of performance measurements and summarizes some of the findings in this area. He includes data from studies of Russian as well as American organizations. See V. F. Ridgway, "Dysfunctional Consequences of Performance Measurements," *Administrative Science Quarterly,* 1 (September, 1956), pp. 240-47.

THE LAST CHAPTER focused on statistical production records, informal practices in crediting production, and effects on major agency operations. In this chapter we shall once again focus on the "shadow-world" of bureaucratic operations, i.e., reporting on records of what was not really so in actuality, but this time in analysis of another agency record known as, "Time Distribution Sheets."

Time distribution procedure required that interviewers record on a daily basis and in units as small as quarter-hours the time spent on every activity performed. Each activity was known by a special code number which interviewers filled in at the beginning of each month on the blank time sheets for all operations that they expected to perform. Each official then recorded the time spent on each coded activity at the end of every work day.[2]

These records in the ideal could serve the ends of facilitating supervisory control over subordinates' work, to ensure a good balance of time spent on various activities, and to provide a record of the number of hours used on different agency operations. Time distribution records thus served as a management tool.[3]

These records were also important as a budgetary tool.[4] This purpose derived from the budgetary procedure instituted by the very top federal echelons of the agency, and has reference to certain formal norms, or in agency terms, "standard time factors," which will be discussed.

The figures, however, that were listed by Agency C interviewers on time distribution sheets came to have little reference to the time actually spent on various operations.

---

[2] These codes were known as "time distribution codes," and are described in the agency manual of procedure as: "A system in which identifying numbers are assigned to each of the functions in a state employment . . . agency, so that these identifying numbers, instead of names of functions, can be used by personnel to identify on a record the functions on which they worked for the amount of time shown."

[3] This purpose on the unmodified level is given in a definition of the time distribution system in the agency manual of procedure.

[4] This is also from the agency manual of procedure.

This was dysfunctional, for officials filled out detailed record sheets, tabulated daily, totaled monthly, but wasted their time, not providing the accurate data originally desired. We shall analyze these records more completely in the following sections.

Standard Time Factors

The time records by themselves could not serve as an adequate control mechanism. It was first necessary to refer to at least generalized norms in order to determine whether or not an official was putting in too much, or too little time on certain operations. There had to be reference to a *standard* of "proper" times.

The standard used referred back to the time that the upper levels decided to allot for each operation after a type of time study analysis, and derived from budgetary procedure instituted by Washington, D.C. headquarters for all state agencies. According to the report of a state governmental commission, the budgetary procedure is as follows:

> Funds for the employment bureau activities of the Division . . . as for its unemployment insurance work, come from Congressional appropriations. . . . The budgetary process can be summed up as follows:
> 1. About one and one-half years prior to the beginning of a fiscal year, . . . [the top level of the bureaucracy] supplies state services with a set of economic assumptions. . . . These assumptions are checked and modified as needed, and are translated by state offices to apply to state conditions. These assumptions are used primarily to determine the suggested stresses on different types of activity rather than upon the suggested total budget request.
> 2. Beginning about 1951, . . . [the bureaucracy] has successively established, in its drive for scientific management, a system of cost accounting to serve as a fundamental guideline for state agencies in the preparation of budgets. The central concept involved is that of "standard time factors." On the basis of a series of nation-wide studies in 1954-55, the. . . [bureaucracy] has allotted a given number of "minutes per unit" of employment service

activities. The standard time factors are applied to each of four basic "pay items": new applications, counseling, testing, and placements. . . . Thus it is estimated by . . . [the bureaucracy on the federal level] that a new applicant should be processed in 19.4 minutes . . . a skilled or semiskilled worker placed in 95.1 minutes.

The man-hours allotted by. . . [the bureaucracy] for other . . . [agency] activities are largely contingent upon the hours allotted to placements. Thus time allotted to employer visits is 23.7 percent of placement-hours. . . .

It should be noted that this procedure is purely administrative, and not required by statute.

. . . .

. . . although an agency has been given a certain sum of money on the basis of an approved estimate that it will make [for example] 100,000 skilled and semiskilled placements at 95.1 minutes per placement, it may either seek to cut down the number of these placements or the time spent on them and divert the man-hours saved to other activities. In other words, the "standard time factor" is a budgetary rather than a work concept.[5]

Operating officials knew what the standards were, but only very generally, for while supervisors often brought wide deviations from the standard to an interviewer's attention, the exact norm was a matter of managerial interest and knowledge only.

Over a period of time, operations varied and by necessity so did times spent on various activities. These variations were often due to chance factors (e.g., many difficult clients appearing in a month by chance), seasonal factors, economic cyclical fluctuations, or sometimes poor work techniques of officials. Thus the interviewer's record of the actual time he spent on work operations sometimes deviated sharply from the standards allocated in the budgetary process. Such sharp deviation was generally brought to the interviewer's attention by the supervisor.

When this occurred, the official did not change working behavior, but changed the time recorded. If, for example, an

---

[5] From a governmental report not cited in full in order to preserve the anonymity of the research locale.

interviewer was spending and recording many more minutes on each placement he made than was standard, and too little time on some other activity, the official did not change his work speed, *nor was he expected to change work.* He changed the time figure on his record, deducted hours from the interviewing-placement code, and added this to another coded activity. The figures were *manipulated* until a balance based on supervisory desires was reached. The records did not serve the real control or information purposes intended, for figures were changed, but daily operations remained the same.

Supervisors were aware of this practice and accepted it; and in fact, demanded it! Exigencies of the clothing industry meant that production figures, as well as time spent on certain activities, normally fluctuated from season to season. It would have been clearly dysfunctional if, for example, section heads had interrupted the progress of interviewing when many clients were waiting for service to tell subordinates that they were interviewing for too long a time, and should proceed to other work. Therefore, work speed was not expected to equal the standard. Indeed, according to formal budgetary procedure, the standard time factors were not a work concept, but were only a budgetary concept, and time could be allocated according to local work needs. Yet the local work-time records were still manipulated because of managerial and supervisory pressures at Agency C to meet the budgetary standard, even though it was not formally expected that work-time should equal budgetary standards.

"Taking Time"

Superiors occasionally returned totaled time sheets to officials, saying, "You did not *take* enough time for . . .," and an activity was mentioned. This in agency argot did not have reference to exactly how long officials actually spent on each activity. If actual figures were the subject of discussion, the supervisor would have said that the interviewer did not *spend* enough time on an operation. The word "take" referred to the times taken, or placed on the records without reference to reality. When supervisors told subordinates that they did not take enough time, officials engaged in manipulation, removing hours from one activity, coding it to another, finally bringing the record into another balance, but in this case with the standards as requested by the superior.

Here there is no doubt that the supervisor knew time records were being fabricated. He himself was asking, not that officials change their working habits, for it was already too late to change what had been done throughout the month, but rather that they change the figures on the record sheets to meet the standards. A superior rarely told an official that he should spend more time on certain activities in the next month through change in operating behavior so he could then better meet the standard time factor total in actuality. He did use these "errors" to show the official how much time he was expected to "take," or record on his time sheet at the next monthly period, regardless of how he performed his tasks, or how much time he actually spent on various duties. If his figures deviated too far from the standard in the monthly period already completed, the official was obliged to change his records for work *already done.*

"Taking time" was no secret at Agency C, but was quite expected and the normal state of affairs. This is illustrated in the case of "conference time." Superiors generally had meetings with their subordinates at least once each week. At the end of the meeting officials were sometimes told by the superior to "take" a certain number of minutes on their time sheets for conference time. This number of minutes sometimes did not equal, but went over the actual time spent in conference. The superior knew this and so did staff, but comment was not made by either for this was so normal; that is, so frequent in so many activities.[6]

---

[6] According to formal procedure the time listed on the records had to be in units of fifteen minutes. For example, ten minutes were recorded as fifteen minutes, and 28 minutes were listed on the records as one-half hour. In the case above,

(continued)

Wasting of Time

At the end of every month there was a flurry of activity as officials sat at their desks, pencils and erasers in hand, trying to bring their time record sheets into balance and deriving totals.

The figures on the records had to balance across the sheet in total for each activity, and down the sheet for each day. Both totals had to equal the exact number of working hours in the month. In dealing with many fractions of hours, it often occurred that officials erred in adding and "lost" or had too many hours (or fractions) which caused the total figures to be in imbalance. In these cases, officials spent much time searching for the error, sometimes with the help of colleagues. This wasted time, because in actuality the records were inaccurate even when a balance was reached.[7]

When an entire section was trying to bring these manipulated and inaccurate record sheets, and other records into balance at the end of the month, reception officials were often forced to turn away many clients because there were too few free officials at the time for interviewing activity.

---

the actual conference time, for example, could have equalled only ten minutes, but the superior might have asked for recording of one-half hour to show that he had spent "sufficient" conference time with staff members during the statistical month, and that subordinates had received the "advantage" of one-half hour of conference.

[7] This inaccuracy is a matter of degree. Although figures were inaccurate in reference to true time spent on various activities, they still grossly and generally reflected actual activities. For example, the time taken for interviewing activities was higher every month than that taken for clerical time, and in reality this was true, for officials spent the bulk of their time interviewing instead of performing clerical chores. However, the time figures listed in *each* of these two categories was not a specific indicator of the time actually spent, nor did it even reach a close approximation to specific times. If an official had too much time in the placement-interviewing code, he frequently subtracted this time and added it to clerical time (or to other minor activities), even if he had performed no clerical chores at all that day.

There were some activities that totaled close to the actual time spent. Aptitude testing, within a very limited range, had to take a certain time, because the actual test was set up to require this time. Recording of such information generally came close to the truth. These activities were unlike the great majority performed, where there was much manipulation.

Further Inaccuracies

Officials, especially in one section, often balanced their sheets a day or two prior to the end of the month by approximating figures for the days ahead. This was to give supervisors enough time to add sectional figures together before the deadline date. This too resulted in inaccuracies.

It should be mentioned that officials could not record accurate times even if they so desired. This was because the time spent per interview or on other activities was not recorded immediately as the task was completed. It was only at the end of the day that officials filled out their time records, and it was indeed difficult to remember exactly how long one had spent per operation throughout the work day. The manipulations already discussed above only made these records more inaccurate than they would have been even in the formal ideal. In other words, the records were not formally meant to be "exact to the minute" for each activity. Formal procedure, which demanded recording in units of fifteen minutes, itself prevented such precision. However, many manipulations on an informal basis deviated so far from formal expectations that it was obvious that the recording procedure itself became more important than the actual information it was supposed to convey.

It is also obvious that time wasted in frequent restrictive practices could not be "coded" into the time records, but had to be "fit" into one or another category, and this yielded even further inaccuracies.

Another Informal Modification

Some few officials were annoyed at having to change their figures at the end of the month to meet supervisory demands, and considered the records to be unimportant. They informally modified to meet this situation, did not fill in these sheets on a daily basis as the formal procedure required, but waited until the *end* of the month. Then they went back in reference to their *production records*—to match production credited with general, standard time factors as they knew them for each item of production—filling in the amount of time supposedly spent for each activity, each day. This was certainly inaccurate, for it was impossible to remember what one had done in terms of units as small as quarter-hours of time as many as thirty days back. The records were filled in according to what the official thought would meet supervisory desires. An entire sheet of figures, totals, and balances was thus filled in, times fabricated, and then passed to superiors for inclusion in sectional totals.

Superiors accepted and indeed demanded manipulations of time records. However, the informal modification just discussed deviated too far from established procedure, for it showed without a doubt that the time records were almost entirely fabricated and meaningless. Supervisors prohibited this activity, but this did not halt some few officials from continuing to covertly engage in such behavior. These people hid their blank time records until the end of the month, and then filled in the hours for the entire month all at once, when the monthly statistical period was at an end.

This shows that superiors required fabrication, so the sectional records could read closer to the standards, but would not allow subordinates to admit through their actions that the time records were *entirely* meaningless.

Ambiguously Defined Categories

There were also certain activities that were ill-defined and ambiguous in daily use at Agency C. Agency officials could have requested clarification from upper levels had they so desired.[8] However, clarification was not requested and

---

[8] The author, after participation was halted, wrote to upper levels in Washington, D.C., and requested among other things the formal definitions of several activities. In response, inserts from an agency manual of procedure were sent that defined these activities quite specifically. If the author, no longer an agency employee, secured these definitions without trouble, then this means that agency officials certainly could have done so if they had desired. The local agency also had manuals defining these activities.

these activities were used by local officials for the end of adding or subtracting times as needed, in order to fill in the important operations (such as placement-time) "correctly."

Conclusions

The time record procedure, including standard time factors set up for scientific management purposes serves as an example of the extreme transformation of a procedure because of managerial and supervisory constraints which obliged local level subordinates to fabricate, and again shows change toward a dysfunctional end. Officials wasted their time and upper echelons received a faulty picture of local level operations. [9]

The "figures" and the desire to meet the standards—even though upper echelons did not intend that standards were always to be met, for the standard time factors were for budgetary purposes and were not a work concept—became more important on operating levels than the actual purposes of the records. Once again there is an indication of bureaucratic dynamism toward a dysfunctional end, when numbers became more important than truth.

The next chapter traces the operation of what was known at Agency C as the *former employer procedure*, its relation to statistical records of operations, and its striking dysfunctional consequences.

---

[9]It is not known how often upper echelons used these records, or how aware upper echelons were of lower level deviations from recording procedure. Upper levels might have made allowances for fabrications, but this must remain a supposition, for information is not available on this point.

CHAPTER NINE

The Former Employer Procedure

Introduction

THE PREVIOUS CHAPTERS in Part Three have presented data derived mainly from participant-observation, and showed the dysfunctional consequences of statistical records as used at Agency C. The present chapter also focuses on this same problem by discussing another procedure, this time using not only observational data, but also quantitative data from actual records of operations.

We begin discussion of this procedure by first presenting Professor Blau's findings in 1949:

> Since interviewers were interested in maximizing their "figures" [on statistical records], they tried to do so by various means. Occasionally, a client who had been temporarily laid off expected to return to his former job within the next few days. After confirming this with the employer, the interviewer made out a job order and referred the client to this job. In this way he improved his number of referrals and of placements (and the corresponding proportional indices) without having accomplished the objective that these indices were designed to measure, that is, without having found a job for a client. Sometimes an interviewer even went a step further; if a client said he expected to

return to his former job in four weeks, the interviewer asked him to return to the office then and "referred" him to his own job, wasting the client's time and his own.[1]

This practice which Blau found at Agency B of referring clients to their *own* jobs after a temporary layoff was known as the *former employer program* in 1956-59 (F.E.'s in agency argot).[2]

Blau believes that this practice was an unofficial one at Agency B in 1949. In a letter to the author, he writes:

I am virtually certain that the practice of referring a client to his own job was not an official one when I studied . . . [Agency B]: I was told that it was something "wrong to do" when my attention was first called to it by some interviewers, nobody who explained official procedures to me ever mentioned it, and I observed it only rarely.[3]

Correspondence with the commissioner, the very top-level state official of the bureaucracy studied, however, yields the inference that the former employer policy was an *official one since 1940*: "The Former Employer Program dates back to the establishment of the Apparel Industries Office [Agency B] in 1940."[4]

It is doubtful that this bureau head, the commissioner, would refer to an unofficial practice in an official communication when dating the start of a procedure.

It is, however, absolutely and certainly known that the former employer procedure *was an official one in 1956-59 at both* Agencies B and C, and a large proportion of

---

[1]Peter M. Blau, *The Dynamics of Bureaucracy* (rev. ed., Chicago: University of Chicago Press, 1963), pp. 45-46.

[2]For ease of reading, the more formal term, "former employer procedure" will be interchanged frequently in this chapter with the more informally used term. "F.E." The related term, "F.E.'s," refers to temporarily unemployed clients, and placements made through referral of these clients back to their former employers. The designations "F.E." and "F.E.'s" were commonly used in agency argot at both Agencies B and C during the 1956-59 time period.

[3]Personal letter to the author dated October 3, 1961.

[4]From a personal letter to the author (dated November 15, 1961) from the bureau commissioner. The commissioner indicates that he secured his information from the local Agency B management.

production credited at Agency C was of former employer type. In addition, the important point is not so much whether the procedure was official or unofficial at Blau's date of study in 1949 (although if we knew for certain we could make interesting interpretations) but rather that this procedure in one form or another dates from 1940, and that it was official at both agencies in 1956-59.

Scope of the Former Employer Procedure at Agency C

Blau found that this practice did not occur often at Agency B, but "quite often" is a better description for Agency C studied years later. At this later date Agency C interviewers produced a good proportion of their placements by referring temporarily unemployed clients to their own employers and crediting rehires as placements. Each time a client was referred back to her own employer, a vacancy (job opening received) was also credited on statistical records, as was a referral. Placements derived from sending clients back to their own jobs (i.e., rehires in actuality) were given the same credit for agency budgetary purposes as that provided for regular, or "real" placements.[5] In other words, "easy" former employer placements (sending clients back to their own employers) counted as much as "real" placements (finding a new job for a client) in the "pay-item" budgetary allocation system for agency operations.

The proportion of Agency C vacancies received, referrals, and placements that were of former employer type are not available in published records of operations. The writer, however, kept a copy of his own production taken from his official, individual statistical records, and these do list F.E. operations.

These records show that in the 31-month period from September 1956 through July 1959,[6] the author as a govern-

---

[5] *Ibid.*
[6] This excludes October 1956, December 1956, June 1957, and July 1957 for which data are not available.

ment official, who worked for lengthy periods in three of the six Agency C sections, had placed a total of 2,105 applicants on jobs (see Table 2). Of this total, 1,082 (51 per cent) were of former employer type, where workers were only sent back to their own employers after a temporary layoff.[7] Table 2 shows that within this period the author's highest former employer placement proportion was 82 per cent of all placements in July 1958. The lowest, in which few total placements were credited, was 9 per cent of former employer type in March 1959.

Some skeptics may think that the writer might not be representative of all other staff members in his production and thus might doubt the value of inferences made here about the scope of F.E. operations. There is, however, another method of estimating the amount of former employer work performed at Agency C, and this method yields figures much in line with those taken from the writer's own production records. The second method of deriving former employer data is to compare operating statistics for time periods in which the former employer procedure was in effect with comparable time periods when it was no longer in effect.

The procedure was drastically modified in July 1960. At that time and thereafter officials were no longer allowed to credit placements for applicants who were rehired by their own employers after a temporary layoff, and after being "referred" to these employers by agency personnel.[8]

Table 3 shows that Agency C production in vacancies, referrals and placements each fell by half (in rough figures) when the former employer procedure was no longer in effect.

---

[7]Recall the discussion in the previous chapters which shows that interviewers' records of production were not accurate. This also applies above. However, the inaccuracy in this case only makes the proportion more outstanding. If there were "broken needle" placements included in the total placement figure above, then this means that the number of "real" placements is lower, and that of this lower number of "real" placements, 1,082 were of applicants only referred back to their own long-term employers (who would have rehired them anyway, as shall be seen, without agency "service").

[8]This drastic modification, which really served to rescind the procedure, will be discussed later.

TABLE 2
THE AUTHOR'S PLACEMENT PRODUCTION FOR 31 MONTHS

Month	Total Placements	Former Employer Placements	Per Cent of Total Placements That Are Former Employer Placements
Sept. 1956	80	50	63
Oct.	(Data not available)		
Nov.	136	108	79
Dec.	(Data not available)		
Jan. 1957	74	23	31
Feb.	143	82	57
Mar.	59	20	34
Apr.	65	21	32
May	78	40	51
June	(Data not available)		
July	(Data not available)		
Aug.	58	23	40
Sept.	72	22	31
Oct.	44	18	41
Nov.	49	15	31
Dec.	68	52	76
Jan. 1958	61	18	30
Feb.	52	8	15
Mar.	68	42	62
Apr.	62	20	32
May	54	10	19
June	55	26	47
July	38	31	82
Aug.	76	33	43
Sept.	98	79	81
Oct.	77	45	58
Nov.	49	23	47
Dec.	82	47	57
Jan. 1959	96	59	61
Feb.	48	11	23
Mar.	33	3	9
Apr.	37	23	62
May	51	27	53
June	63	49	78
July	79	54	68
TOTALS	2,105	1,082 *	

*Former employer placements therefore comprise 51 percent of total placements.

TABLE 3

AGENCY C PRODUCTION FIGURES FOR ALL SECTIONS COMBINED, WITH AND WITHOUT THE FORMER EMPLOYER PROCEDURE*

With F.E. Procedure	Without F.E. Procedure	Per Cent Decrease
July 1959-Dec. 1959:	July 1960-Dec. 1960:	
Total Placements 14,631	Total Placements 6,522	55
Total Openings+ 24,998	Total Openings 11,482	54
Total Referrals 23,309	Total Referrals 10,816	54
Jan. 1960-June 1960:	Jan. 1961-June 1961:	
Total Placements 15,688	Total Placements 7,786	50
Total Openings 27,118	Total Openings 13,451	50
Total Referrals 24,708	Total Referrals 12,296	50

—Taken from published agency records of operations.

*The time periods used have been chosen to give comparability by holding seasonal factors constant. This is attained through using the same half-year periods for different years, both before and after the change in procedure.

+It will be recalled that openings are another term for job vacancies received.

It follows that one-half of Agency C vacancy, referral and placement totals were credited for sending temporarily unemployed clients back to their own employers prior to the period when the procedure was rescinded.

It is evident that former employer activity was frequent at Agency C and certainly was not "occasional" as Blau observed at Agency B. Since a roughly estimated one-half of major Agency C operations were taken up with F.E.'s, it is important to trace this entire procedure in terms of causes, formal goals, and dysfunctional consequences.

The Former Employer Practice as a

Formal Procedure at Agency C

The F.E. practice where a client was referred to her former employer was a formal, rather than an informal modification at Agency C. According to formal procedure this practice worked in the following manner:

The benefit client was generally seated for an interview if she stated at the reception counter of the clothing agency that she expected to return to her former employer but she did not know exactly when. It was necessary to check the veracity of this client's assertion that she would be recalled, and also to find out exactly how soon. A telephone call to the employer determined the recall date, and if two weeks or less, with provision of an exact recall date, the client was referred back to her own job. If rehired within two weeks, placement credit was taken.

The commissioner of the State X Employment Bureau summarizes the overt reasoning behind the establishment of the former employer procedure:

It is traditional in the apparel industry for many workers to return to the same shop each season. The [labor] union [for clothing workers] protects these workers by providing contractual rights binding upon employers. On the other hand, workers have the right to return to their shops but are not obligated to do so. Such workers are designated as assigned workers.

Because the apparel industry is characterized by this "assigned worker" relationship between an employer and an employee, it was often necessary to check the availability of a worker for referral. In general, if it was established that a worker was to return to his former employer within two weeks, he was not exposed to a job offer with another employer. If, however, a worker's establishment did not resume its activity within a two week period or the worker was uncertain as to the date of recall, he was available for possible referral to jobs other than his assigned shop.[9]

It is important to note that clothing industry conditions

---

9 From the commissioner's letter, *op. cit.*

played an important part in the establishment of this procedure. The highly seasonal nature of the clothing industry meant that there were wide fluctuations in employment. As a result, this branch serviced many benefit clients who were only on short-term layoffs, and who were reporting to the agency as part of their obligations under the unemployment insurance law to search for employment, even during a temporary period of layoff. The two clothing agencies dealing with a highly seasonal industry (and hence many temporarily unemployed clients), of the many agencies in City X, were the *only two* allowed to use the F.E.'s as a formal procedure.

In the ideal, the former employer procedure could serve several functional ends. First, the former employer procedure could help the agency get temporarily unemployed workers back to their former jobs as soon as possible. This point is confirmed by the commissioner:

The Former Employer Program fulfilled the Employment Bureau responsibility to protect the Unemployment Insurance Fund by seeing that seasonally unemployed workers returned to gainful employment as promptly as possible.[10]

Second, the procedure allowed verification of the client's assertion of rehire, making certain that she was not a malingerer. The third ideally functional end requires some elaboration.

Many temporarily unemployed clients misinterpreted the unemployment insurance law and believed that they were fully entitled to benefits during seasonal layoffs, but without job search obligations. On occasion, temporary jobs were available, and offers were made to clients on temporary layoff. These clients frequently argued with officials or complained about agency interference with the period of temporary unemployment. These people already had jobs to which they intended to return, and were not inclined to search for others when on short-term layoff. This was in spite of legal requirements to the contrary.

---

10 *Ibid.*

The former employer procedure allowed a client on a very short layoff to be sent back to her own job when the firm resumed operations. This avoided the time-consuming and annoying task of having to send a client to a temporary job, when the former employer would recall her within a very short time. Scarce time could then be spent with other clients whose temporary unemployment period was lengthy, or with those who had no jobs at all.

This is what the procedure could have ideally functionally provided.[11] Let us now turn to *actual* operations under this procedure as observed and practiced at Agency C.

Dysfunctions of the Formal F.E. Procedure

Statistical records pressured officials to maximize their production figures, and as Blau says, they tried to do so by various means, which improved placement and referral totals without accomplishing the objective which these records were designed to measure.[12]

A 1959 report of a governmental investigating commission also notes that on an agency-wide basis in City X, the budget and personnel evaluation systems press toward cutting corners by emphasis on easier placements.[13]

Modification of generic placement procedure at Agency C allowed referral credit for sending people back to their

---

[11] There may have been other more personal motives too, which accounted for the establishment of the former employer procedure, not necessarily functional for the agency as a whole, and that are not available in the data. An example is the possible desire of upper-level officials to immediately raise placement totals for increased budgetary allocations. It should be emphasized, however, that there is no proof at hand for this latter statement.

[12] Blau, *Dynamics . . ., op. cit.,* pp. 45-46.

[13] From a governmental report not cited in full to preserve anonymity of the research locale. This governmental report and others in the series used in this work were written by a commission which investigated Agency C and six others in City X in 1959. The information above is therefore derived from several agencies and is not limited to the ones upon which this work places major attention. The commission's findings are not limited to, and in fact do not mention, former employer activity but focus on cutting corners through discriminatory policies. (Discrimination will be discussed in Chapter Ten.) While the findings do not focus on F.E.'s they can still be applied to the subject at Agency C.

own employers, and rehires by former employers yielded statistical placement credit. This type of placement is extremely easy to make. All the interviewer had to do was telephone the employer, determine the recall date, fill out a brief record sheet, and provide a card with the client's own employer's name and address (as an "introduction"). [14] This counted statistically as an interview, a solicitation to an employer (when the employer was contacted by telephone to determine the recall date), a referral (if the employer could give an exact recall date within a two-week time period from the date of the telephone call), a vacancy (when an exact recall date was secured), and placement credit was recorded for a hire if the client was rehired within two weeks' time. Experience did not have to be matched with the employer's requirements, matching the client's access to transportation with the location of the employer was avoided, wages did not have to be discussed, nor union factors, type of work, skill level, or related matters. A client was merely being introduced to her own employer and was being sent to her own job. This was an exceedingly simple method of increasing figures on records.

The statistical records pressured toward easy placements. Staff moved toward emphasis on former employer placements at Agency C because these were the easiest placements to make. Supervisors and managers also constrained subordinates toward increased F.E. production because it maximized total sectional and agency records.

According to a former interviewer: ". . . the management was so much more interested in statistics and F.E.'s than in anything else. . . ." [15]

---

[14] Sometimes the interviewer did not even have to telephone the employer. If it had been determined after one telephone call for one worker, that the entire plant would resume within two weeks, all other workers from that plant reporting to the agency could be referred back to the former employer on the basis of this information. In this case the interviewer only had to fill out the record card for all subsequent workers and had to provide introduction cards to the former employer.

[15] From the letter of the former official quoted extensively in Chapter Seven. This quotation ends with reference to the testing program. The statement on the subject of F.E.'s is unsolicited, for the writer merely asked this person to comment

(continued)

In addition to pressures of statistical records, another reason why officials came to emphasize former employer operations was because it helped avoid frustrating conflict with clients. An argument was likely to follow when a client who was temporarily unemployed, or sometimes when a client who had no position at all, was offered a job. The client frequently wanted to wait until rehire by the former employer or sometimes to avoid employment altogether. There was little such conflict when the interviewee was being sent back to her own employer (except where she had been kept waiting too long for an interview).

Officials under these constraints came to emphasize this easy work to such a great extent that they were spending a good proportion (roughly one-half according to Tables 2 and 3) of their major working energies on this practice. This caused neglect of other clients as well as neglect of the major placement and unemployment insurance goals. Instead of providing more time for long-term temporarily unemployed clients, and those who had no jobs, officials actually neglected these clients in the press for more F.E.'s. Records were certainly maximized but officials were often achieving such maximization at the expense of *real* employment service. Former employer clients, in addition, were frequently being seated for interviews and serviced even when there were *no* temporary jobs available, and therefore, when there was no question of malingering, but only for the purpose of maximizing statistical records.

Dysfunctions, however, were not limited only to the neglect of real employment agency service (i.e., finding real jobs for the unemployed). There were other dysfunctions

---

on the testing program. The former official, however, found it necessary to comment on the effects of F.E.'s on the testing. The former employer procedure permeated Agency C operations to such a great extent that discussion of almost any aspect of Agency C in 1956-59 must return again to the emphasis on F.E.'s. This is, of course, connected to emphasis on maximization of statistical records.

It should also be mentioned that many of the clients seated for interviews when supervisors or others "stuffed the box" (discussed in an earlier chapter) were of F.E. type.

too, within the former employer procedure as it was used at Agency C.

One such dysfunction observed by Blau was also repeated very frequently at Agency C. If a former employer referral could not be made (e.g., if the employer or applicant insisted that he did not know exactly when the plant would resume operations but thought that it would be perhaps in three or four weeks) officials sometimes avoided referring the client to a temporary job even if such vacancies did exist. This was in order to avoid conflict and the trouble of matching a temporary job with an unwilling client. As observed by Blau, the client was given a reappointment date close to the period of anticipated recall, and a former employer referral was attempted at the next time the client visited the agency.[16] This met the needs of the officials to avoid trouble and met desires of clients to avoid temporary jobs, but this deviated dysfunctionally from the unemployment insurance as well as placement goals. In addition, Blau notes that when the client had to return to the agency only to be "referred" back to his own job, he was wasting his own time and the time of the official servicing him was also wasted.

Interviewers were so highly pressured toward achieving good production records at Agency C that they sometimes even went several steps further.

At times of layoff, employers advised their workers that they would be rehired when seasonal activity again made recall possible. Generally this would be "in a few weeks." The clothing industry fluctuated widely in activity. Rehire dates depended on the changeover time to new clothing styles, receipt of goods from manufacturers, delivery of material from other sources, negotiations with suppliers, manufacturers and customers, the state of the economy, and a whole host of other contingent variables. Employers frequently did not know exactly when they would recall employees, for it depended on many different factors. It was only very shortly before rehire that most employers could

---

[16] See the quotation from Blau (*op. cit.*) pp.45-46, on pp. 144-45.

say exactly when operations would resume, and even here last minute contingencies often caused further delay in rehires. It was for this reason that employers generally told their workers that recall would be made in a few weeks instead of giving an exact date. Employers tended to contact workers for provision of recall information shortly before the rehire date, when the exact date was more certain.

Temporarily unemployed workers tended to report to the agency with their employers' information of "a few weeks layoff" (or with similar information). A reply of a few weeks was generally insufficient for the receptionist, and the client was often seated for an interview. The interviewing official then telephoned the employer to determine exactly when he would rehire this worker.

The employer often answered that which he had told the worker and the truth to the best of his knowledge: "A few weeks." The official was pressured to maximize figures and a reply of "few weeks" meant that a former employer referral could not be made. According to formal procedure, the employer had to provide an *exact* recall date within a two-week time period before a former employer referral could be made.

The interviewer felt obliged to improve his record if his proportion of referrals to total interviews was low. In such a situation he sometimes probed more deeply and put words into the employer's mouth. For example, an inexact employer reply of, "Perhaps two or three weeks until recall" sometimes led the official to write on the employer's record card, the "exact" information, "rehiring all workers in two weeks," and this client as well as other workers from the same firm were referred back to their own jobs. Sometimes the employer was pressured by the official into saying, "two weeks," by repeated probing, when he really did not know exactly when he would rehire his workers. Here real employment agency operations were being neglected only to give temporarily unemployed workers faulty information!

Clients on short-term layoff did not want to be sent to temporary jobs, and were likely to complain if this occurred.

On the other hand, clients also often made negative comments when they were sent back to their own employers, for they had waited for interviews, only to be told what they already knew: that their employer would rehire them; and they were given introduction cards to their very own shops! Some employers, in addition, were annoyed at frequent agency telephone calls, both at time of original verification, and then at time of rehire when officials read off long lists of names to determine former employer placements. Thus the former employer procedure as used at Agency C was also adversely affecting public relations.

What makes the dysfunctional consequences extreme to the ultimate degree is that employers called their workers back to work *themselves,* even when agency officials were informing workers of recall dates. All workers were not eligible for, nor did they wish to collect, unemployment benefits, and therefore did not report to the agency. All workers from a particular plant did not report to the agency at the same date, and not all were interviewed, so certainly all were not informed of the recall date through the agency former employer procedure. The employer could not rely on the agency for the recall of workers because he could not risk missing the recall of essential employees. Since the great majority of employers did not rely on the agency for this recall service, and contacted their workers themselves (some workers contacted their employers by prearrangement or otherwise), government officials were not performing a special service for the benefit of clients and employers under the former employer procedure, nor were they meeting unemployment insurance obligations. They were only performing work that was not required, detracting from other goals as well.

Another. dysfunctional aspect of this procedure, and an unanticipated consequence, was that it also created conflict between staff members because of the procedure of calling former employer clients to interviews.

Pressure toward maximizing records was so great, and

former employer activity was so easy, that some officials in competition with co-workers, arranged the timing of their work so they could manage to interview easy former employer clients instead of more difficult "regular" clients. Other staff members were inclined to become annoyed at this practice for they had to interview the more difficult cases left.[17]

The bureaucrats were busy about half of their work time with a procedure that in reality had turned into generally useless paper work, created antagonisms, and deviated far from the requirements of employment agency operations.

An interviewer sums up the futility of the former employer work when he sarcastically writes: "Yes, things are certainly humming at . . . [Agency C]. Busy, busy, busy. Oh how those F.E.'s keep rolling in."[18] In the case of F.E.'s, Agency C was indeed "a magnificent navy on land."[19]

A Halt to the Former Employer Procedure

The former employer procedure in one possible form or another had been in effect since 1940. However, it was only in July 1960, twenty years later, that a formal adjustment was made by upper bureaucratic levels which counteracted the dysfunctions observed at Agency C in 1956-59, and refocused placement procedure on its intended objective, i.e., to find real jobs for unemployed persons. The formal former employer procedure was discontinued, and placement, vacancy and referral credit could no longer be taken for sending clients back to their own employers.

Even the commissioner of the State X Employment Bureau notes that the procedure was rescinded because it

---

[17]Some officials arranged work to service other types of easy clients too, and to avoid the more difficult and troublesome. This entire matter, with analysis also applicable to the easy F.E.'s, has been discussed in Chapter Six.

[18]The letter from which this is taken, and the remark about the F.E. procedure were unsolicited.

[19]C. Northcote Parkinson, *Parkinson's Law* (Boston: Houghton Mifflin, 1957), p.7.

became time consuming and costly; perhaps referring in a general way to the very same conditions already discussed in this chapter:

> . . . the program was time consuming and costly. Although it was recognized as a valuable service [ideally?], because of the cost involved it was decided in July of 1960 to discontinue it. This decision was made after many discussions with the Regional Office of the Bureau of Employment. . . .[20]

Ultimate effects of this change cannot be fully discussed because participation was terminated in 1959. Consultation with some local agency operating officials in 1960 served to bring this change originally to this writer's attention.

It is known, however, that agency placement, vacancy and referral statistical records immediately dropped by about one-half as a result of this change (see Table 3). It should be mentioned that this is not dysfunctional, for the records are now a more accurate indicator of service, and this also means that officials are no longer wasting their time and that of clients on the most often useless former employer procedure.

One former interviewer (but temporarily assigned as a supervisory official at the time of conversation in August 1961), in response to the question of how operations are without the F.E.'s, sums up the functional aspects of this change when she states that it is better, but only "for those who want to do a satisfying day's work." This official means that time is not now being wasted by interviewers on the F.E. work, but implies that those interviewers who emphasized the easy F.E.'s, and relied on it to boost their production records, do not find operations better.[21]

---

[20]From the commissioner's letter, *op. cit.*

[21]In sociological argot this official's evaluation can be translated as: The modification is functional in terms of organizational service-oriented goals, but dysfunctional in the eyes of those officials who emphasized former employer activity, and who can no longer rely on this easy work to maximize records.

Conclusions

Special local conditions where most clients reporting to the clothing agency were only temporarily unemployed pressed toward a departure from generic agency procedure. A modification of generic placement procedure, called the former employer program, was made to meet this special local condition. This procedure, however, caused extreme deviation from the major organizational goals, and again there is indication of dysfunctional pressures deriving from statistical records.

The bureaucracy studied here was not static. Staff on various levels of the agency modified formally and informally to meet special local needs, as well as the effects of prior changes (although they did not always do so). That there was sometimes a dysfunctional lag in time before a needed formal modification was made is illustrated by the F.E. procedure. This practice had been in operation in one form or another for *twenty years* before upper hierarchical levels adjusted placement procedure as specially applied to the clothing agencies by rescinding the former employer procedure in 1960.[22] This caused a halt to the dysfunctional operations under the former employer procedure and brought Agency C closer once again to generic organizational goals.

---

[22] This change applied both to Agencies B and C at the 1960 date.

* * *

Conclusions to Part Three

THE CHAPTERS in Part Three showed how a series of modifications caused by an original change to detailed recording procedure caused dysfunctional consequences. The records came to have more importance to the government officials than the activities and performance that these records were designed to measure, control, and improve. There was a displacement of goals.

A roughly estimated 50 per cent of Agency C major production credited was of former employer type. We can then surmise that at least half of Agency C work in referrals, vacancies and placements credited were not of "real" employment agency (service-oriented, job-finding) nature, but only led to more "numbers" on records. Within this percentage, there were other inflations, such as recording of "broken needle" placements. This means that *less* than 50 per cent (roughly estimated) of production of major items credited was of real employment agency activity. Dysfunctional competition of various types must be added as a consequence of production stress and of visibility of work on the records. Haphazard referrals to jobs and tests, the wasted time maintaining inaccurate records, the possibly faulty budgetary allotments because of inflated records, restriction of output, the effects on clients who had become secondary in the "numbers game" played by officials (for the goal of maximizing records), useless field visits, losses in terms of public relations, lack of protection of the unemployment insurance fund, and lack in providing employers with the desperately needed workers they had to have for efficient production (when such workers were available, of course), also are dysfunctional consequences. These losses defy measurement.

It is evident that dysfunctional consequences of these records as used at Agency C were great indeed. Of course, full blame cannot be placed on the records. Other factors were interacting here too (e.g., the highly seasonal nature of the clothing industry, and the many clients who preferred not to find jobs and who made difficulty for the officials). But then again, here is a government agency that received a full budgetary allotment for less than 50 per cent of *real* employment agency work!

To be sure, the agency did provide service to clients and emphasis in the previous pages on dysfunctions should not lead the reader to think that clients received no employment service whatsoever. But while the agency often provided service, often it did not, and it was on this latter point that Part Three has focused.

Statistical records certainly affected job applicants and clothing employers at Agency C, because it affected the agency operations. It is obvious that bureaucracy and clientele (including special local conditions) are closely entwined.

Agency emphasis on quantity, and cutting of corners in response, decreased service. Examples of decreased service to employers are useless field visits; and former employer activity, among many other matters, for job applicants. But difficult clients, in connection with pressures of statistical records, also caused officials to emphasize easy as well as needless activities and to inflate records instead of troubling themselves with such clients. This emphasis only adversely affected the applicants and deviated from organizational goals. In short, both formal agency procedures and related pressures, as well as more informal client pressures, caused officials to deviate from organizational goals and to emphasize matters which ironically led to decreased service to clients.*

To sum up and to conclude briefly, formal procedures such as the budgetary procedure on upper levels, and the related statistical records of production on lower levels, were formally designed to attain better operations, better service to clients, and increased achievement of organizational goals. However, these procedures led to pressures which in conjunction with client demands and behavior, and local conditions, caused Agency C to deviate to an extreme degree from service-oriented organizational goals.

Part Three has thus traced a formal procedure (statistical recording procedure) and its highly dysfunctional consequences.

Part Four will focus on the agency anti-discrimination policy, and will trace dysfunctions on an agency-wide basis, and on various bureaucratic levels.

---

*It should be recalled that decreased service is defined in relation to organizational goals. Clients who were "sneaked out," for example, were satisfied with "service." Repeated difficulties with temporarily unemployed clients who did not want temporary jobs and who wanted to be "sneaked out" led to dismissals of some such clients without the service demanded by organizational mandate. But this led the official to "make-up" for the other service not provided by emphasizing needless work and cutting corners, and only added to pressures for interviewer emphasis on the easy former employer referrals to maximize records, even to the extent of sometimes providing faulty information. The client in the case of former employer activity (emphasized in part because of ease of this operation as compared to finding temporary jobs for unwilling clients), often had to wait for interviews when no temporary jobs were available. This was decreased service in relation to client *and* agency goals.

PART FOUR

AGENCY-WIDE DYSFUNCTIONS

> *The radiation of control from the elders is
> limited by the reaction of the young men,
> that from the priests is limited by the reaction
> of the laity, that from the bureaucracy is
> limited by the reaction of the citizens. . . .*
> —EDWARD A. ROSS*

---

* *Social Control* (New York: Macmillan, 1901), p. 84.

CHAPTER TEN

The Discrimination Case

> *. . . the legislature hereby finds and declares that practices of discrimination against any of its inhabitants because of race, creed, color or national origin are a matter of state concern, that such discrimination threatens not only the rights and proper privileges of its inhabitants but menaces the institutions and foundation of a free democratic state.*
> —From the Anti-discrimination Law enacted in State X.

THE EMPLOYMENT BUREAU in State X had a special policy against discrimination in its operations. This non-discrimination policy was in effect in 1949, and Blau noted that it was a pervasive principle taught to new employees.[1] In 1956-59 this anti-discrimination policy was still in effect, operating in conjunction with a state law which acted to

---

[1] Peter M. Blau, *The Dynamics of Bureaucracy* (rev. ed., Chicago: University of Chicago Press, 1963), p. 22.

forbid biased practices in employment agency referrals and in employers' hiring practices.

Employment agencies, private and public, as well as employers, were not allowed to list applicant racial characteristics on job application cards, and were not allowed to discriminate in referrals, hires, or employment. Public Employment Bureau agencies, in addition, were to act as an aid to the State X Anti-discrimination Commission (set up to implement the state law against discrimination) by reporting violating employers who indicated bias in their requests for workers from the agencies.

The law, however, was one thing, but what was actually practiced at some City X agencies and some business firms was yet another. These deviations form the main subject matter of this chapter.

Other chapters have dealt mainly with Agencies B and C. Data, in good part derived from the reports of a governmental commission, are extended in the following pages to cover not only Agencies B and C, but also other agencies in City X. It will be seen that events at other locales corroborate the findings of deviation from goals at Agency C. It will also be seen that deviations were not limited to the interviewing level, but occurred on other higher levels of the bureaucracy as well.

The Flagello case [2] begins an account of a situation that started with internal determination of an illegitimate practice by one interviewer, but which mushroomed into an agency-wide affair which was brought to public attention.

The Flagello Case

Special employment interviewers were assigned to

---

[2] It should be recalled that fictitious names are being substituted for all real names in this book. It is important to specify that Mrs. Flagello and some other persons discussed were *not* assigned to Agency C, but to another agency in City X. Some upper level officials, to be discussed later, had a measure of control over all City X agencies, but some were managerial officials immediately in charge of only one local agency other than Agency C or Agency B.

various high schools in City X as an expansion of agency service to meet employment needs of students. In February of 1958 one of these special interviewers, Mrs. Flagello, was scheduled to take an extended leave because of illness. Mrs. Flagello trained a replacement (Mrs. Angell) and during training she advised this replacement of an informal modification.

Agency rules and state law flatly prohibited discrimination in agency referral policies or in employer hire policies. This law also prohibited employment agencies, private and public, as well as employers, from listing applicant racial characteristics on application cards. This was designed to avoid referral or placement only on the basis of race, which was felt to be a variable best excluded from consideration in referring and hiring suitable workers.

Mrs. Flagello, however, found it convenient to make such notations and informally modified this formal requirement. She did not overtly list racial characteristics on the application cards because this could obviously be seen by supervisors and checked. She rather devised her own "dot" system to indicate race of students. Those cards that had a dot placed in a specific space signified nonwhite applicants while absence of dots indicated white students.

While training Mrs. Angell as the replacement, Mrs. Flagello informed her of the illegal dot coding system and asked that she maintain this informal modification. Mrs. Flagello was also purported to have requested the replacement, "not to refer the students with the dots on their cards during Easter for employment in June after graduation."[3]

It has been seen that informal modifications of various types were frequent at Agency C and the data here show that there was an informal modification by an interviewer at another locale too. The "dot" system was only one of

_____

[3] From one of a series of eight governmental reports by the State X Antidiscrimination Commission not cited in full in order to preserve anonymity of tne research locale. All further references to any of the eight reports will be treated in the same manner.

very many changes that dysfunctionally deviated from major agency goals and policies. [4]

Mrs. Angell, however, refused to maintain Mrs. Flagello's dot system which deviated so broadly from agency policy and state law. Mrs. Angell reported this matter to her superior, also telling him of information she had received from students while she had been working at the high school which led her to believe that Mrs. Flagello, "had taken credit for several placements for which in fact she was not responsible." [5]

The superior reported this to an upper level official in April 1958, and this official in turn reported the matter to a yet higher level in the bureaucracy, the superintendent of the division under whose jurisdiction the special interviewers in this case were assigned. [6] Various bureaucratic levels were now apprised of the informal modifications on the matter of discriminatory coding and improper crediting of placements on records.

Emphasis of the agency on placements and crediting on statistical records to the detriment of other goals is strikingly shown when the superintendent focused attention on the charge of fabricated placements, but neglected the discriminatory action. The superintendent said that she was aware of the charge of discrimination, but that in her view improper crediting of placements was a much more serious breach of agency regulations. [7] Hence Mrs. Flagello's (and

---

[4] The agency anti-discrimination policy is tied to the major placement goal by partly specifying the manner the placement goal was to be reached. This anti-discrimination policy, backed by law, required that suitable candidates should be referred to openings on the basis of qualifications and not either preselected or denied full service because of race, creed, color, national origin, or age. Age was a later addition to the anti-discrimination law, and aimed within certain age limits, at eliminating restrictive hiring practices because of this factor. The relation of the anti-discrimination policy and the placement goal will be discussed further in the pages ahead.

[5] From governmental report.

[6] *Ibid.*

[7] Data for Agency C discussed in Chapter Seven show that deviation from placement crediting procedure (although not in the same manner as Mrs. Flagello's deviation) was not unusual.

at this time Mrs. Angell's) superior was instructed to make an investigation into the improper placement claims.

The superior made his investigation and reported the results to the manager (his superior). According to the superior's report, the charge of fabrication of placements was substantiated. The superior also found, incident to his investigation, that one of the application cards that had a dot was that of a Negro student.[8]

This report was sent to other upper-level officials who discussed the findings considerably and then decided that they would let the entire matter rest because Mrs. Flagello was on extended sick leave which was forecast to end in complete resignation from her position. Mrs. Flagello's physician also said that her condition was so serious that she could not be talked to about anything. In addition, the agency superintendent felt that nothing more could be done about the fraudulent placement charges, and that there was insufficient evidence for action on the application dot charges.[9]

In January 1959, however, the entire case had to be reopened, when contrary to expectations, Mrs. Flagello requested reinstatement to her position with the agency. This request resulted in further hearings by upper-level officials on the charges of fabrication of placement records.[10]

It was decided to reinstate Mrs. Flagello, after consultation and approval by various upper hierarchical levels. Mrs. Flagello was allowed to return to her position as a regular employment interviewer, but not to return to her former special assignment at the high school.[11] However, there was still a void because other interviewers had to be apprised of the agency action in this situation in order to avoid misinformation:

It was feared that Mrs. Flagello would spread untrue stories

---

[8] From governmental report.
[9] Ibid.
[10] Ibid.
[11] Ibid.

about the situation and mislead . . . [other special interviewers] still in the program. 12

The superintendent met with several supervisory staff members to decide what information about Mrs. Flagello should be given the other officials. This interviewer had fabricated placements and illegally coded race on application cards, but she was being reinstated to her position, and as a result an official upper-level stand had to be taken for the information of other interviewers. It is important to mention that one of the supervisory officials present at the meeting (Mr. Glass), was also head of the local Civil Service Employee's Union. During the meeting:

After the superintendent reviewed the charges concerning the placements and had stated the results of the investigation and the decision of the administration, that in view of the time lapse and the small number of cases which could be verified, charges could not be sustained and that Mrs. Flagello should be reinstated with a reprimand, Mr. Glass raised the question of what had been done about the discrimination charge. The superintendent said she thought it had been covered in the investigation but wasn't sure, and went on to explain to Mr. Glass the reasons why primacy had been given to the charge of fraudulent placement. Besides the reasons previously expressed, the superintendent mentioned that the investigation of the placement charge was easier to conduct since it involved interviewing only a group of 20 students, while an investigation of the charge of discrimination would involve every student registered in the school. Mr. Glass disagreed with the superintendent's position.
It was decided at the meeting, according to the superintendent, that the State X Employment Bureau should not take any action which might be construed as administering additional punishment; that the two counsellors to whom Mrs. Flagello had given misinformation should be given a short statement of the correct information by the superior, that Mrs. Angell should also be informed by the superior as to what had happened and that any comment in regard to Mrs. Flagello's relationship to

---

12 *Ibid.*

the school program would be met by a statement that she is not returning and will not return to the school program. It was thought, the superintendent declared, that, "The least said the soonest mended." 13

Mrs. Flagello was reinstated, albeit with a reprimand from an upper-level official in relation to the fraudulent placement claims. This action was taken only on the basis of the improper placement claims, and the reprimand made no mention of the unlawful coding of application cards.

This handling of the case caused Mr. Glass (the agency supervisor and union official) to protest, for the deviation from the anti-discrimination law and policy had been treated rather mildly. Mr. Glass thereupon *in his capacity as union head* requested a meeting with a high-level official (the Director of State X Employment Bureau Personnel). The request was granted and Mr. Glass, together with a committee of the union local, met with the director. The union committee stated its opinion that the State X Employment Bureau should pursue further the charges of discrimination against nonwhite students. As a result of this meeting the director requested the Bureau's Department of Counsel to make a further internal inquiry into the discriminatory coding. 15

Thus the pressures of the union president-agency supervisor led to a more complete investigation, whereas previously the entire matter, according to upper-level decision, was to be dropped without further disposition. It is important to note this reversal of internal agency decision-making when external pressures in the form of the union acted on the organization. Another point worthy of comment is that in this case an agency supervisor also has a dual role as local union president. Supervisory officials in private businesses are generally considered manage-

---

13 *Ibid.*
14 *Ibid.*
15 *Ibid.*

ment oriented and often do not become members of unions. [16]
The effect of the dual role is evident when Mr. Glass abruptly switched from agency supervisor included in private, internal upper-level deliberations, to union president in his request for a meeting with a higher-level official. In this meeting the purpose was to secure reversal of an internal decision already made by managerial personnel and this was achieved.

As a result of the union pressure, the agency counsel's office examined application files containing Mrs. Flagello's work. Referral records were also checked.

The findings of this *internally conducted* investigation showed that application cards of nonwhites were indeed dotted, but that students whose cards were marked and those that were not dotted were referred almost equally to jobs. [17] The internal investigation by the counsel's department also took sworn testimony from Mrs. Angell in which she told of her training by Mrs. Flagello, and the related matters. This was presented before the agency general counsel, the associate counsel, with Mrs. Angell's superior also in attendance. Mr. Glass, however, was barred even though Mrs. Angell requested his presence as union representative. Mrs. Flagello then testified:

. . . [that she] did not remember telling Mrs. Angell about the dots and claimed that she had separated the cards of the

---

[16] According to the National Labor Relations Act as amended by the Taft-Hartley Act (The Labor-Management Relations Act of 1947):

"Nothing herein shall prohibit any individual employed as a supervisor from becoming or remaining a member of a labor organization, but no employer subject to this Act shall be compelled to deem individuals defined herein as supervisors as employees for the purpose of any law, either national or local, relating to collective bargaining." (Section 14a.)

In other words, employers are no longer *required* (under the act) *to bargain* with supervisors, but supervisors can become members of unions, and employers can, if they wish, regard supervisors as employees for bargaining purposes.

The bargaining issue is not the main one at the State X Employment Bureau because wages and other major issues were set by the legislature and were not subject to bargaining.

[17] From governmental report.

students to be sent out at Easter in Mrs. Angell's presence so that she would know which students to send out at Easter and which to send out in June. . . .

. . . [also] there was absolutely no distinction in referrals as to whether a person was a Negro or a white or a Puerto Rican. She claimed that the students she worked with, if they had an adequate I.Q., could be placed anywhere, into any training program. . . .

. . . [she] denied that she put the dots on the cards of Negroes. She claimed that she put the dots on the cards of students that needed special attention . . . of course there were a lot of Negroes. . . .

. . . .

Mrs. Flagello was . . . handed 15 cards that were dotted and that were marked for Easter referral and she was asked to explain why she dotted each card.

As she read the cards she explained that one had asthma, two needed dental work, one had transferred from the West Indies, one was taking home economics, one was an academic student, two wanted a job in a particular field, one overestimated her abilities, one was good but quiet, and one was an exceptional student Mrs. Flagello wanted to get into a training program. Mrs. Flagello was unable to explain the existence of dots on four cards.

Mrs. Flagello then acknowledged that there were good students whose cards were dotted and stated it was for the purpose of calling their qualifications to the attention of prospective employers.

Mrs. Flagello was then handed the cards of 35 students whose cards were not dotted and was asked to explain the absence of dots from their cards.

In most cases, she claimed that the students were superior and didn't need any special attention. It was pointed out to her that some of the students in the group were academics, or had asked for a special field or position and that she had not dotted their cards, although she claimed that she had dotted the cards of other students for the very same reasons.

She was then asked to explain why practically 100 per cent of the dotted cards were cards representing colored students.

She stated that the colored children probably needed her more to make a special call for them because of their personality or their abilities. She said, "The colored children have difficulty with English often but lots of them are good at math. Well now you can put them in a math. [*sic*] job and they won't ever have to use their English."

She denied categorically and emphatically that she had placed the dots on the cards because the students were colored. [18]

The internal hearings were closed, and the agency counsel presented his findings. This was March 11, 1959, about one year after the case was first brought to light by Mrs. Angell. The report stated:

If discrimination against nonwhites was intended for the purpose of not referring them for good jobs, the record does not support this result. . . .

The counsel also indicated . . . that in view of the testimony which indicated that the population of the schools was from 40 to 50 per cent nonwhite, only a small number of the cards were marked.

He also indicated that although Mrs. Angell was positive that Mrs. Flagello had trained her for a week or two, a check of the personnel records of the superior's office established that the only association between Mrs. Flagello and Mrs. Angell was on February 21, 1958 and February 24, 1958. [19]

He also found that Mrs. Angell did not report the substance of the conversation until two or three weeks thereafter. . . . [20]

The counsel found that Mrs. Flagello was an experienced, educated, mature woman and stated that it does not appear probable that she would make the statements attributed to her by Mrs. Angell during an acquaintanceship of less than two days. [21]

It is interesting to note that Mrs. Angell who originally brought the entire case to light, and who had already been

---

[18] *Ibid.*

[19] We have already seen that agency production and time records were inaccurate. However, information on the accuracy of training records is not available.

[20] Governmental report. There is a discrepancy here, for the governmental commission from whose report this quotation has been taken finds that:

"The record does not appear to have any evidence to support . . . [the] finding [that Mrs. Angell did not report the substance of the conversation until two or three weeks after she had been trained by Mrs. Flagello]."

[21] *Ibid.*

corroborated at the least in terms of the *presence* of dots on the cards, as well as in the matter of Mrs. Flagello's false placements, here is being put on the defensive instead of being commended for her action. Indeed, Mrs. Angell was forced to give testimony without the presence of Mr. Glass as her union representative. The counsel or other upper-level officials for some reason—perhaps because they thought that he would once again disagree with decisions made or object to the line of questioning taken in the testimony—did not allow Mr. Glass to be present.

When the counsel evidenced doubt that Mrs. Flagello would, as a mature, experienced, and educated woman, tell Mrs. Angell of the informal modifications in an acquaintanceship of less than two days, he seemed to be unaware of the great number of changes in daily operations on the local level. At Agency C, various modifications were quite "natural" to interviewers, and newly hired officials soon learned how to cut corners too. There was no great secret among interviewers about many informal modifications, and sometimes even supervisors, as we have seen, themselves requested such change. This information is based on Agency C participation. Since the participant-observation data does not cover that area emphasized by the counsel's investigation, he could well have a point, although this writer is more than skeptical of the validity of the counsel's assertion that it is improbable an interviewer would request continued informal modification by a colleague after only a brief acquaintanceship.

While Mrs. Angell is put on the defensive in the statements quoted above, the counsel reversed himself and contradicted his previous position:

He also found that Mrs. Angell, while apparently much younger and less mature [than Mrs. Flagello] did not appear to be untruthful or given to exaggeration.[22]

---

[22] *Ibid.*

The counsel in this statement appeared to be acting more as an intermediary in bringing two dissenting parties together again by showing both to have some good qualities, than in his role as a legal expert. Finally, he concluded:

> It would appear that when Mrs. Angell had occasion to examine the dotted cards after Mrs. Flagello's departure on leave, she noticed that practically all of the cards appertained to non-whites. However, the factual analysis indicates that Mrs. Flagello did not in fact discriminate against nonwhites. She gave them as good, if not better, service than she did the white applicants. . . .
>
> From all of the foregoing I come to the conclusion that the dots were placed on the cards by Mrs. Flagello as a "short-hand" method of identification of cards that required particular attention and not for the purpose of discriminating against any of the applicants.[23]

Hence the counsel's internal investigation ended on a "good note," reconciling Mrs. Angell's and Mrs. Flagello's testimony without difficulty to either one. The case does not end here, however, for there later was a striking public pronouncement of discrimination at the Employment Bureau. Mr. Glass was still dissatisfied with the handling of this case, and this led to further events.

It should be emphasized that the counsel had concluded that the cards were indeed marked, but without discrimination. However, he failed to take into account the fact that state law *prohibited any notations whatsoever* that would indicate race of an applicant. According to law, this coding itself was a discriminatory practice.

External Pressures

Once the agency completed its own investigation under the prodding of Mr. Glass, the dissenting parties still felt that the matter had been handled improperly in the study, the findings, the final disposition of the case, and the treat-

---

[23] *Ibid.*

ment of Mrs. Angell who appeared to be put under pressure instead of being commended for calling first attention to the deviating informal modification.

Under this situation, the assistant regional director of the union sent a letter to the state governor, repeating many of the issues already taken up in this chapter, and others which shall be discussed. This provided another external pressure on the agency upper-level officials to treat this matter with better regard for state and agency policy. This letter of protest, dated March 16, 1959, is reproduced in full in the appendix. One section, however, is most interesting for this study and is repeated here:

> The superintendent was reminded that the . . . [agency under her control] has a low proportion of nonwhite employment interviewers as compared with other offices throughout the city and that . . . [this agency] does not have a single nonwhite account interviewer while other offices have 20-30 per cent. Account interviewers are charged with maintaining relations with specific firms and [are] responsible for providing workers for these same firms. To this the superintendent replied, "What do you want me to do, hire Negroes?" [24]

Discriminatory hiring policies were illegal under state law, and this state agency was supposed to help another governmental department, the Anti-discrimination Commission, by reporting violating private employers. The letter above alleges that the superintendent, a higher-level state official, indicates the same discriminatory feeling that can lead to biased hiring and assignment practices that the agency is duty bound by law to help erase in *private employers!* [25]

---

[24] The source from which this letter has been taken for research purposes is the governmental reports *(ibid.)*.

[25] This is not the only example of its kind in American public bureaucracy. Bernard H. Baum, for example, writes in his study of decentralization of authority at the U.S. Civil Service Commission:

"Agency F [Agency F referred to by Baum has no necessary connection or relationship with employment agencies in general, or with Agencies B or C in

(continued)

Another external pressure was placed on the agency when charges of discrimination were vividly brought to the public in a front page article in a March 17, 1959, newspaper (reproduced in full in the appendix). On March 18 this same newspaper published yet another article under a striking front page banner headline covering the width of the paper:

BIAS COVERUP LAID TO STATE [26]

The first article reported on a study that the newspaper itself had made as a check on agency job bias and indicates that informants, probably union or unofficial agency sources, brought the case to the attention of the newspaper:[27]

---

particular], like all other agencies being considered, had clerk-typists certified to them from a centralized [Civil Service] Commission Register. On the other hand, they had their own board of examiners to fill their own professional positions. The head of this agency, who was also the chairman of its board of examiners, said to the author, who was at that time a Commission representative, 'If you send us any more of those "niggers" and try to make us hire them, I'll set up a separate office for them in another building and send the typing out to them and have them send it back.' This statement was made a matter of record in a memorandum retained in the Commission files for several years. No formal action ever resulted." See Bernard H. Baum, *Decentralization of Authority in a Bureaucracy* (Englewood Cliffs, New Jersey: Prentice-Hall, 1961), pp. 108-9.

For similar cases see: William C. Bradbury, "Racial Discrimination in the Federal Service: A Study in the Sociology of Administration" (unpublished Ph.D. dissertation. Dept. of Sociology, Columbia University, 1952).

26 This entire article is reproduced in the appendix.

27 The first newspaper exposé was published just *one day* after the date of the letter to the governor, and the March 18 article which mentions the union letter was printed another day later. This is too soon for the information to have come from official government sources. The newspaper article itself states: "The persons giving information to this newspaper said they had not used official channels for their complaints because they feared retaliation from superiors. They insisted that any investigation by the Division into its own practices would result in a 'whitewash.'"

There is some discrepancy, however, in the newspaper account. The March 18 newspaper article mentions that: "The union's action [the letter to the governor?] came *after* the . . .[newspaper] yesterday [March 17] reported the existence of 'gentlemen's agreements' between some business firms and the Division under which the Division referred only whites or only Negroes for certain positions." (Italics added.) Yet the union's letter to the governor was dated March 16 and the first newspaper article was dated March 17, *one day later.*

To spot-check the stories told by the informants, this reporter posed as an employer and telephoned six . . . [agency] account interviewers recently.

Only one interviewer flatly refused to take my order for two white clerical workers and heatedly informed me that my request was against the law. [28]

The newspaper thus found informal modification of the anti-discrimination law, agency policy, and agency procedure for dealing with discriminatory orders. This modification by different interviewers, coupled with the Flagello case, was now no longer an internal agency affair, but was made public.

After this initial disclosure, other newspapers rapidly followed suit and also reported the charges. The governor, the press, and now the public had dramatically been apprised of the deviation from law and generic agency policy. An independent (external to the agency) governmental commission (the Anti-discrimination Commission), already established for implementation of the anti-discrimination law, immediately entered the situation and launched an intensive investigation. We shall see that the commission did not reach the same mild conclusions that the counsel's office did in the internal investigation. External independent investigation was made of the charge:

. . . that a significant number of . . . placement interviewers and . . . [superiors] will discriminate in making referrals of job applicants on the basis of race if an employer asks the interviewer to do so or the interviewer thinks the employer wants him to do so. This, in essence, is the charge encompassed in the phrase "gentlemen's agreements" [of interviewers with biased employers]. [29]

---

[28] Maintenance of anonymity of the research locale and principals in this case dictates the need to avoid reference to this newspaper by name. The reader is also cautioned to recall that this article is referring to an agency other than Agency C.

[29] From governmental report, *op. cit.*

Here the charge is well expanded from the original under which the agency itself undertook its internal investigation because of the prodding by Mr. Glass. The original charges investigated by the agency itself, concerned the deviating actions of one individual interviewer, but the investigating commission was probing a complaint of discrimination among "a significant number" of interviewers in the entire state employment bureaucracy (as well as upper-level deviations from law in the agency's own assignment policies).

Findings of the Anti-discrimination Commission

The commission performed an investigation by checking agency records and by interviewing 97 interviewers and superiors in seven City X agencies. The commission found that:

. . . [the] charge [of discrimination] is justified by the evidence produced in the investigation.

The State Employment Bureau policy against discrimination is explicitly stated in its various manuals. It is communicated to the personnel . . . through orientation classes upon employment and is again stated to the professional staff in the course of in-service training programs.

In my view there is a clear break between these precepts and the actual practice. [30]

---

[30] *Ibid.* At this point it is fruitful to present some information on the study methods, the sample, etc. used in the investigation. The commission itself gives an account of these matters:

"The phase of the investigation which is reported here consists of the findings of interviews with 97 employment interviewers and senior interviewers [supervisors] in seven different locations of the City X area . . . of the State X Employment Bureau. This constituted about one out of every eight persons assigned to placement duties in the area. The placement personnel interviewed were given full assurance of anonymity to encourage them to speak freely." *(Ibid.)*

To interrupt briefly, it is interesting to note that the author was one of the officials interviewed by the commission. This might have somewhat biased the study toward replication of the results reported on the basis of his participant-observation. However, it is obvious that one respondent of 97 is not sufficient

The chairman of the commission, speaking on the basis of data collected by his organization, took note of the fact that generic agency policy had been informally modified which caused extreme deviation from basic agency precepts. We have seen that participant-observation data and use of agency records of production showed many informal modifications at Agency C. This is a case that corroborates findings of many deviations that were previously presented. However, the deviations here are unlike the others discussed because they are brought to the attention of the *public.*

To continue with the commission's findings:

In many cases, the lowest personnel echelon—the placement interviewer—does not believe that supervisory personnel up the line . . . [are] entirely committed to the policy of non-discrimination.

The placement interviewer has no conviction that he will have crisp and clear backing if he undertakes to enforce the policy directions given to him with respect to discrimination because of race, creed, color or national origin. In fact, he suspects that he may be considered a bit of a "troublemaker" if he does try to enforce the policy. These seem, inescapably, the conclusions to be required by . . . [the data in the report made by

---

to cause significant change in the final results of the investigation. Also interesting is that the author as respondent in this sample was given assurance of anonymity. Nevertheless, a supervisor who escorted the writer into the room in which the interview was to be held, introduced him to the commission representative by name, which could well inhibit responses. However, the writer never experienced any "repercussions" as a result of responses.

To continue with the report:

"These interviews were supplemented by a review of approximately 100 rating sheets of persons in the training program which leads to interviewer status. These reports include comments by both the trainee's supervisor and the trainee.

"Interview questions were of two major types. One revolved around the procedures for annual ratings, the importance of production achievement, and chances for promotion in the Employment Bureau. The second set of questions were aimed at determining any difficulties encountered by placement personnel in placing minority persons and the role of discrimination." *(Ibid.)*

the commission]. [31]

Conversely, it must also be concluded that the placement interviewer has some specific evidence that the use of race as a criterion for distinction among applicants will not be stringently regarded or promptly proscribed by supervisory discipline. This it seems to me is a major effect of the Flagello case which is . . . concerned with the use of a system of discriminatory "dot" coding by a placement interviewer. . . .

The recommendation which flows from these findings is self-evident. Supervisory personnel must make it unequivocally clear to each and every succeeding echelon down the line that one price the Employment Bureau will not pay for meeting any real or fancied quota of placements, or establishing or maintaining a "cordial" relationship with employers is the price of tolerating or assuming limitations or specifications based on race, creed, color or national origin. [32]

In our terms, the commission is saying that redefinition of the anti-discrimination law in order to increase placements and to maintain better relations with employers (which ideally should lead to increased placement totals) is forbidden, and the agency supervisory staff should make this clear to operating officials.

The commission also indicts the agency for its handling of the Flagello case:

The procedure followed was not so much "cover-up" as a display of weakness and indifference to the implications of discriminatory employment practices in the operations of the State X Employment Bureau.

---

[31] *Ibid.* These conclusions are based on a study of seven agencies, including Agency C. Discriminatory orders were at a minimum at Agency C, for reasons to be discussed. Therefore, conclusions do not follow completely for Agency C. There is, however, no reason to doubt the findings of the commission in this regard. Participant-observation shows that these findings do apply (although not so extremely to Agency C), and the conclusions moreover fit all the other findings made thus far about deviation from agency goals. In addition, it was common knowledge among personnel that discrimination was prevalent in placement activity, and most interviewers even at Agency C, where such orders were minimal, were known to act outside the strict provisions of the anti-discrimination law on occasion, and for one reason or another.

[32] *Ibid.*

The information relating to the "dot" coding was brought to the attention of the State X Employment Bureau in conjunction with information that the same interviewer had also claimed credit for placements which she had not made.

What then happened strikingly symbolizes the degree to which the State Employment Bureau seems to emphasize the importance of placements and warrants the belief by its own staff and the public that it is willing to temporize with its responsibility to enforce anti-discrimination policies and legal requirements.

Specifically, the State Employment Bureau moved relatively quickly with an initial inquiry into the improper claims on number of placements: it continued and completed its investigation when reinstatement was requested after extended sick leave; and it reinstated the interviewer with a change in assignment and reprimand after an informal hearing. It did all this while ignoring almost completely the associated charge of the discriminatory "dot" code which the employment interviewer was alleged to have used to distinguish between white and nonwhite students.

It was only after the union protested that any investigation into this phase of the interviewer's activities was initiated; and when the State Employment Bureau did finally move on this subject it did so in a manner which could hardly impress any member of the State Employment Bureau's staff with a feeling that supervisory personnel regarded this type of issue as one of paramount importance. 33

The commission also criticized the disposition of the Flagello case on other grounds:

The report of the Commission's investigation notes that there is room for a difference of opinion as to what finding the evidence will support as to the use which the interviewer [Flagello] made of the coded cards; and the Commission would not at this late date suggest that it would be in any way useful to contradict the finding of the State X Employment Bureau that the "dot" system was not used to the disadvantage of the colored students involved or that additional or different punishment is required.

At the same time, I should like to note that I am inclined to the utmost skepticism whenever I am informed that the basis

33 *Ibid.*

for separating colored and white job applicants is a desire to "advantage" rather than "disadvantage" the colored applicants.

Over and above all such questions, however, is the very clear objective fact that the act of coding was unquestionably on the basis of color. No one of the students whose card was coded was other than a Negro or Puerto Rican student; and such a coding practice by any employment agency or place-ment interviewer, in private or public employment, is in itself an unlawful discriminatory practice. On this point the State Employment Bureau records show a complete absence of any official comment. Certainly, the disposition of the Flagello case, at a minimum, should have included some very pointed and unqualified remarks which would make it quite clear that such a coding is flatly prohibited and what will be entailed if there is any use of it.

I think it also worth observing that the procedure which was followed, namely, a kind of informal hearing before the General Counsel of the Employment Bureau, after much faltering up and down the supervisory ladder does not represent a de-sirable method or forum. It assuredly could not have helped foster any belief that State Employment Bureau disapproval of discriminatory practices is a major premise of that organiza-tion's policy and procedure.

Finally, it is apparent that both the budget procedure and the personnel evaluation system used by the State Employment Bureau create pressures on many of its professional employees to make placements. . . . The problem requires, at a minimum, clarification to the entire staff that placements must not take precedence over a non-discriminatory policy. [34]

Here there is a conflict between bureaucratic goals. The agency's major goal is that of providing a placement service, but another goal is to operate that placement ser-vice with regard to the anti-discrimination law. Operation with such regard, however, might yield *reduced placement levels* by alienating employers who desire discriminatory referrals. This conflict in actuality is resolved, however, because both the placement goal and the anti-discrimination law are related. The agency has the provision of a place-

---

[34] *Ibid.*

ment service as its major goal, but is proscribed, being required to meet this goal only in certain ways. Army-type conscription of applicants into employers' establishments to meet the shortage of skilled help in the clothing industry certainly would aid employers and would yield increased placement levels. However, as is quite evident, the agency was not free to engage in any such activity in order to make placements. Placements were the major goal, but operations had to be carried on toward this end within a specific framework. One of the limitations on the method of making placements was the anti-discrimination law, and the commission, finding that placements were taking precedence over this law in actual agency operations, demanded that clarification of agency obligations to the law be made.

Differences Between Agency C and Other City X Agencies

The pressures to make placements deriving from the personnel evaluation and budgetary systems (reflected on the local level in detailed interviewer statistical records of operations) were quite likely to cause discriminatory referrals. However, this occurred for the various City X agencies servicing traditionally "all white" industries, which unlike the clothing producing industry serviced professional, sales, clerical help, etc.

Referral of nonwhite clients to an employer who does not want them can cause complete halt of all future placement operations with this employer. If placements are hard to come by (i.e., if conditions are such that few applicants are being hired), and the industry is one in which many employers desire discriminatory referrals, then this pressure is likely to cause "gentlemen's agreements" where agency staff do not refer nonwhite clients to such employers, and do not report these discriminatory requests to the Anti-discrimination Commission as obliged under the law. Placements are important to interviewers, but employers control placements by hiring or rejecting referred applicants. Hence, interviewers follow predominant employer desires rather than anti-discrimination procedure in order to maximize statistical placement records. According to the commission:

> Many State [X] Employment Bureau interviewers and . . . [supervisors] report feeling pressure toward quantity of placements to a degree which may cause them to neglect other aspects of the job—including precautions against discrimination. [35]

This is corroborated in one of the newspaper articles mentioned earlier:

> The account interviewers who "co-operate" with the biased employer have equally simple motives, this reporter was repeatedly told. Their efficiency ratings are determined by the number of placements they make. Federal aid is also allocated to the division on this basis. [36]

It is most important to note that pressures of records on maximization of placements leading to bias in referrals did not for the most part apply to Agency C servicing the clothing industry, and likely not at Agency B either in 1959, which serviced the same industry. This is because most clothing employers in 1956-59 did hire nonwhites, but when an occasional discriminatory order was received, most officials neglected agency procedure for reporting such employer actions. This was not so much the result of placement pressures on statistical records at Agency C. Many nonwhites were already being hired without problem and it was relatively easy to place available skilled workers regardless of race because of extreme demand. Some officials told those few employers who indicated job bias of the anti-discrimination law, and generally an employer relaxed (dropped) his biased request immediately. However, the form that the interviewer was still required to fill out in such cases was rarely filled out. This meant that the Anti-

---

[35] *Ibid.*

[36] Newspaper article dated March 17, 1959.

discrimination Commission did not have a complete record file of discriminatory requests relaxed for specific employers. This is dysfunctional for the commission *to the extent* that it used these records to keep track of, and to control employers who repeatedly requested biased referrals, relaxing specifications when by chance an interviewer refused service, but still later attempted to secure similar referrals from *other* officials.[37]

If the employer still requested a discriminatory referral and did not relax his biased specifications, or sometimes if he explained the reason for his biased request "rationally," some few Agency C officials allowed the order to stand, although they did not list this discriminatory information on the order. (Some officials did not even *attempt* a relaxation of the employer's biased request.) A notation was likely to be placed on the order, reading for example, "Use extra care in selection. This is not the ordinary 'floorgirl' [an unskilled position in the clothing industry] job," or other variations on this theme, such as, "Be selective." This was a hint to other interviewers that the employer did not desire the usual unskilled client reporting to Agency C (who was often nonwhite) but likely preferred a white person with special ability, and for "rational" reasons, e.g., the job might have had promotion chances where even a nonwhite with special skill would likely not be accepted by co-workers.

It is important to note, however, that there was no established informal norm in this regard. The notation on the order was not a precise indicator of the desire for a discriminatory referral, but served as a *hint* to the official that a nonwhite was *likely* not wanted. This entire situation is vague at Agency C because few discriminatory orders were received, many officials were consciously liberal in attitudes toward nonwhites, and many clients reporting to the agency were nonwhite. The problem of discrimination

---

[37] It is not known how the Anti-discrimination Commission *actually* used such records.

was not a severe one at Agency C, and thus precise informal norms did not have the chance nor the need to develop on this matter. It is known however, that some few discriminatory requests were received, but that employers making these requests were very rarely reported to the Anti-discrimination Commission, and that some officials did meet the employer's discriminatory desire.

There were also certain limited fields in which many interviewers tried to avoid referral of nonwhites because these clients most often were not hired, and probably for many varied reasons, but which the interviewer *thought* were the desires for white clients. The Anti-discrimination Commission makes a relevant point in this connection:

> . . . it is reported that interviewers sometimes fail to refer minority applicants to firms where they believe they will not be accepted because they wish to spare the applicant's feelings or carfare. [38]

Many Agency C officials engaged in one or more of the types of behavior discussed above at one time or another in their careers, *not because of the pressures of records,* which could be relieved in other ways, especially since few employers discriminated in the first place, but rather because they did not want increased visibility of work (which occurred when forms had to be filled out and cleared through supervisory and managerial levels). A related reason was lack of knowledge of procedure involved. So few discriminatory requests were received, and so few "discrimination" forms filled out, that most interviewers had not seen a form for reporting discrimination with the exception of their initial training (which had long since been forgotten). These forms had to be secured from the supervisor, and the entire case discussed with him, as well as the procedures involved, and this relates to the visibility factor.

---

[38] From governmental report, *op. cit.*

Another reason was to avoid giving an employer trouble by reporting him to the Anti-discrimination Commission, as well as to avoid arguing with a biased employer. In addition, some employers' reasons for biased demands were so "rational" (in relation to pervasive cultural tendencies toward relegation of nonwhites to a secondary position), that officials generally preferred not to give an employer trouble and avoided the reporting procedure. Where the official's own feelings of bias, or of the uselessness, or unenforceability of the law, coincided with that of the biased employer, a report was also likely to be avoided. [39]

It is interesting at this point to present the findings determined through the investigation performed by the Anti-discrimination Commission on the subject of reporting of violating employers. The reader is first cautioned to recall that the findings presented below have been derived from an interview sampling of seven agencies and are not confined to Agency C. There is, however, no great disagreement between findings applicable to Agency C and those of six other agencies in City X. According to the commission:

> Nearly all of the interviewers as well as the . . . [supervisors] in all of the offices [local agencies] covered disclaimed any knowledge of widespread discriminatory practices in the industries they service. A sizable minority did state, however, that they had received discriminatory job orders or that they had observed situations which appeared to be discriminatory.
>
> In cooperation with the Anti-discrimination Commission, the State X Employment Bureau has set up a procedure for handling job orders which specify preference for a particular racial, religious, national, or age group. According to policy— and all interviewers appear to understand the policy—should an

---

[39] Only one overtly biased interviewer was observed in three years of participation, but he too referred nonwhite clients to the many employers who would accept them. It should also be mentioned that these reasons above for lack of compliance with anti-discrimination procedure do not apply in equal force to all Agency C interviewers, and the constraining factor for some was not the same for others.

interviewer receive a job order which contains discriminatory specifications, he must attempt to persuade the employer to remove (or "relax") them by pointing out that the State Employment Bureau cannot accept his order as it stands. . . . Should the employer agree to remove his discriminatory references, his order is accepted and applicants are sent to him solely on the basis of their qualifications for the job. A special reporting form, known as . . . 510.1, is to be filled out by the interviewer and given to his supervisor as a record of the discriminatory job order. Should the interviewer be unable to get the employer to remove the discriminatory specifications, however, his order must be refused, and a second form, known as . . . 510 must be filled out giving the details

Only four persons, out of the 97 interviewed, recalled receiving discriminatory orders during the past six months in which they had been unable to persuade the employer to remove the offending specifications. About a fourth stated that they had received such orders, but had obtained removal of the discriminatory specifications. Seldom did any interviewer report receiving more than two or three. But one, himself somewhat balding, said: "If I had a hair on my head for each time an interviewer got a discriminatory job order, I'd have a full head of hair."

Nearly all of the interviewers as well as the senior interviewers indicated that they had received thorough instructions during initial training on proper procedures for handling discriminatory job orders. Many indicated, however, that they were now unsure of the exact method for making out both the 510 and the 510.1 forms. Many of these said that they could not remember the last time they received a discriminatory job order.

And even of those who said they had been given such orders, a number admitted that they had neglected to fill out the required forms—especially when relaxation of the [discriminatory] specifications had been obtained. One interviewer admitted frankly that he had received five or six discriminatory job orders in the past six months. In all but one case, he had convinced the employers to remove the discriminatory phrases. "But I haven't sent in any 510.1's, though. They're required, yet it doesn't seem worth anything more than just another statistic." He added, however, "But the 510 form is another matter." [40]

---

[40] From governmental report.

It is worthwhile to interrupt here, because this official makes a statement that emphasizes well a point made in other chapters. This official remarks about the uselessness in his eyes of the discrimination reporting procedure (dealing with "relaxed" specifications), and he says that the form required is just another *statistic*. This is an excellent example of the way many Agency C staff members felt about statistical records. The records, or "statistics" were felt to be worth more to management than the procedures or work involved. This is also an example of how the uselessness of many of the statistics-based emphases overflowed into even other procedures. This official did not fill out the required form, because he felt that the agency desired this work only for the sake of statistical records, and not for the real work concerned. To continue with the commission's study findings:

A . . . [supervisor] said that he had never received either a 510 or 510.1 from any of the interviewers under his supervision in the year since he had been promoted to a supervisory position, although he was aware that some interviewers had received discriminatory job orders. "I've never filled one out, either," he added.

More than ignorance or negligence is said to be involved. A few persons indicated that the filing of reports on discriminatory job orders was frowned upon by State X Employment Bureau personnel higher on the status ladder. [One official at Agency C justified his deviation from procedure by saying that upper levels desired a cover-up of discriminatory job requests which he provided. This will be discussed.] Said one . . . [supervisor] bluntly: "It's a sin to send through a 510 in this building. For every 510 that goes through a dozen don't." He continued, "If the interviewer asks if he should fill out a Form 510, he's told by his supervisor or upstairs [top management at his office] not to be silly. I'll bet half the interviewers don't know how to fill out a 510. 510's make the State Employment Bureau look bad."

Two interviewers in another office felt that they had been frustrated by their supervisors when they first came on the job because they were "overly crusading or idealistic." One of these stated that she had filled out a 510 form, but had been "as much as told by my supervisor to 'Get smart! This one won't stand up.'" The matter did not end there. "They called me a crusader, and I was very unpopular for awhile." Another interviewer reported filling out a 510 form and having trouble getting it through his supervisor for what he believed were picayune reasons. He said that he did not know what had finally happened to it, but that it was the last one he ever filled out. 41

It should be evident at this point that the establishment of formal procedure for a certain end is one matter, but securing compliance on various levels with requirements of formal procedure and policy is yet another.

Discrimination in the Bureaucracy's Own Operations

The commission found even more cause for comment, when the investigation inferred that the State X Employment Bureau discriminated, not only in referral of clients, but also in its *own* operations in policies dealing with assignment of interviewers! According to the commission's report:

It is a fact that in the early history of the Division . . . [there were] devised special procedures to insure . . . equality of opportunity; but here again we have a tradition of leadership in policy and procedure which has, I think, less than fulfilled its promise.

I should first like to deal with one specific charge which was brought to the attention of the Commission. It is [the charge] that in the . . . [local agency servicing commercial and sales help] about which much of the controversy has occurred regarding "gentlemen's agreements" and the like, there are no nonwhite employment interviewers.

This is not the fact . . . 10.7 percent of all employment interviewers at . . . [this agency], or twelve persons, are reported to be nonwhite. This undoubtedly is a short and explicit answer to the charge but I did not consider it a complete answer, nor do I now. The commission's investigation sought to deter-

_____

41 *Ibid.*

mine the functions of the twelve nonwhite employment interviewers.

Eleven of the twelve nonwhite employment interviewers are
Negroes. Three of these are on reception desks where they
handle no placements. Three more are assigned to special
services where they counsel and refer workers with special problems [e.g., the handicapped]. One handles part-time employment
in a variety of industries. Another is one of two interviewers
in the . . . [another area of the city] branch of the office handling
a variety of assignments. Two more are trainees not yet assured
permanent employment or assignment.

Only one of the eleven Negroes is assigned permanently
to a desk where he handles full-time employment in a specific
set of industries or jobs. This is the kind of assignment in which
the interviewer must establish working relationships with a particular group of employers; and it is the type of assignment
which is held by well over half the white employment interviewers
at the . . . [office handling commercial and sales help]."

In offices with 20 or more interviewers, there is a striking
parallel between the proportion of nonwhite persons applying
to an office [clients] and the proportion of nonwhite interviewers
employed there. Of the five offices with the highest percent of
nonwhite applicants, all but one rank among the five with the
highest proportion of nonwhite employment interviewers. Of the
four offices with the lowest rankings in nonwhite applicants, all
but one rank among the four lowest also in percent of nonwhite
interviewers.

. . . The . . . Office [serving commercial positions and sales
help] ranks lowest of all the offices in proportion of nonwhite
applicants and next to the lowest in proportion of nonwhite
interviewers.

This kind of information can, of course, be said to be inconclusive, but it does raise questions. When coupled with the
equally inconclusive picture of the promotional opportunities
which have been filled by nonwhite persons in . . . [City X]
offices, it gives rise to some feeling of unease among those
members of nonwhite groups who wish to make the State X
Employment Bureau their careers.

Except for a few positions at the top managerial level in
the State X Employment Bureau, all supervisory positions are
filled from the ranks of the title immediately below it. Of 48
persons certified in recent years for promotion to senior employ-

ment interviewers (the lowest ranking supervisory title), 40 whites and three nonwhites have been appointed. Five persons, all white, have been rejected. For promotion to employment manager and senior employment manager in recent years, 21 whites have been accepted and two rejected. The two Negro candidates have been rejected. . . .

Out of 190 persons holding supervisory titles in local offices in the . . . [X] City area of the Employment Bureau, 18 are nonwhites. This is less than 10 percent, compared to 17 percent among employment interviewers.

There is no simple solution or easy recommendation in this area.

The statutory prohibitions against discrimination of course provide procedures and forums for specific individual complaint cases.

As to the overall problem, the competitive civil service is one part of further assurances toward equality of opportunity. Insistence on non-discriminatory attitudes on the part of appointing personnel is another. And, finally, I think, the Advisory Council [established to maintain equality of opportunity in this bureaucracy]—and particularly its public members—must again assume and maintain a very high degree of continuing interest in this field of the State X Employment Bureau's operations. [42]

A case dealing with an informal modification by one interviewer thus led to evidences of informal modification on an agency-wide basis, and on several hierarchical levels. A government bureaucracy, charged with the responsibility of reporting violating private employers, was found to practice policies which inferred discrimination in its very own operations!

Another Finding of the Commission

The governmental findings indicated that upper levels on an agency-wide basis also de-emphasized agency responsibilities to the commission until at the date of 1959 there was a breakdown in efficient liaison procedure between the two

---

[42] *Ibid.*

governmental organizations: the Anti-discrimination Commission and the State X Employment Bureau. According to the investigating commission's report:

> The program includes the designation by the State X Employment Bureau of a liaison officer to the commission to function on a staff level. Originally a full-time operation, this position is now filled on a part-time basis. The result has been a very substantial reduction in the activities performed both within the State Employment Bureau and in liaison with the commission.
> I have previously indicated that the total impression which the investigation leaves is a picture of a steady and progressive decline in emphasis on the incidence of discrimination by the . . . [State Employment Bureau] over the last few years. This opinion is necessarily buttressed by the steadily diminishing activities of the liaison officer designed to work with this commission. [43]

Formal Amplification and Further Modification at Agency C

After the commission exposés, upper-level agency personnel amplified and began to stress the need for compliance with the law, and the need for more extensive reporting of employer discriminatory requests. Closer liaison was established by upper levels to the State Investigating Commission, and refresher training sessions on the subject of the law and procedures were given to officials. In addition, a most unusual city-wide meeting was held one afternoon of all interviewers of all public employment agencies in City X. Agency employment operations were terminated for the entire afternoon while upper-level officials made speeches referring to this case. This was on the formal level, and overtly indicated more compliance with agency goals and state law. The dysfunctional informal modifications were to be broken completely in the ideal.

After this new emphasis, there was evidence at Agency C of a heightened sensitivity to the anti-discrimination law.

---

[43] *Ibid.*

Officials were more careful to report discriminatory practices. However, modification of anti-discrimination law and procedure was so pervasive that some continued their previous practices (e.g., not reporting employer discriminatory requests).

A most interesting example of the pervasive modification of this procedure and deviation from law was brought to the writer's attention two years after participation had been terminated (and over two years after the State X Employment Bureau formally modified its stand). A day-long association was arranged with an Agency C official who was not aware of the author's study. During the course of conversation this official volunteered the information that he had at one time been assigned to visit an employer who had discriminated in hiring.

This employer had telephoned Agency C for a worker; the order was accepted, and by chance a nonwhite applicant was referred to fill the employer's vacancy. The employer did not accept the applicant, and told the interviewer who telephoned to check results of the referral that there was no hire because the applicant was a Negro.

The interviewer filled out a required report of discrimination and thus maintained the formal agency procedure. Procedure then required that a visit be made to the employer to determine full facts of the case, and to attempt, in a face-to-face discussion and explanation of the law, to secure relaxation of the discriminatory policy.

The informant, rather than the interviewer making out the report, was sent to the employer. The employer indeed admitted to the visiting official that he had discriminated, but said that if he hired a Negro, he would lose all other long-time skilled employees who would resign in protest. At this point the informant (the visiting interviewer) told the employer, "We must all live under the law," but deviated far from procedure by telling him how to violate the anti-discrimination law without sanction! The employer was advised by the official never to tell an interviewer that he did not hire someone because of race, but merely to say that the client was "inexperienced" for the job. In this way the client could be refused because of race, but without the knowledge of agency personnel and without the risk of being reported to the Anti-discrimination Commission. In addition, he advised the now grateful employer to compose a letter to the proper bureau to the effect that he was not aware of the law at the date of refusal, but that in future dealings he would act in accordance with anti-discrimination requirements. Sanctions generally were not applied when an employer was educated to the requirements of the law and relaxed the discriminatory policies. This employer was "educated," but on methods of discriminating and avoiding sanctions at the same time!

The Anti-discrimination Commission itself found through its own study of seven agencies that some interviewers believe employers "get around" the law by finding "legitimate-sounding" excuses to avoid hire of nonwhites. According to the commission:

A number of interviewers suggested [to the commission representative] . . . that few employers of any size in State X are naive enough to think they will not be chided if they announce preference for certain groups to the interviewer. But there are other ways in which discrimination may be practiced. One interviewer explained it this way: "With larger employers, they are too sophisticated and too conscious of public opinion. They would not come out and say it. They have more subtle ways of discriminating." Another said: "What happens is that most employers will not openly state discriminatory orders. He just turns down referrals. [The employer does not hire nonwhites referred by the State Employment Bureau but does not mention discrimination.] In these cases, you just can't prove it. You may have a hunch, but you don't really know." Still another interviewer said that she had encountered employers who, when called back in reference to a discriminatory request, denied that they had placed it. Other employers, it was reported, will inevitably find something wrong with any Negro applicant sent to him: "They haven't uniforms to fit him, he drinks too much, or they will find one bad spot on his record.' [44]

In the case described by the Agency C interviewer, the employer that he had visited was unlike the employers discussed above, and did admit a biased hiring policy, but the interviewer gave him advice on how to avoid hire of nonwhites without the risk of being chided by the government. This employer was now, as those discussed above, no longer naive.

In the Agency C case, we see that one interviewer followed formal procedure and wrote the required report about discriminatory hiring policy when it was necessary. Another official, assigned to visit the firm for the prime purpose of following up this report, redefined procedure to secure good relations with the employer.[45] This visiting interviewer was sensitive and responsive to the employer's needs and desires (the employer claimed that hire of a Negro would result in loss of other workers difficult to replace because of the shortage of skilled workers). This responsiveness, however, deviated from agency procedure and law.

The informant told the author that all parties were satisfied with the outcome of the case, except the official who had filled out the report, but who in fact, "should have known better," than to have reported the employer.[46] This reporting official, according to the informant, created difficulty for the agency and employer, which he, as an interviewer skilled in employer relations then had to handle. This interviewer in fact believed he would be sent to handle

---

[44] *Ibid.*

[45] It is interesting to note that unlike the predominant situation as discussed in Chapter Seven, the field visit here had a definite purpose. However, even in this case the purpose was informally modified and limited the intended effect of the visit, i.e., there was no attempt by the interviewer to eliminate discrimination at this firm, or to secure employer acceptance of the law.

[46] Recall the plaint of the "crusading" interviewer in the Anti-discrimination Commission's report. See the quotation on pages 193-94.

other reports of discrimination because of his "skill" in employer relations.

The informant said that his behavior was desired by the manager and upper levels of the agency, because a report of discrimination in which no relaxation could be secured had to be handled by upper levels. This showed lower level inability to secure relaxation and made trouble for all concerned. According to this official, upper levels desired a "cover-up," which he provided, at the same time maintaining good relations with the employer.[47]

It is not known whether managerial and other upper levels in this case indeed desired "cover-up." However, the important point, sociologically speaking, is that the official assigned to visit this employer *attributed* this desire to the upper echelons. This belief, whether or not true in factual terms, then led him to certain action which only frustrated the attempts of another official who had followed procedure.

*"If men define situations as real
they are real in their consequences."* [48]

The person who visited the employer confided that he also did not report discriminatory practices as determined through telephone conversations with employers, and this is *even after* the obvious heightened sensitivity to the anti-discrimination law and procedure after the exposés.

As a note in passing, the reader should not think of this official as an "ogre." This man had a family, hopes and dreams (most unfulfilled) as many other people in our population who are not bureaucrats. This official's deviation from policy and law came as a result of responsiveness and sensitivity to employers' needs, as well as a result of his inter-

---

47 The use of the word "cover-up" is interesting because this is one term used in the earlier charges against the agency. The commission also found that placement interviewers feel that upper levels do not stringently enforce the anti-discrimination law. This agency interviewer feels the same, even after the commission's findings, refresher training sessions, etc.

48 This is the well-known theorem by the sociologist, W. I. Thomas.

pretation of upper-level agency wishes in this matter. This, of course, is what most of this book is about—local conditions and constraints as causes of informal modifications of procedures, rather than the popular view of bureaucrats as rigid, unyielding gargoyles. Yet, if this interviewer's actions look bad in the public eye, it is not because of rigidity and conformity to all the rules, but because of responsiveness and flexibility to an extreme degree; and here this is dysfunctional in relation to organizational goals of both the Anti-discrimination Commission and the Employment Bureau.[49] It should be mentioned, however, that the employer discussed did not see this as dysfunctional and this is why the author earlier took extreme care in the delineation of the criteria used in appraising functions and dysfunctions.

We see then that this one situation illustrates well the thesis of the *Demonics of Bureaucracy:* that flexibility and modifications can cause dysfunctional results.

Robert K. Merton, in his article, "Bureaucratic Structure and Personality" has emphasized imperfections of bureaucracy as a result of *overconformity to rules,* which is certainly opposite to the tendency of flexibility as discussed here. However, Merton does mention a tendency comparable to the one discussed throughout this volume, although he uses different terminology. Merton's statement provides a good analysis of the dysfunctions caused by the flexible bureaucrat who breaks rules to meet personal demands of clients, and how this, as well as overconformity to rules, is an imperfection of bureaucracy:

---

[49] There is a problem in terminology here which applies not only to this point, but elsewhere too in reference to similar conditions. When we say "rigid" we usually mean in bureaucracy lack of responsiveness to client requests and needs, and "always following the book." In this sense, which is the way this term is being used in this book, the informant above was not rigid, but he was flexible, responsively and informally modifying procedures to meet the employer's needs and desires. On the other hand, we have to recognize an ambiguity in this term, for the official *was* "rigid" in the sense that he *persistently* refused to change his behavior to meet the formal provisions of the anti-discrimination law.

. . . with respect to the relations between officials and clientele, one structural source of conflict is the pressure for formal and impersonal treatment when individual, personalized consideration is desired by the client. The conflict may be viewed, then, as deriving from the introduction of inappropriate attitudes and relationships. Conflict with*in* the bureaucratic structure arises from the converse situation, namely, when personalized relationships are substituted for the structurally required impersonal relationships. This type of conflict may be characterized as follows.

The bureaucracy . . . is organized as a secondary, formal group. The normal responses involved in this organized network of social expectations are supported by affective attitudes of members of the group. Since the group is oriented toward secondary norms of impersonality, any failure to conform to these norms will arouse antagonism from those who have identified themselves with the legitimacy of these rules. Hence, the substitution of personal for impersonal treatment within the structure is met with widespread disapproval and is characterized by such epithets as graft, favoritism, nepotism, apple-polishing, etc. These epithets are clearly manifestations of injured sentiments. The function of such virtually automatic resentment can be clearly seen in terms of the requirements of bureaucratic structure.

Bureaucracy is a secondary group structure designed to carry on certain activities which cannot be satisfactorily performed on the basis of primary group criteria. Hence behavior which runs counter to these formalized norms becomes the object of emotionalized disapproval. This constitutes a functionally significant defence set up against tendencies which jeopardize the performance of socially necessary activities. To be sure, these reactions are not rationally determined practices explicitly designed for the fulfillment of this function. Rather, viewed in terms of the individual's interpretation of the situation, such resentment is simply an immediate response opposing the "dishonesty" of those who violate the rules of the game. However, this subjective frame of reference notwithstanding, these reactions serve the latent function of maintaining the essential structural elements of bureaucracy by reaffirming the necessity for formalized, secondary relations and by helping to prevent the disintegration of the bureaucratic structure which would occur should these be supplanted by personalized relations. This type of conflict may be generically described as the intrusion of primary group attitudes when secondary group attitudes are institutionally demanded, just as the bureaucrat-client conflict often derives from interaction on impersonal terms when personal treatment is individually demanded.[50]

Indeed, the bureaucrat in such cases can do no right for he is *damned* if he follows rules to the letter, and *damned* if he deviates from the rules to meet personal demands of clients. The case of the official at Agency C who told the employer how to break the law without sanction serves as only one example. Had this official followed the rules to the letter he would have alienated an employer, and when he met the employer's personal desires he violated the law and still looked bad in the eyes of other clients and members of the public.

Blau's 1949 Findings Contrasted to the 1959 Findings

In 1949 Professor Blau found that discrimination was practiced by Agency B clerks at a reception desk:[51]

The ethnic affiliation of the receptionists, in principle irrelevant for bureaucratic operations, evidently did in fact influence official decisions. Either Miss Degraff [white clerk] discriminated against Negro clients or Negroes tended to be less qualified, since their educational and vocational opportunities in America are inferior, and Mr. Dill [Negro clerk] treated them preferentially.[52]

The *reception clerks* above *did* allow ethnic affiliation to influence their operations. However, *interviewer bias was*

---

[50] Robert K. Merton, *Social Theory and Social Structure* (rev. ed., Glencoe: Free Press, 1957), pp. 204-5. Footnote omitted.

[51] It will be recalled that interviewers performed reception work in addition to their normal interviewing work at Agency C. *Clerks* were receptionists at Agency B.

[52] Blau, *Dynamics . . ., op. cit.,* p. 88. See his pp. 87-90 for a full discussion of reception desk discrimination.

neutralized because these officials had to contend with improving their placement records. Blau writes:

> Since the performance of clerks [at Agency B] was not evaluated on the basis of statistical records, personal considerations had wider scope for influencing their operating decisions. Interviewers, on the other hand, had to set aside these personal considerations in order to make placements. Even if they were not particularly worried about productivity, their satisfaction at work was largely derived from helping clients find jobs, not merely from talking to them. The chances of helping Negroes were much better, as one interviewer explained: "We get only very low-paying jobs, and the salary requirements of Negroes are much lower. . . . They're willing to accept less, because they're forced to do so." This must not be interpreted to mean that only Negroes were interested in the jobs this department had to offer. Many white as well as Negro clients who were anxious to get jobs could not be referred on account of the shortage of job openings. However, the greater alacrity with which Negroes accepted the poorly paid jobs available made them preferable clients and thus tended to neutralize any bias against them that might otherwise have existed.
>
> Great concern with making a good showing on the production records constrained interviewers even more effectively to exclude all considerations that had no bearing on maximizing placements from their official decisions.[53]

Blau concluded that:

> Equitable treatment of clients was an important latent function of statistical records of performance in Department X.[54]

Blau found that statistical records served the latent function of neutralizing interviewer bias at Agency B. However, the intensive governmental investigation in 1959 finds, mainly on the basis of its data derived through interviews, that there were agency-wide discriminatory practices by personnel on various levels caused in good part by the *em-*

---

[53] *Ibid.,* pp. 92-93.
[54] *Ibid.,* p. 94.

phasis on placement production, and by the pressures of statistical records!

The findings of the governmental commission and the conclusions drawn point to the fact that the budgetary and personnel evaluation systems, which are connected intimately with statistical records of production, press toward cutting corners. According to the report of the commission:

> This phase of the investigation indicates that there is an unwritten, unspoken "quota" of placements to be made which is the backbone of the State Employment Bureau. Cutting corners by making the easier placements is the direction toward which both the budget and personnel evaluation system press. To the extent that strong safeguards do not exist to counterbalance these pressures, temptations to discriminate do exist.
>
> . . . it is apparent that both the budget procedure and the personnel evaluation system used by the Employment Bureau create pressures on many of its professional employees to make placements. . . . The problem requires, at a minimum, clarification to the entire staff that placements must not take precedence over a non-discriminatory policy.[55]

How are the paradoxical findings of Blau and the commission resolved?

It must be recalled that Agencies B and C serviced the clothing industry and that most employers in the City X clothing industry did not discriminate in hiring. This is because of the industry's long history of accepting minority group members, the lower pay provided by clothing firms which nonwhites are more willing to accept, the poorer working conditions and low status occupations which, again, more established groups do not wish, as well as the extreme shortage of skilled help in 1959 which meant that employers were often pressed to accept anyone with skill, regardless of race or personal feelings of bias.

Where employers will accept nonwhites, interviewers are also pressed to refer qualified clients whether white or nonwhite, regardless of their own personal bias, in order

---

[55] From governmental report; *op. cit.*

to maintain good production records. Employers in the clothing industry generally (with exceptions) accepted nonwhites. In addition, many clients reporting to Agency C were nonwhite. Thus, if an interviewer referred no nonwhites at Agency C, his records on various counts could be low enough to cause supervisory complaint. Furthermore, as Blau says, Negroes are often more willing to accept the poorer pay and poorer working conditions prevalent in the clothing industry than are whites. For this reason it is often much easier to refer Negro clients to jobs. As we have seen, the budget and evaluation systems (tied to statistical records of production on the local levels) pressed toward emphasis on easy placements. Among other things, more cooperative, less demanding, and therefore easier Negroes (e.g., nonbenefit clients who were Negro) were referred, neutralizing possible overt or latent bias.[56]

At agencies handling traditionally "all white" fields (e.g., sales help and commercial positions), employers were more likely not to want Negro referrals. Referral of a Negro for a certain commercial position, for example, might well have resulted in a no-hire and loss of placement credit for the referring interviewer. Too many such referrals might alienate an employer completely; an account might be lost, and all further placement activity with this employer could end. Therefore, in cases where employers desired only white

---

[56] The placement and statistical recording pressure discussed above is connected with *referring* clients according to ability regardless of race where *employers tend not to press for discriminatory referrals.* The discussion on pages 188-91 showing that Agency C interviewers were pressured more by desire to avoid visibility, trouble, etc. in making *some few discriminatory referrals and not reporting such demands to the Anti-discrimination Commission, than by statistical records and placement pressures,* refers to *reporting* situations where employers *do press for biased* referrals. At Agency C few employers requested biased referrals and many hired nonwhites. In addition, many clients were nonwhite. Thus interviewers were pressed to refer qualified people *regardless* of race, and despite possible overt or latent bias. This is an extremely elusive, but *most basic point* to be considered in the discussion above.

It should also be mentioned that the discussion above is emphasizing discrimination against Negroes. The same discussion applies to other nonwhite groups serviced at the agency too.

applicants, or were thought to have so desired, "gentlemen's agreements" might have been reached where no nonwhite clients were referred. This was in order to maintain high production figures on statistical records and to maintain good relations with these employers.

This is opposite to Blau's conclusion that attributes neutralization of interviewer bias to the pressures of production records, and illustrates that bureaucratic procedures do not operate in a vacuum. Pressures toward maximization of records led officials to neutralize their bias for the pragmatic end of good records. However, this is only where employers in a group, as another organizational participant, will accept nonwhite clients. Where employers desire to violate the law, agency personnel have been found to cooperate, dysfunctionally deviating from law and agency policy, *again because of the desire to maintain good production records.* In addition, once employers bolster the conscious or unconscious bias of certain interviewers, there may well also be decreased service to nonwhite clients for this reason, whereas when employers will accept these clients, the need to maintain good records will override personal interviewer bias.[57]

Employers, in the ultimate sense, control the number of placements an interviewer can make, for it is the employer who finally accepts or rejects the applicant referred. Employers control the socially valued object (placements) in this case. Hence different employer demands and actions at various agencies lead interviewers to differentially modify to meet the employer wishes. This in turn affects the operation of agency procedures.

Professor Blau discussed implications of his Agency B findings for neutralization of bias:

---

[57] The use at this point of the terminology and idea of conscious and unconscious, and earlier of overt and latent bias ("latent" and "unconscious" referring, for example, to bias of even consciously liberal whites) is not original. Blau *(Dynamics . . ., op. cit.)* had earlier referred to this on his pages 82-83 and on his page 95.

These findings have some implications for social action intended to change discriminatory practices. It is often held that it is impossible to abolish discrimination against minorities in a specific institutional setting until the prejudiced attitudes that prevail in our culture have disappeared. The data presented suggest a way to accomplish this supposedly impossible task. If objectives of overriding importance can be made to govern organized activities, discrimination will be eliminated regardless of the presence of prejudice. Concentrating all their energy upon maximizing placements, interviewers ignored the skin color of their clients. . . . The crucial point is not that the given objective is valued more highly than prejudice but that preoccupation with reaching this objective precludes the intrusion of prejudice in a particular social situation.

These findings also raise a problem that has implications for functional theory. Why was the bureaucratic requirement designed to assure equitable treatment of clients less effective in doing so than statistical records, which were not intended for this purpose? The rule to treat Negroes and whites alike directly conflicts with a deep-seated preferential attitude toward whites in our society. The fact that this attitude is largely unconscious for liberal whites, including most of the officials in Department X, makes it especially difficult to check its influence. As a result, individuals resist even their own deliberate efforts to treat whites no better than Negroes. Statistical records, on the other hand, did not arouse this resistance, precisely because officials were not aware that their concentration on making placements had any bearing on the problem of discrimination.

In functional terms, a social pattern with the latent function of impartiality, statistical records, was more effective than a different pattern with the same manifest function, antidiscrimination rules. Since latent function is defined as an unintended consequence, the concept implies that the social behavior involved is motivated by factors other than the function under consideration. The efforts to maximize productivity engendered by statistical records were not motivated by attraction to, or resistance against, the principle of impartiality, as relative conformity with antidiscrimination rules was, but by the appeal of a good rating and other factors. These extraneous motives made performance records a powerful force against discrimination.[58]

---

[58] *Ibid.*, pp. 94-95. Footnote omitted.

While this seems to be verified by Blau's findings, the later findings as presented in this book in part show that where employer wishes oppose the bureaucratic rule, then this latent function no longer exists. [59] The very same procedure (statistical records in this case) may only reinforce the dysfunctional bias when other participants press toward such bias.

These findings make it appropriate to make an addition to Blau's treatment of how to curb bias. It is necessary to:

1. Establish a pervasive bureaucratic policy against bias. Establish, in other words, a bureaucratic procedure with the *manifest function* of curbing bias. This has been done at the State Employment Bureau.

2. Institute another procedure and emphasis, such as the need to maintain high-level records of performance, that also serves the *latent function* of curbing bias. [60] This is the point of Blau's discussion about the latent function of statistical records. The Employment Bureau already has such records, as has been indicated.

3. Receive cooperation from other participants in the bureaucracy (such as employers). This is the present author's addition to Blau's formulation and makes the problem of curbing bias, at least for this agency, a more difficult one. Once employer cooperation and compliance is secured, it is then necessary to follow points one and two above for employers; that is, *within the employer's organization* (e.g., his plant). This is because the employers now have to worry about the effects of hiring Negro help on other of *their own organizational participants;* e.g., on consumers, as well as on their other workers who might resign in protest against hire of a nonwhite co-worker. If employer compliance is secured, then attention must be focused on

---

[59] It will be recalled that the conclusion of the Anti-discrimination Commission's investigation found poor upper-level backing of the policy and law too. This can also affect personnel actions on the lower levels, as do employer demands.

[60] It should be recalled, however, that the strain to maximize records was found to be dysfunctional in other agency operations. See Part Three.

gaining compliance of workers and consumers.

It was stated earlier that one employer claimed that he would not hire a Negro because his other employees would react adversely. In such a case (if this is a true assertion) it is not enough to effect a law only curbing bias of employers, or using statistical records with the latent function of curbing bias for employment interviewers. The interviewer must deal with employers, and the employer must deal with his own organizational participants, such as employees and consumers in public contact work.

It is very interesting to note that the anti-discrimination law is not oblivious to this matter but takes this problem into account. According to the law:

> Any employer whose employees, or some of them, refuse or threaten to refuse to cooperate with the provisions of this article, may file with the commission a verified complaint asking for assistance by conciliation or other remedial action. [61]

It should also be mentioned that the law, which intends to constrain an employer to hire without regard to race, also constrains employees to work with nonwhites if all employers in a particular industry are also obeying the law and the protesting workers cannot find other employment to their satisfaction; that is, meeting their prejudice—and surmising, of course, that the workers need jobs—meaning that they *must* have work for support. This again has reference to the power structure. The same point applies to interviewers. Where employers were hiring without regard to race, interviewers had to refer without regard to race, or

---

[61] From the anti-discrimination law enacted in State X. It is significant that the writer had not been aware of this important provision until he had decided to read the law in its original form, and this was when this chapter was being written (after termination of participation). This lack of information occurred despite agency training and refresher training sessions on the subject and the law. Either the provision was not mentioned in the training, or it had been, and the author as a government agent had not been attentive. In either case this is sociologically significant. Here we have a provision of the law which in the ideal case was intended to counter employer rebuttals against the intent of the law. However, at least one bureaucrat was not aware of this provision because of lack of knowledge or remembrance.

they could not have maximized production records.

The point is that there is strain to discriminate, despite law or agency policy, because of the same desire on the part of various organizational participants with power over a socially valued object, and on various hierarchical levels.

We have seen that the formulators of the law were aware of this problem and did not only focus on employer acceptance of the law without regard to workers. The law also allows employers to bring complaints against their employees who do not wish to obey the anti-discrimination provisions, e.g., those who threaten to resign if a nonwhite is hired as a co-worker. In these cases the commission may attempt through conciliation or other means to gain employee acceptance of the new nonwhite employee. However, we see that it is one thing to have a law on the books, but yet another to make agency personnel suffer trouble and bring employer discrimination to light. It is one thing to give employers the right to bring employee stubbornness in the matter to the attention of the commission, and another to have employers do so, instead of accepting employee threats as a guide to action. It should also be realized that the law is formulated in ideal terms. A biased employer might only be supported by biased employees, using his workers' threats more as an excuse to maintain his own biased hiring policies. In addition, it is difficult to have even liberal employers risk failure of the commission to secure acceptance of this law by employees through conciliation or other means, and thus to risk the loss of worker allegiance; or more severe in this case, to risk the loss of workers and possible loss of the entire organization. It is one thing to offer conciliation service, and another to make even the liberal employer believe it will work instead of affecting his business adversely. The problem is a difficult one indeed. Blau presented an hypothesis, based on his Agency B findings that:

. . . a social pattern that has a latent function is more effective than a different pattern that has the same manifest function if conscious or unconscious resistance against attaining this objective can be expected.[62]

To this hypothesis, we ought to add the words (derived from the Agency C findings):

> . . . provided other relevant third parties (other organizational participants) with power do not act as a confounding variable, and do not themselves resist attaining this objective.

Blau has written, after reading of the difference between his findings and those of the governmental commission:

> I would think that the general principle is that if you are working within a power structure where the more powerful persons discriminate, the path of least resistance is to conform to their practices, i.e., to discriminate, and the more pressure there is on workers, the more they have to discriminate (contrary to their own convictions; i.e., even Negroes would be expected to discriminate against Negro applicants in this situation). But if this is not true, discriminating is a luxury you can afford only if there is little pressure.[63]

This summarizes well the major conclusion of this section.

Conclusions

Several important conclusions and implications can be drawn from data presented in this chapter.

First, we have further evidence of informal modifications with dysfunctional consequences at Agency C and elsewhere.

---

[62] Blau, *Dynamics . . .,* *op. cit.,* p. 95. This is a difficult hypothesis to comprehend at first reading because this is taken out of the explanatory framework provided by Professor Blau in his work. Tracing his general hypothesis to the specific case from which it originated, "the social pattern that has a latent function," refers to statistical records. "A different pattern that has the same manifest function," refers to the anti-discrimination policy of the agency. In the case described by Blau, "the conscious or unconscious resistance" refers to the resistance of personnel against treating whites and nonwhites equally.

[63] From a personal letter to the writer from Professor Blau (dated October 3, 1961).

Second, there is independent substantiation of information derived through participant-observation of stress toward maximization of statistical figures on records, and some inflation of records to show a high placement total.

Third, there is the implication that informal modifications, to be maintained, must receive at least implicit cooperation from colleagues. Mrs. Angell, the replacement, did not desire to continue the informal modification made by her predecessor, but in addition, she felt that similar modifications made in the past should be brought to the attention of her superior. Had the replacement desired to informally modify as her predecessor did, or at the least to do her work according to procedure, allowing the past modifications to remain secret, the entire series of events leading to a break (although not a complete one, as has been seen) in the agency-wide discriminatory policies would never have occurred. In addition, the initial desire to bring a colleague's deviation from law and agency policy to the attention of a supervisor, served to at least partially break the chain of informal modifications in this matter, not only for the local level, but for other levels and agencies in the entire Employment Bureau in State X.

Fourth, deviation from law and agency policy was treated rather mildly by upper levels and did not match the emphasis given to the subject of discrimination by legislators as well as in agency training sessions. What was written in the law, and taught to new interviewers, and the actions of upper levels (and in fact of lower levels too) did not match.

Fifth, the importance of the role of sources external to the agency, and their operation in bureaucracy can be traced. One of the supervisors present at a meeting discussing the charges was also a union official. This supervisor did not agree with other top-level officials in their disposition of the case. His request as the union head for further investigation yielded a reversal of decision and such a probe was made by internal agency sources. Subsequent handling of the case, however, prompted a further external pressure through a letter to the state governor by another union official.

Internal operations became a matter of public knowledge when the press wrote about the issues involved. An independent commission, established for the prime purpose of maintaining the anti-discrimination law, apprised of this situation by the press and later by the governor, launched an immediate investigation. This provided another external pressure. The results of this investigation and effects of these external sources on the bureaucracy were presented.

These pressures led to formal amplification serving to at least partially break dysfunctional informal modifications. The bureaucracy, now under attack, amplified its training program on the subject of discrimination, tied itself more fully by liaison to the Anti-discrimination Commission for further aid in countering these matters, and made an anti-discrimination stand clear to lower levels.

In this case an internal complaint of deviation from law and policy did not serve to cause formal modification. When outside, external sources focused on operations, only then was formal modification made. This shows the role of external sources as checks and balances on a public bureaucracy.

Sixth, bureaucratic secrecy has also been traced, for an upper-level official believed that, "the least said the soonest mended," and upper levels refused to allow the union representative to be present when Mrs. Angell, the interviewer reporting the malpractice, was being questioned. Breaking of this secrecy resulted in exposés uncovering malpractices well over and above the charges made originally.

Seventh, the pervasiveness of discrimination as well as modifications of procedure are also illustrated, when deviation from the law was still evident even after the investigation, increased sensitivity to the law through refresher training sessions, etc.

Finally, Professor Blau's 1949 findings on the latent

function of statistical records in the neutralization of interviewer bias could be said to have been reversed on an agency-wide basis in 1959, although corroborated in situations where most employers did not press for discriminatory referrals.

At Agencies B and C other participants of the organization (employers) with control over a socially valued object (placements) themselves often followed the dictates of the law, and frequently hired on the basis of merit rather than race. At these agencies statistical records served the latent function of neutralizing interviewer bias, for even officials with conscious or unconscious bias had to refer Negroes in order to maximize records.[64] Conversely, this very same statistical reporting procedure served to dysfunctionally reinforce discriminatory practices by officials in agencies where employers were not willing to comply with the law.

This leads to the revised Blau hypothesis that depending on the role of other participants, a single bureaucratic procedure can have latent functions, or dysfunctions. This means that it is not enough to deal only with paid employees, such as the interviewers at the bureaucracy, in order to halt discrimination. It is necessary to deal with the bureaucracy as an open system (or if not as an open system, then certainly including employers as clients, in addition to officials as participants), with bureaucratic operations and procedures affecting and being affected by operating officials, upper-level officials and clients.[65]

---

[64] It should be recalled that even Agency C interviewers did not follow reporting procedure and law in relation to discrimination at most times when employer actions and requests did make use of this procedure necessary.

[65] Some students of organization do not limit the boundaries of an organization to include only the paid employees. According to March and Simon: " . . . we must necessarily be somewhat arbitrary in identifying some particular individuals as participants in a given organization. A number of individuals other than those we will identify as principal participants in a business organization receive inducements from the organization and provide contributions to its existence, and under special circumstances such 'participants' may assume a dominant role in determining the equilibrium of the organization. But when we describe the chief participants of most business organizations, we generally limit

The power structure affects bureaucratic operations. In this case the employers had the power, i.e., employers controlled the socially valued objects (placements). The bureaucrats in turn were pressed to act in accordance with illegal employer demands to meet the organization's placement goal rather than meeting this goal in the formally approved manner, i.e., with regard to anti-discrimination procedure.

The functional or dysfunctional use of a specific procedure depends on many contingencies. A change in one

---

our attention to the following five major classes: employees, investors, suppliers, distributors, and consumers." From: James G. March, Herbert A. Simon, *Organizations* (New York: John Wiley and Sons, 1958), p. 89.

Clients have the same relationship to government bureaucracies as consumers have to business organizations. As chief participants at Agency C, both clothing workers and employers acted to mold to a good extent the behavior of the bureaucrats.

Other scholars perceive clients as *outside* the system, but the organization is seen as an *open system* which means that the clients as participants certainly do have an effect on the organization. Chris Argyris, for example, in his study of the organization of a bank says in discussing customers that: " . . . here is an example of people who are not formally employees, but who are permitted to perform organizational tasks. Their control over activities of these processes stems not only from the organization's basic need for the customer but from their continuous contacts with the regular employees. Clearly, without customers the organization would collapse and without their frequent appearance on the scene, the employees' tasks could not be performed. Data of this type confirm our assumption that organizations are open systems and are affected by others outside them." Chris Argyris, *Organization of a Bank* (New Haven: Yale University Labor and Management Center, 1954), pp. 55-56. Public employment agency clients and bank customers are not completely alike, although there are similarities. However, the point is that Argyris, conceiving of customers as outside the system, nevertheless sees the system as open, and finds that customers had a definite effect on the organization. This latter is the same point as that drawn by March and Simon *(op. cit.)*. Simon also discusses this point in his book, *Administrative Behavior* (2nd ed., New York: Macmillan, 1957), p. 113 (footnote), and discusses C. I. Barnard's thoughts on this matter in 1938: "Barnard, in *The Functions of the Executive,* was perhaps the first writer to insist that the customers must be considered as part of the system of organization activity in any theory of administration. His views on this point have still apparently not gained wide acceptance among writers on administration. As pointed out earlier, the important question here is not how 'organization membership' is to be defined but whether or not the behavior of customers is to be included in the analysis of the organization."

factor, a change in the attitude of one set of participants with power, can yield a shift in the balance of functional or dysfunctional consequences of an operating procedure used by officials, as the bureaucrats' actions change in response. The sensitivity of bureaucratic operations to various local influences is thus illustrated.

PART FIVE

FINAL CONSIDERATIONS

> . . . *the wise man despises no one. Instead,*
> *he watches . . . closely and tries to discover*
> *the roots of what he sees.*
> —NIKOLAI GOGOL*

---

*Dead Souls (New York: Signet, 1961), p. 272. Published originally in 1842.

CHAPTER ELEVEN

A Last Analysis

SPECIFIC CONCLUSIONS have already been presented chapter by chapter; it would be redundant to repeat them all here. Nevertheless, it is relevant at this point to state propositions and general conclusions about bureaucracy and bureaucratic behavior that can be derived from this study.

Let us realize that we cannot overgeneralize results because of the limitations of the case-study method (as discussed in Chapter One); however, it is important to state general propositions and conclusions that can be placed into the framework of the theory of bureaucracy to be tested further by others in future research. In this context it must be said that while we must be cautious about overgeneralizing, the replication with Blau's study does provide one more level of generalizability than only a single case-study of a single agency at a short and fixed period of time.

Conclusions

Bureaucracy is a form of organization based largely on rationalization and routinization of tasks, emphasis on rules, impersonality, and the other efficient aspects so well stated by Max Weber, and discussed in Chapter Two of this book. Nevertheless, scholars have found that informal changes and interactions occur, and these are part of the informal organization that arises when people begin to work in the formal organization. Blau studied bureaucracies, concluding that bureaucracy is dynamic and that the changes made, the informal changes and activities, "are not simply idiosyncratic deviations but form consistent patterns that are new elements of the organization."[1]

The first proposition about bureaucracy then is that bureaucracy is dynamic, so aptly stated in the title of Blau's book, *The Dynamics of Bureaucracy.*

This later study of a bureaucracy related to the one Blau studied years earlier replicates Blau's findings of dynamism. Rules, procedures, and formal interactions at Agency C were changed in response to various constraints. The changes did become part of the organization in Blau's case, as well as at Agency C. Nevertheless, we must carry Blau's findings one step further, presenting another proposition about bureaucracy, derived from the study of Agency C.

The changes made build upon one another, are affected by changing local conditions and client demands, the desires and conceptions of work of operating-level bureaucrats, supervisory and other upper-level officials, in such a way as to lead to pathologies of various types. Bureaucracy is dynamic, but in a way that may best be called demonic, referring to change (dynamics), but in a dysfunctional direction. The many and broad deviations from official goals induced by the original change to a detailed statistical recording procedure, as described in the various chapters of this book, certainly provide evidence for this proposition. This proposition of *demonics* helps us to understand why it is that an ideally efficient organizational system should stand in such great public disrepute; so much so, that the

---

[1] Peter M. Blau, *The Dynamics of Bureaucracy* (rev. ed., Chicago: University of Chicago Press, 1963), p. 3.

word, bureaucrat, has become an odious term.

The major conclusion of this Agency C study then, is that of the demonics of bureaucracy; however, this is not the only conclusion, nor the only generalization that can be made about bureaucracy. There are other related and important conclusions that can help us understand the *processes* leading to the demonics of bureaucracy. At this point let us turn to these conclusions.

Bureaucracy does not operate in and of itself, as if in a sterile atmosphere or a vacuum. *A bureaucracy is a social system immersed in an external environment, and is closely interrelated with numerous forces ordinarily considered external to the system.* Local conditions such as economic factors and client desires and demands did influence bureaucratic behavior at the agencies studied.

The comparisons with Blau's study provide proof for this proposition. There were certainly replications between findings of Blau's study in 1949 and the ones reported in this book, based on 1956-59 participation; however, specific observations in the two studies did at times conflict sharply, so much so, in fact, that at times it made for the reporting of exactly opposite findings by the two researchers. Such discrepancies can be blamed on faulty observations of one or both of the observers (Blau or the present writer), but evidence points strongly to shifts in local conditions as the cause of most of the discrepancies in findings between the two researchers. Local conditions shifted in time; in turn, so did the behavior of the bureaucrats in response, leading again to the conclusion of the dynamics of bureaucracy. An example is Blau's observation of mostly "sneaking in" in 1949 and the later finding of mostly "sneaking out" in 1956-59, both actions made in response to specific and repeated client demands, and availability of time and personnel, which were different on the average at the two agencies.

If bureaucrats are human and not the robots so many think they are, then indeed clients are also human, and are affected the same way as the bureaucrats by shifting local conditions. Most interesting to note in this example of "sneaking in and out" is that the client demands in general also changed as did local economic and other conditions impinging upon clients. These conditions led clients to make specific requests and demands of the bureaucrats at the two locales; the bureaucrats were influenced by these demands, as well as by the very same conditions affecting clients (such as the job market), and changed their work behavior in response. Note how closely the bureaucrats, clients, and local conditions are intertwined.

To continue with our example of the tendency toward "sneaking in and out" in response to client demands, let us recall that "sneaking in" detracted from the aims of the reception procedure to limit the flow of clients at Agency B, and "sneaking out" caused Agency C officials to neglect their unemployment compensation function, as well as to neglect responsibilities to employers who at the time were desperately seeking skilled employees. This example helps us to understand the processes involved in leading dynamism to dysfunctional results.

We can study the inner workings of bureaucracy as a separate entity only as a scientific abstraction, but to neglect the more "external" influences of clients and other impinging conditions coming from outside the bureaucracy is to neglect, as we have seen, a very important part of bureaucracy. We are inclined to study the effects of teachers upon students, but often forget that which students know so well: that teacher cannot fail them all; hence, students have an element of power over their superordinates in the hierarchy. Many businessmen have found to their dismay that they no longer can maintain power and control when subordinates strike. Nor has the lesson been lost on union officials when workers hold a wildcat strike without the consent or even prior knowledge of union leaders. We study leadership, but without followers the leader has no one to lead.[2] In the same way we must not neglect the

___

[2] See George C. Homans, *The Human Group* (New York: Harcourt, Brace and World, 1950), pp. 418-19 for a discussion of this issue.

strains and various other influences from clients and other conditions that subtly (and sometimes not so subtly) impinge upon the bureaucrats and the bureaucracy which, as found so often in this study, turned the *dynamics* of bureaucracy into the *demonics* of bureaucracy. Let us trace again the processes leading to the demonics of bureaucracy, but this time from another direction.

Officials were dynamic in their behavior and tended to informally modify rules and procedures in order to meet client demands which conflicted with the rules, and often did so to avoid conflict with clients, rather than attempting to meet the major formal organizational goals. More specifically, the officials were often found to be sensitive to pervasive client desires as part of the local conditions on the operating level, even if these desires conflicted with formal organizational goals. Closely related to this is the conclusion that *the power structure constrains officials to informally modify procedures* (to meet demands of participants with power over a socially valued object).

At Agency C, where employers as clients with power over a socially valued object—placements in this case, and job satisfaction in this case and in others—desired discriminatory referrals, officials tended to yield to their demands, in this way breaking official rules, which eventually led to a state-wide scandal. If employers as clients did not demand discriminatory referrals and in fact obeyed the law to the letter, the desire to make high placements recorded on statistical records would likely have pressed even biased officials to comply with anti-discrimination rules. Somewhat hard to swallow is the conclusion that *clients themselves can press the bureaucracy toward a pathological direction;* and if one set of clients succeeds and is satisfied with the results (e.g., biased employers), then others (e.g., liberal white and nonwhite clients and citizens) rail against what they see as corruption and bureaucratic inefficiency. In the same manner, job applicants "sneaked out" at Agency C were satisfied, but employers as another set of clients became angry at "bureaucratic inefficiency" when they heard that large numbers of people were collecting unemployment compensation at the very same time these employers were desperately in need of skilled help. The process continues: these feelings are made known to the officials in field visits, in part (among the other factors discussed) making these visits distasteful for officials who then perform "quickie" visits and spend the rest of their "visiting" time at a racetrack, swimming, running personal errands, or just returning home from "work" early.

A bureaucracy is an intricate social system with interrelated, interdependent parts. For the sake of simplicity many of the issues discussed here and elsewhere have been handled separately, but in the example immediately preceding (in fact also oversimplified for the sake of brevity and to avoid repetition) we can see processes, *the chains of events, one building upon another, pressing the bureaucrats toward deviation from formal organizational goals.*

Really, it is no wonder that bureaucracy has fallen into such popular disrepute. If the bureaucrats rigidly follow the rules, they are criticized; and if they meet client demands which often request special treatment or breaking of the rules (as in the cases just mentioned) then these clients are satisfied, but others again criticize the bureaucrats for inefficiency. Data in this study showed that the bureaucrat suffers an intolerable human strain of client requests for rule breaking on the one hand, and on the other hand, the strain of formal rules and procedures, and pressures for high statistical records. To escape this strain, bureaucrats often perform "nonsense" work (such as former employer referrals, or "quickie" field visits, or fabricate records) which again leads to public criticism when brought into the realm of public knowledge. Bureaucrats are in an unenviable position indeed.

The problem of bureaucracy can be analyzed from two directions: the preceding discussion shows that local conditions and the power structure deriving from clients are important, but on the other hand we must not forget the *internal hierarchy and power structure either. The bureaucrats themselves also have a hand in the processes of change, as well as in change towards a dysfunctional direction.*

The Agency C study found that where the managers and supervisors (as part of the internal hierarchy) pressed for high records of production, lower levels often modified to meet this demand, but not always in the direction leading to attainment of the organizational goals. An important conclusion is that *managerial actions and desires do not always lead to attainment of the formal ends, because lower-level operating personnel informally modify to meet their own conceptions of work, their perceptions of importance of the tasks and procedures, as well as the constraints of local economic conditions and local client demands.*

As already discussed in this chapter and in another context, sometimes lower-level officials were faced with a dilemma: the requirement that they attain certain managerially desired ends, as well as the actual contingencies of work. This study finds evidence leading to the conclusion that *where there is a conflict between demands of formal procedure and exigencies or conceptions of work on the operating level, operating-level bureaucrats meet the constraint by fabricating or manipulating information on records and forms, and by acting as if they follow procedure when they do not.* The officials do not always follow the rules and procedures in the manner requested by upper levels, but they do not always openly refuse to follow them either! Some examples as evidence for this conclusion are the many manipulations of statistical production records, "made-up" field visit purposes, manipulations of time distribution records, and failure to use "demand sheets" at Agency C. Related to this conclusion is the finding that demands of work and exigencies of work in relation to pressures of records also led officials to perform useless work to maximize these records. This is an example of displacement of goals. Records, an instrumental device, a means to an end, became a terminal value, an end-in-itself.[3]

The conclusion of change toward a dysfunctional direction reflects only a *tendency*. Not all changes were dysfunctional. The Agency C study did indicate functional halts to some series of formal and informal modifications that had caused wide deviations from organizational goals. These halts may be a result of formal action taken by upper levels internal to the agency (for example, the formal halt to the F.E. procedure at Agencies B and C). However, if those inside the organization do not modify, external organizations and sources (for example, unions, newspapers, investigating agencies, administrative and/or political figures such as a state governor) can *force* a return to maintenance of organizational goals. Here again we see that the power structure, both internal and external to the agency, is important, not only in helping to cause chains of informal modifications leading to dysfunctional results, but also in forcing a halt to these changes. Yet, although there were halts to dysfunctional series of changes, the tendency toward changes leading to deviation from formal goals was at times stronger still; as, for example, in the one case of continued discrimination even *after* the statewide discrimination scandal, and the strong formal upper-level move to return to the formal goals and procedures related to the anti-discrimination law.

The conclusions and processes discussed here show us that we are faced with an important problem. Our society needs bureaucracy, but the question of how to control bureaucratic pathologies is a difficult one indeed. The factor of unanticipated consequences of social changes; the tendency toward displacement of goals; the influence of the internal and external power structure, client desires and demands; and other local conditions, when coupled at the start with a tendency toward dynamism or change, often yield results which at best might be called dysfunctional;

---

[3] This is a paraphrase of Robert K. Merton, *Social Theory and Social Structure* (rev. ed., Glencoe: Free Press, 1957), p. 199.

at worst, corrupt and pathological.

Thus far the discussion has been on a scientific and, in this chapter, theoretical level. What are the practical applications of these study results for the goal of improvement and control of bureaucracy? This issue is discussed in the next chapter.

CHAPTER TWELVE

Implications of the Study

THE AGENCIES DISCUSSED in this work had been organized within a large-scale bureaucratic structure for the attainment of specific goals. Let us now trace some implications of this major finding for bureaucratic operations in a democracy. [1]

In our modern-day society we cannot completely do away with bureaucracy, despite its shortcomings, as one last, drastic solution to its ills. For example, a large-scale bureaucracy is needed to administer a mammoth, nation-wide system of public employment and unemployment compensation offices. Bureaucratic organization is needed to administer a whole host of other public as well as private operations too.

If there seems to be no escape from bureaucracy, then what, at least according to the findings of this limited study, can we do to solve its ills? How can bureaucracy be im-

---

[1] There are limitations of the case-study method. Briefly, we must be careful not to *overgeneralize* from a single case. However, with this in mind, it is interesting to widen the scope of this work and to present broad suggestions for the improvement of this particular bureaucracy, and *implications* of the study findings for other bureaucracies.

proved so that it maintains its organizational goals and serves the citizens, instead of, for example, its own voracious appetite for "statistics"?

The following proposals are presented:

1. Bureaucratic rigidity in all cases would be dysfunctional, for changing conditions *require* changing procedures to keep pace. Dynamism, and not total inflexibility, is the solution. This research does find many evidences of dynamism. There are many formal and informal modifications of various sorts, one building on another, in response to local conditions. However, many of these numerous modifications lead to deviation from major organizational goals. If this is so, then the first step is to control this dynamism, this series of modifications, in order to focus them on, rather than away from organizational goals. The next proposal deals with the problem of how to achieve this control.

2. We have seen that bureaucratic operations are highly sensitive to specific local conditions, such as the actions and desires of various organizational participants. For example, at the study locale employer pressures toward violation of the anti-discrimination law (when coupled with other internal agency pressures and strains) led to informal modification of procedures and deviation from major organizational precepts. Client desires to be "sneaked out" led to dysfunctional deviation from reception sifting policy and from more generic placement and unemployment insurance goals. The desire of officials to cushion themselves from conflict with clients again made for deviation from organizational goals. Supervisory desires to have high "figures" on sectional statistical records ironically led to restriction of output by subordinates, which again deviated from major organizational goals. These are only some examples of how participants at the study locale—employers and job applicants as well as superordinate and interviewing officials—through selfish personal wishes caused

strains for dysfunctional bureaucratic operations. And then, having in good part caused the problem, employers and applicants as a group complain of lack of service and bureaucratic nonsense, officials of client hostility and "numbers games," managers of restriction of output, etc.

Job applicants and employers look for the speck in the bureaucrat's eye, and it is most certainly there, but they pay no attention to the beam of law violation in their own. Since they cannot see properly because of the beam in their own eyes, they blame the bureaucratic organization for inefficiency, nonsense, and red tape, when all the while they themselves are in good part the cause. The bureaucrat, on the other hand, looks at the beam in the client's eye, and forgets about the speck in *his* own.[2]

The answer to the problem of how to control the dynamism of bureaucracy so it leads toward functional ends lies with removing the strains caused in part by clients, as well as officials, that lead change toward dysfunctional consequences.

The method of achieving the elimination of such strain is simple and yet not so simple; an easy proposal to present in writing, but a difficult one to put in practice. It is the proposal made time and time again for the solution of various kinds of societal ills. It is a solution proposed by men as diverse in generation, veneration and vocation as Jesus Christ and Pitirim Sorokin. The proposal is *altruism*.[3]

There are various organizational participants who, with a good measure of altruism, could halt many strains toward bureaucratic deviation from goals. Let us first take the officials. Loyalty to the major organizational placement

---

[2] "Why do you keep looking at the speck in your brother's eye, and pay no attention to the beam that is in your own? How can you say to your brother, 'Just let me get that speck out of your eye,' when all the time there is a beam in your own? You hypocrite! First get the beam out of your own eye, and then you can see to get the speck out of your brother's eye." From Christ's Sermon on the Mount, Matt. 7:5.

[3] See Pitirim A. Sorokin, *The Reconstruction of Humanity* (Boston: Beacon Press, 1948).

and unemployment insurance goals, the will not to allow client anti-organizational desires to interfere with bureaucratic operations despite resulting personal trouble, as well as cognizance of the role of a government worker in a democracy not to allow *all* bureaucratic operations to go unquestioned are necessary.[4] Thus a good balance of *autonomy* and *loyalty* in officials is needed—a most difficult combination and balance to secure and maintain—but nevertheless needed. According to David Riesman:

> The "autonomous" are those who on the whole are capable of conforming to the behavioral norms of their society . . . *but are free to choose whether to conform or not.*[5]

In other words, strict conformity is not desired; but rather flexibility (i.e., the ability to follow procedures but also to be able to deviate from them), as well as a measure of loyalty to organizational goals.

This leads to a moral issue for it cannot always be assumed that organizational goals are always morally correct. The problem is, when is loyalty to organizational goals morally sound? In exactly what situations should the bureaucrat maintain organizational goals and when should he deviate from the goals? In other words, he should be autonomous, but when should he conform and when should he not conform to organizational goals?

In the case of the employment agency the problem is not as severe as that arising in other bureaucracies dealing with items having greater moral overtones, such as birth control, eugenics, armed services, political ideologies, etc. But problems did occasionally arise even at the employment agency.

The unemployment insurance law, democratically en-

---

[4] Some men in their role as bureaucrats have performed horrible atrocities but have often given as defense the fact that they were only cogs in a bureaucratic machine, and were *only* following *orders* leading to their numerous misdeeds. Taking humanitarian values as the criterion, they were *too* loyal to bureaucratic rules and goals.

[5] David Riesman *et al., The Lonely Crowd* (New Haven: Yale University Press, 1961), p. 242. (Italics added.)

acted, required that *all* clients collecting unemployment insurance benefits accept suitable employment, or the insurance benefits could be halted. On occasion, the official was confronted with a moral problem. For example, a very aged applicant might admit overtly or otherwise that she did not want to find work but needed the benefits to help maintain herself. The official was faced with a dilemma: a humanitarian desire on the one hand to allow this very aged and obviously physically weak client to collect the needed benefits, or on the other hand the organizationally oriented desire to maintain the unemployment insurance law. What should the official do? There is no simple answer and to avoid the issue, let us say that this is not a sociological, but a moral question. Sociologically, it can only be said that it was observed that an official would often allow such clients to collect the benefits without making a job offer (i.e., "sneaking the client out"), but sometimes he did not do so, and suffered pangs of self-doubt as a result (especially when colleagues disagreed with the action taken, thereby not providing the support the official needed for the soothing of a guilty conscience).

The discrimination issue is a more clear-cut case, because discrimination conflicts not only with agency procedure and law but also with democratic precepts of equality. But even here there is a conflict. In a specific case, should an official maintain the law and help a Negro applicant, or should the official help an employer who says he will suffer if he does obey the law? Of course the answer will be different depending on the side of the fence from which the problem is viewed.

To continue with the major point, a degree of loyalty is needed for focus on major organizational goals, even if sometimes with the result of personal difficulty. Autonomy is needed to avoid misuse of bureaucratic power under the guise of being just a cog in a machine. Autonomy is also needed in order to be able to refuse to maintain dysfunctional informal modifications, as did Mrs. Angell at the employment agency, for example.

This proposal is a difficult one to achieve, and frequently falls into the sphere of moral judgements and evaluations, but it is no use crying out against the pain of the illness if one will not take the bitter medicine to cure it; and our citizens, including some bureaucrats, have been too eager to cry out against the sickness of bureaucracy, but have not been overly eager to take the difficult but necessary cure of altruism and autonomy.

Let us trace the operation of altruism for participants other than the bureaucrats. It is necessary for clients to become aware of generic agency goals as set by law, and to altruistically accept them, even when it presses against individual desires. For example, argumentation and conflict with the bureaucrats might lead to avoidance of a temporary job referral, and might meet personal desires. However, the client should not be surprised when at some point in long-term dealings with the bureaucracy, changes caused by such pressures cause the client to be confronted with "nonsense" procedures.[6]

---

[6] An example as discussed in Chapter Nine is requiring a client to wait for a long period of time for a needless interview and only to be given an introduction card to his own employer, at the same time that there is a slack season and no available temporary jobs at hand.

If all clients had told the truth, there would have been no strain for officials to check the veracity of the client assertions by calling employers (which helped toward emphasis of these former employer operations). If temporarily unemployed clients would accept temporary job referrals without complaint, then regular work would not have been as difficult and troublesome to officials as it was, and it is hypothesized that the officials would not have emphasized the F.E. procedure to the extent that they did.

Changing to another bureaucracy, there are also frequently heard complaints against the picayune and often most difficult to comprehend rules and regulations of the United States Bureau of Internal Revenue. In the same breath, however, many people boast of how they fail to pay their full income tax. The picayune nature of many of the procedures, as well as the occasional disliked call-ins to the Office of Internal Revenue requesting defense of deductions made, expenditures listed, etc. are probably in response to the actions of the citizens. Around the year 330 B.C., I think it was Plato who wrote: "When there is an income tax, the just man will pay more and the unjust less on the same amount of income." If all men were just, then the Internal Revenue bureaucrats would not have to engage in the behavior and promulgate those procedures that so
(continued)

The cure for this situation is for clients to take the bitter medicine of recognizing obligations under the law, and of not applying for benefits if they do not feel like searching for employment during a temporary layoff, or of accepting without complaint temporary job referrals when made. However, in a democracy it is not necessary for the citizen to accept all that government bureaucracy imposes. If the client disagrees with the officials, there is a complete step-by-step appeal procedure at this agency and many others in the United States, handled by neutral referees. If the generic goals conflict with the client desires, the method in a democracy is not to pressure the government bureaucrat to deviate from these goals, but rather to pressure the legislature (under the "rules" of democracy) to formally change the organizational goals.

Some employers, another set of participants, want to violate the law by discriminating in employment. If this is so, then there is little reason to place full blame on the bureaucrats when exposés are made, showing the government agency itself dysfunctionally deviating from anti-discrimination policy (in order to meet employer constraints). The cure for this bureaucratic illness is altruism on the part of the prejudiced employer who must accept the bitter pill that the law, democratically enacted, forbids discrimination in employment. At the point that all employers accept this law, and all workers accept nonwhite colleagues, and all consumers accept nonwhite sales help, etc., the government bureaucracy would then itself be forced to operate similarly.

To summarize then, altruism on the part of officials, applicants and employers is necessary to cure the ills of at

many citizens find so obnoxious.

On the other hand, the procedures in use at this bureaucracy may make some citizens unwilling or unable to properly pay their full tax honestly. Client and bureaucracy are closely entwined.

At Agency C, client actions and pressures caused dysfunctional modifications. Various formal and informal agency procedures, however, made it difficult for many clients to *avoid* pressuring the bureaucrats.

least this bureaucracy. Bureaucratic change leading to deviations from organizational goals is started in part by sensitivity to the actions of the participants in the bureaucracy. A halt to this sensitivity only leads to dysfunctional rigidity, another ill. In this case the cure lies in a change of attitude on the part of the participants so the bureaucracy would be pressed toward, instead of away from organizational goals.

3. The third proposal concerns the role of checks and balances, and is perhaps the easiest of all the proposals made thus far to implement. The role of parties interested in but yet outside the bureaucracy, such as the investigating commission, the press, the governor, and a union, in forcing a return to organizational goals was evident in the discrimination case. These outside parties functionally helped to control the mushrooming modifications that so few inside sources originally seemed willing or able to control.

Internal upper-level checks against lower-level deviations from goals are also needed. We saw, for example, the functional effect of an upper-level modification to halt the former employer procedure in July of 1960. Conversely, we saw how upper-level deviation from the anti-discrimination law and its relegation to a secondary position only reinforced lower-level deviation.

To summarize these three points very briefly, the implications of this limited study for improvement of this bureaucracy in our democracy are as follows:

1. Encourage flexibility and dynamism, but focus this toward the major organizational goals.

2. Achieve loyalty to the goals of the organization, but also autonomy and altruism on the part of all participants in order to avoid strains for dysfunctional modifications, and as another side of the same coin, to focus dynamism toward organizational goals.[7]

---

[7] There is a whole series of proposals that must be made to achieve loyalty to the organizational goals on the part of participants at Agency C. For example,

(continued)

3. Maintain checks and balances of internal and external sources against misuse of bureaucratic power and deviation from goals.

These comprise the proposals suggested for curbing bureaucratic ills of the type illustrated in this book in reference to Agency C. Undoubtedly, however, these proposals will be met by outcries of impractical ivory-tower daydreaming. To this charge, I, as the author of the proposals, also agree; for I too am a pessimist. While I vouch for the principles and study findings underlying the steps listed for the improvement of this "ill" bureaucracy and others like it, I do not and cannot vouch for the human behavior necessary to carry these steps to fruition.

One reason for my pessimism is that in order to meet ideal ends all the proposals must be undertaken simultaneously and then maintained over a long period of time. There is some question about whether these simultaneous changes can be achieved. First, it is doubtful that all applicants, all employers, or all officials (or even a majority of them) will subvert their own immediate desires to more altruistic ends, regardless of how often they are urged to do so.

Second, the problem becomes even more complicated because many of these desires have connections on the *unconscious* level, such as unconscious bias of even some overtly liberal whites.[8] Third, this proposal is especially difficult for Agency C and others like it where so many clients because of limited educational background and/or language difficulty cannot understand many of the basic

---

improvement of the morale of officials would first be a necessity. Focus has not been made in this work on such problems which would comprise a book in itself.

It should also be mentioned that the discussion above is on a very general level. It does not deal with needed internal reforms, such as change of the statistical recording procedure, changed supervisory selection and training, etc. that are needed for improvement of this bureaucracy.

[8] This thought and example has been derived from Peter M. Blau. See *The Dynamics of Bureaucracy* (rev. ed., Chicago: University of Chicago Press, 1963), p. 95.

requirements under the law, or realize the need for altruism.[9] Fourth, there are other factors that are contingencies difficult to control, such as seasonal fluctuations, economic cycles, etc. which can cause the strain for series of dysfunctional modifications, even if complete altruism were achieved for participants. Since we have seen that bureaucracy is so sensitive to such factors, then it appears that the strain will always be present for a dysfunctional series of changes.

---

[9] For example, Agency C clients are frequently told that only employers contribute to the unemployment insurance fund and that employees contribute nothing. However, many clients think that they too contributed to the fund and therefore see no reason why they should not be able to take advantage of their contributions according to their own desires. Erwin O. Smigel also finds this in an independent study of attitudes toward "chiseling" of unemployment compensation. See his "Public Attitudes Toward 'Chiseling' With Reference to Unemployment Compensation," *American Sociological Review,* 18 (February, 1953), pp. 59-67. According to Smigel:

"While 82 per cent of the sample did not know who paid for the compensation, the more significant figure is that 69 per cent thought the worker paid or partially paid for his own benefit. These people not only did not know who paid for . . . [unemployment insurance] but 'knew' incorrectly. Most of these individuals confused . . . [unemployment insurance] with Old-Age and Survivors Insurance to which the employee does contribute. Ten per cent of the sample who knowingly approved of illegal application for or receipt of . . . [unemployment insurance] also thought the worker paid all or part of his benefit. The point of view of these people is that the employee buys at least a part of his own insurance and he should therefore be allowed to withdraw the money he put in for that protection." (p. 63.)

Some comments in a study of problems arising under the "availability for work" provisions of the unemployment insurance law (benefit clients must be ready, willing, and able to work) also are appropriate to the discussion:

". . . it must be recognized that some benefit claimants who restrict their availability are trying to 'ride' the program. They seek to collect benefits when they are actually not interested in working. Such claimants are a drain upon the resources of an unemployment compensation agency—its time, its money, and its prestige. To keep out all the work-shy claimants is difficult, if not impossible, without hurting many honest claimants who are anxious to go back to work. . . . The result is that often we must depend upon a slower method, of weeding the malingerers out after they are inside the system and drawing benefits. This is expensive and can be damaging.

"The unemployment compensation agency can do this necessary policing job. Education can, however, in time, reduce the size of that job. We accept the need to teach school children their rights and duties as citizens in a political democ-
(continued)

Now these proposals by some odd chance just might be achieved completely. Yet difficulty would still be hypothesized in the control of the dynamics of bureaucracy, for these dynamics appear to be so sensitive, times so changing, human interrelations so frail, and misconceptions of intent and meaning so easy.

Yet there is no reason for the patient to be confined to the bed for life, because conditions are not ripe for complete cure, when with *some* attention he can walk again, albeit with a limp. Just because it seems impossible to achieve complete cure, does not mean that we have to allow complete unchecked dysfunctional bureaucratic operations. We saw that only one autonomous person, a lower-level interviewer at a local City X agency, caused a whole series of events that finally led to the breaking (although not completely) of an entire dysfunctional series of modifica-

---

racy. Similarly, we need to teach them their rights and duties as participants in an economic democracy. Among the duties we must teach is the duty of the citizen, when he is a benefit claimant, to aid in protecting the unemployment benefit fund. Although the training of our people in economic citizenship ought not to end with their formal schooling, it ought to begin there. If the schools will accept this responsibility we may be able to reduce the number of the unemployment benefit 'chiselers.'" Ralph Altman, *Availability For Work* (Cambridge: Harvard University Press, 1950), pp. 256-57.

I am somewhat pessimistic on these grounds too. Too much reliance is placed on "education" to cure too many ills, with the result that it sometimes fails in many areas, and sometimes even in the areas in which its prime organizational goal lies (e.g., teaching children to read and write). In addition, lack of altruism is not limited only to the uneducated. Numerous cases of cheating behavior on college campuses are vivid examples. But while education in the ideal could help clients to at least become *aware* of the need for altruism, there is also the problem of coping with those who do not or cannot secure the advantages of education (e.g., many of the foreign-born clientele of Agency C), and many who do receive a public school diploma but are of low intellectual and reasoning capability (although they have found their niche in the City X clothing industry or in other industries of this type).

To sum up, very frankly it is doubtful that education or any other cure is evident for a good portion of the population which will make them wish to shoulder responsibility in the realm of economic democracy. Education might help somewhat in avoiding misinformation (e.g., as to who contributes to the insurance fund) but yet clients are *already* told, and still misinterpret the law according to their own needs and desires. In the terms above, it is doubtful that all participants (or even a majority of them) will subvert their own immediate desires to more altruistic ends, regardless of how often they are urged to do so.

tions.[10] If *one* can do so much, imagine then how much several can do. The path is clear. Complete cure is improbable, but shall the word "bureaucrat" be an epithet forever? Must we allow bureaucracy to run wild, or shall we, as we did with many physical matters, such as the atom, bring it under control? And to show the ticklishness of this problem, the direction of control can be dangerous too, as witnessed in the physical science sphere by control of the atom for destructive war purposes, and in the social science sphere by the cases of war criminals who accepted organizational goals too blindly, were too loyal, performing as a result most hideous acts against humanity![11] But this then, is where autonomy is important, and this is where the role of checks and balances in the proposals become important.

Bureaucracy should not resist such increased autonomy and checks and balances in its operations. It has been said that:

"Democracy, if it knows its business, has no reason to fear bureaucracy."[12]

This can be turned around:

Bureaucracy, if it knows its business, has no reason to fear *democracy!*

---

[10] This refers to Mrs. Angell's actions in the discrimination case.

[11] Examples are Nazi concentration camp masters, Nazi gas chamber operators, etc.

[12] Sir William Beveridge, *The Public Service in War and Peace* (London: Constable and Co., Ltd., 1920), p. 63. Quoted in William E. Mosher, Donald J. Kingsley, Glenn O. Stahl, *Public Personnel Administration* (3rd ed., New York: Harper, 1950), p. 3.

APPENDICES

A Note on Method

This appendix is prepared for those who are interested in the steps taken in deriving the data and analyses, and in various methodological problems and issues.

A History of the Study

The study began as the result of an accidental assignment to Agency C. Originally there was no idea in mind to perform a sociological study. Employment with the agency was solely for the sake of earning a living.

The relevance of various experiences and observations became apparent when an employee of the bureaucracy at a local agency in another part of the city indicated in conversation during a chance meeting that the agency at which he was employed had been studied by Professor Blau. A close reading of Blau's book began to yield insights into observed and experienced behavior, and a sociological study was born.

The method used was necessarily much more participant than pure observation in nature, since this researcher was also a full-time employee of the agency. Extensive notes were not taken while in the employ of the agency.

There are some, in this modern age of precision and statistically based research, who look down upon this method. Indeed, the participant-observation approach has the problem of possible subjectivity even under the best of circumstances. In this study, mostly participant, and the result of an accidental assignment, the disadvantages appear greater than those arising even in the ideal use of the method. Yet there are also advantages of this method which are usually neglected by critics. In addition, safeguards were taken to help ensure objectivity. These and related issues will now be discussed.

Advantages of the Method

One advantage of the participant-observation approach as used in this study is that I was a full and accepted participant. Thus, actions of the other participants in the situation remained free and "normal." This sometimes is not so when the participant is also known to be a recording observer. Much was learned when officials confided information of various kinds, including illegitimate behavior which most likely would not have been given to a known observer, or even to a short-time full participant who could not have had a chance to make lasting friendships. Information was thus gathered which might otherwise have been closed to a usual "notebook" type of researcher, or even to a short-term participant who was not known to be studying the agency. Blau himself indicated that:

> Observation is not a reliable method for determining illegitimate practices, . . . since they are concealed from the observer, as the following statement made to him [Blau] by one of the special interviewers [for handicapped clients], shows: "Oh, they [other interviewers] hide everything from us [meaning that colleagues compete by hiding job orders instead of filing them as required, and thereby monopolize job vacancies]. We got more orders when you [Blau] sat in the middle of that section than ever before. We laughed about it. Interviewers would hand us

orders asking whether we can use them—when you were looking. That had never happened before."[1]

Yet in my case, I myself engaged in illegitimate practices as a full participant (of course such practices are now no secret to me), and colleagues frequently did the same in my presence, repeating such behavior in my presence even when I returned to the agency after terminating my employ as a government worker. Some colleagues, as personal friends, confided their use of additional illegitimate practices even two years after participation ended. These are definite advantages of studying behavior as a full participant, colleague, and personal friend of the various actors.

Extensive note-taking, "pure" observer techniques, as well as formal interviews and questionnaires would likely have yielded greater *accuracy in recording,* but there is doubt as to whether this would have made for greater accuracy of observations of the type reported in this book in the first place. What people say and what they do are not always the same, and what they do in front of a known observer is not necessarily what would be done when the observer is not there.[2] I was not an "outsider" and therefore had a better chance to observe "natural" behavior.

[1] Peter M. Blau, *The Dynamics of Bureaucracy* (rev. ed., Chicago: University of Chicago Press, 1963), p. 59, footnote 2.

[2] A study of medical students using several research methods found that the more formal interviewing method was less satisfactory for the problems the researchers were dealing with than was participant-observation. See Howard S. Becker *et al., Boys in White* (Chicago: University of Chicago Press, 1961). See especially their Chapter Two and more specifically their pages 29-30 for a discussion of this issue.

Also see Howard S. Becker and Blanche Geer, "Participant Observation and Interviewing: a Comparison," *Human Organization,* 16 (Fall, 1957), pp. 28-32. Comments on the position taken by Becker and Geer are presented in Martin Trow, "Comment on 'Participant Observation and Interviewing: A Comparison,'" *Human Organization,* 16 (Fall, 1957), pp. 33-35. This statement brought a rejoinder from Becker and Geer in *Human Organization,* 17 (Summer, 1958), pp. 39-40.

Dean, in a labor union study, found that participant-observation determined some respondent misrepresentation on questionnaires, a more formal and "precise" method. See Lois R. Dean, "Interaction, Reported and Observed: The Case of One Local Union," *Human Organization,* 17 (Fall, 1958), pp. 36-44.

Blau's method was one of observation and formal interviews which enabled him to acquire systematic information. Such information could not be acquired in the same way in my study; to provide formal interviews would have indicated to officials that I was not merely a colleague. On the other hand, my three years of intensive participation provided detailed inside knowledge about unofficial patterns of behavior which could not be acquired by an outside observer during only a brief period. For example, illegitimate practices were not concealed from me; in fact, I engaged in such activities myself, as did my colleagues. Thus the method of participation used in my study yielded data of a type that complements data secured by Blau through his method of study.[3]

Depth of perception is an advantage of the intense level of participation. I was intimately involved in the work of an employment interviewer, and was a fully accepted member of the work group, interacting intensely with staff members of the agency as well as with clients. For example, very conservatively estimated, the number of face-to-face client contacts made ran well over ten thousand! Such intensive participation over a period of three years yielded many observations and insights which the usual observer might not have been able to secure.

I believe that the three-year time period of participation, intensity of participation and observation, and combined use of this method with the other sources of data discussed, yield advantages which well override the original disadvantages of methodology deriving from the unplanned and impressionistic nature of the original research. It is significant that many observations made as a participant have been substantiated by other sources.

---

[3] Blau, *Dynamics* . . ., *op. cit.,* pp. 32-33. This section in Blau was written in collaboration with the present writer.

Verification Through Other Sources

It must be emphasized that this study was not based merely on participation. Additional sources were also used to supplement and verify data. My own memory bank was first used, and this is based on three years of participation. This was then checked when applicable and possible by later occurrences observed when no longer in the employ of the agency, by reference to my own statistical records of operations as an interviewer, by reference to complete agency-wide records of production (1945-1961), and by reference to training manuals as well as to inserts in the Employ-ment Bureau Manual of Procedure. Letters were written to upper-level officials, including top-level officials, state and federal, for clarification as required on certain formal procedures. Requests for information on occurrences under the aptitude testing program were made to a local-level former colleague who had worked closely in this program. Various local-level employment interviewers in repeated written, telephone and personal contacts also provided information about changes (such as the modification of the former employer procedure) which occurred after employ with the agency was terminated. Original observations were also verified by information gathered through these contacts. In addition, much use was made of eight reports by the State X Anti-discrimination Commission which presented results of the commission's independent study. Newspaper articles on the subject of the discrimination case added data, which also verified observations.

It is evident that personal experiences were basic in the study, but supplementation and verification through use of other sources were also important. Exact areas in which verification through nonparticipant sources was made need not be enumerated, for they have been repeated and identified at appropriate points throughout this entire work.

A Note on Note-Taking

Extensive notes weιe not taken while in the employ of the agency, and as a result some sociologist-colleagues wondered whether this could possibly affect reporting of true and accurate data. The possibilities of lags in memory seemed pertinent on an intuitive basis, but most of what has been reported was so pervasive and firmly imbedded in memory that for quite some time I could not understand why lack of extensive note-taking should cause real concern. However, two years after resignation from the Employment Bureau, a situation was experienced that provided insight into the real reasons behind concern about note-taking. Only then did I understand fully why some sources were troubled by the possibilities of memory lags, while I was not.

This insight occurred when a meeting was arranged with a former colleague who was and still is a personal friend. The former colleague and I discussed agency matters during an automobile trip, later at a picnic, and then throughout the return trip. Officials were not aware of the research and I could not inform the colleague of this study despite qualms and a guilty conscience about the matter.[4] A day-long running conversation was providing an abundance of data on events and situations that occurred both before and after employ with the agency was terminated, but recording the information as it was being received was impossible because notes could not publicly be taken.

---

[4] It should be obvious at this point that agency management on upper as well as other levels would be highly interested in the findings. Knowledge of the study might well reach upper levels through a reverse kind of grapevine if lower-level officials knew of it. It would then be relatively easy for managerial officials to connect certain behavior discussed to some of the officials who engaged in forbidden actions. Some of the information in this report is enough to result in another exposé on the subject of discrimination, as well as loss of job for at least one official. Protection of informants was essential and therefore it was decided to hide the actual nature of the study. This secrecy in relation to former colleagues and personal friends was not pleasant, but was a necessity for the protection of these very people. This problem also made it impossible to embark on a more formal interviewing or questionnaire program of research to verify original observations. Data had to be "caught" as they came.

This was the first time that I ever had to remember so much data, given so profusely in so short a time, for later recording. I was confined to an automobile for the greater part of the trip and could take no notes in that situation. In fact, there were few other times during the day when notes could be made, especially since my hosts had taken my carrying case in which I had left my pen and paper, and removed it to an inaccessible place. So much information was being received, that despite efforts at concentration and memorization, much that had been said was lost. This was especially so in relation to certain quotations that were desired at least near verbatim in illustration of points made in the text of this work.

It was only then that I realized through insight why some sociologist-colleagues were so troubled about lack of extensive note-taking over a three-year period. They had been used to occurrences of rapid forgetfulness when they themselves were interviewing for various studies. If such forgetfulness could occur within a few hours, then what could be remembered over a period of years?

Some thought, however, shows that the two situations are not comparable. I had been trying to recall specific words for purposes of quotations, and to remember certain remarks which were both verifying and adding data to my own work. Information was coming so fast and with such abundance, that during the approximate twelve-hour-long association with the colleague, the greater part of agency operations had been covered; not in a predetermined orderly manner, but as conversation runs, skipping here and there. Recall was indeed difficult when I finally could write my notes. On the other hand, discussion in the major part of the study covered three years of *daily* work-week participation, *daily* observations at the office, and discussion of agency matters with colleagues during informally taken work-time "social hours" (as a result of restriction of output), at rest periods, lunch hours, after work while walking to various transportation points, and with some officials on public transportation while riding home, and at various times on weekends too. Most of the occurrences reported in this study repeated themselves and were discussed time and time again, hour after hour, day after day. The fact that placements and other "statistics" were emphasized by management to the detriment of actual service to clients, for example, was so pervasive that no recording of this fact was needed for recollection. The same applies to "quickie" employer field visits, restriction of output, and operations under the former employer procedure. Recall of these pervasive matters is not subject to the forgetfulness that occurs when an informant roams *once* over a range of subjects, including unfamiliar information, and then when after several hours the researcher tries to record all that was said, and as accurately as possible. Documentary sources, it should be reiterated, were used for verification where applicable.

The *Post Factum* Nature of the Research

The sequence of research was such that participation was first completed, data were collected, and *then* the interpretations were made. Interpretations of this type are called *post factum.*

Professor Merton discusses this procedure:

It is often the case in empirical social research that data are collected and only then subjected to interpretive comment. This procedure in which the observations are at hand and the interpretations are subsequently applied to the data has the logical structure of clinical inquiry. The observations may be case-history or statistical in character. The defining characteristic of this procedure is the introduction of an interpretation *after* the observations have been made rather than the empirical testing of a predesignated hypothesis.

. . . .

A disarming characteristic of the procedure is that the explanations are indeed consistent with the given set of observations. This is scarcely surprising, in as much as only those *post factum* hypotheses are selected which do accord with these observations.[5]

It is for this reason that the reader is cautioned to treat the interpretations in this study as only introductory. This study can stand well as a descriptive account, but since the interpretations were not fully tested because they were *post factum,* the evidence thus remains in Merton's words, ". . . at the level of *plausibility* (low evidential value) rather than leading to 'compelling evidence' (a high degree of confirmation)."[6]

In other words, the research report must at the first level remain as a description of events at a specific locale, tracing functional and dysfunctional consequences of modifications of procedures through a period of time, and comparing and analyzing differences between Blau's work and observations ten years later. The interpretations derived stand as plausible, but must now be studied further by a new set of observations for the explicit purpose in mind of testing for *compelling* evidence.

There is no harm in using this mode of procedure, provided the nature of the interpretations are made clear to the reader, and this has been done.

Sociological Research and "Defects" in Method

There are some who might question the value of a study using methods that are as gross as those in this one, and with interpretations that are *post factum,* therefore needing retesting.

It is my point that it is better to perform a study with defects (provided the defects are brought to the reader's attention) than to have no study at all. It is my view that the data presented and the events discussed, derived through participation, are sociologically relevant in and of them-

[5] Robert K. Merton, *Social Theory and Social Structure* (rev. ed., Glencoe: Free Press, 1957), p. 93. Italics in the original.

[6] *Ibid.* Italics in the original.

selves, despite problems arising from *post factum* interpretations.

To be sure, one tries to perform the best study possible and does not use inexact methods when exact are available. However, the methods could not have been more exact because accidental assignments and chance information led to this study. If the data had not been reported at all because of fear of not meeting strict methodological prerequisites, much information would have been lost because of timidity.

It has been said that:

> The difficulty of coping with sources of error should not be allowed to discourage us to the point of denying the possibility of being *much more objective* than the average observer. . . . all craftsmanship is a matter of doing something *better* than the uninitiated. The counsel of perfection is the enemy of such achievement as might be possible. [7]

The defect, I firmly feel, would be in not reporting the data, even if only for descriptive purposes. The fault would be not warning the reader of defects, or eliminating this study because it could not be exact, thus losing the data. As long as the reader accepts the study in the proper cautionary light as warned in this appendix, then it is useful, if only at hinting at certain processes in bureaucracy that need further study, and if only descriptive of occurrences at one particular bureaucracy.

If I had my life to live over again, I would first become highly trained in sociology, *then* I would read Blau thoroughly, and only then would I become an employee, not at Agency C, but at Blau's Department X at Agency B. I would have my hypotheses before I began participation and I would have recorded a full set of notes even during the period of participation.

Unfortunately, however, it occurred that accident, not design, led to employment at Agency C. It is too late to

---

[7] Carl J. Friedrich, *Constitutional Government and Democracy* (Boston: Little, Brown and Co., 1941), p. 577. Reprinted by permission of D. C. Heath and Company. Italics in the original.

change this course of events now. Very frankly, it must be said that had I not worked as an official at Agency C for three years, it is difficult to know whether I would have become interested in sociology, or in bureaucracy. I have only tried in this study to make good use of observations that arose through a chance assignment. The approach might be considered by some to be unorthodox; but really, let us be somewhat less bound by convention in sociology. Let us not allow "method [to] be a tail that wags the dog."[8] There is more than one way toward knowledge of society, its parts and its workings, and all the ways do not lie only in questionnaires, formal interviews, note-taking, or IBM machines.

---

[8] Melville Dalton, *Men Who Manage* (New York: John Wiley and Sons, 1959), p. 274.

Supporting Data

I. This is the letter sent to the State X governor by the Civil Service Union (See Chapter Ten). All names have been changed for provision of anonymity. The letter was reproduced in a governmental report written by the Antidiscrimination Commission.

March 16, 1959

Dear Honorable Governor:

The following is a narrative report of discriminatory practices in the Employment Bureau of State X. We consider this matter to be so grave and such a stain on State X that we are taking this matter to you directly for your information and correction. We ask for an immediate investigation.

February 1958

Mrs. Flagello, employment interviewer assigned to the . . . High School Program of the X Employment Bureau and the City X Board of Education went on sick leave due to a respiratory ailment. Mrs. Flagello was the assigned counselor at X High School . . . and Y High School. . . . Both schools have a heavy nonwhite student enrollment. Mrs. Flagello was instructed to give orientation to her successor, Mrs. Angell. Mrs. Flagello showed Mrs. Angell two piles of application cards. . . . Mrs. Flagello pointed out that in one pile of cards there were heavy pen ink dots under Item . . . 22. This part of the application card records the personal appearance of the applicant—speech, dress, mannerisms, etc. Mrs. Flagello told Mrs. Angell that each application card with the dot represented a nonwhite high school senior. All of the other cards in the other pile were without dots and represented white seniors. It is the normal practice of the . . . counselor to refer these youngsters to job opportunities during the Easter vacation period with the hope of securing job promises and commitments for June after graduation. Mrs. Flagello advised Mrs. Angell not to refer the children with the dots on the application cards.

February 1958

Later, during the same month, Mrs. Angell interviewed students for whom Mrs. Flagello had recorded previous placements. Many of these youngsters stated that Mrs. Flagello had never referred them to jobs. They stated that they had obtained jobs through friends, relatives, private agencies, etc. From this time on, until the end of the term in June, Mrs. Angell noted that in all cases the dotted cards matched nonwhite students and the cards without dots matched white students. Mrs. Angell reported this matter to her supervisor, Mr. Lifeman.

April 1958

Mr. Lifeman, . . . [supervisor], reported the information that Mrs. Angell had given him to his manager, Mr. Olds.

May 1958

Mr. Lifeman, having been ordered by Mr. Olds to make an investigation, went to X High School. . . . He interviewed 20 students. Each of these students was supposed to have been placed by Mrs. Flagello, according to the records. Mr. Lifeman found that 13 of the alleged placements by Mrs. Flagello were fraudulent. The only Negro student interviewed (a fraudulent placement) by Mr. Lifeman had the telltale dot: the others did not.

May 1958

Mr. Olds forwarded the report from Mr. Lifeman to Mrs. Hammer, Superintendent of . . . [the agency to which Mrs. Flagello and Mrs. Angell were assigned]. Mrs. Hammer sent the report on to Mr. Berg, Area Director, X Employment Bureau, City X.

January 1959

Mrs. Hammer called a meeting at Mr. Olds' office. . . .
Those attending in addition to Mrs. Hammer and Mr. Olds were
Mr. Lifeman, Mr. Lavalle, Mr. Glass—the three supervisors of
the . . . High School Program. Mr. Glass is also the President
of Local 1692 of the Civil Service Union in the X Employment
Bureau. Mrs. Hammer stated that the purpose of the meeting
was to determine how much information concerning Mrs. Flagello
was to be given to the remaining counselors. This was necessary to decide because Mrs. Flagello had been reinstated and
was to return to work within a few days. Mrs. Hammer stated
that Mrs. Flagello would not return as a high school counselor
but would be an account interviewer in another section of Agency
Y. Mrs. Hammer further stated that investigation revealed that
Mrs. Flagello had recorded seven fraudulent placements and
had been given a written reprimand by the Director of Employment Bureau Personnel, Mr. Spitz. Mrs. Hammer asked for
comment. Mr. Glass stated that he had charge of the application cards from X High School and Y High School over the
summer months of 1958 and had seen the dots on the cards.
Mr. Glass asked whether this matter had been investigated, in
addition to the fraudulent placements. Mrs. Hammer stated that
Mr. Spitz, Mr. Berg together with the Assistant Counsel to the
Employment Bureau, Mr. Thorne, had decided that there was
not enough evidence to warrant an investigation. Mr. Glass
heatedly questioned this determination and was told by Mrs.
Hammer that "discrimination was not important." Mr. Glass
asked permission from Mrs. Hammer to quote her on that statement. She then said, "Let us say that it is less important than
fraudulent placements. You feel more strongly about discrimination than I do." Mr. Glass said that this kind of thing must
not be covered up. He pointed out that Agency Y is reputed to
be discriminatory in referrals by all other placement offices
throughout the area and that this is a golden opportunity to
assert our efforts in a constructive anti-discriminatory manner
on a policy level. Mrs. Hammer was reminded that Agency Y
has a low proportion of nonwhite employment interviewers as
compared with other offices throughout the city and that Agency
Y does not have a single nonwhite account interviewer while
other offices have 20-30 per cent. Account interviewers are charged
with maintaining relations with specific firms and responsible
for providing workers for these same firms. To this Mrs. Hammer
replied, "What do you want me to do, hire Negroes?" She then

added that she thought Mrs. Flagello ought to be fired for the fraudulent placements—a personal opinion.

January 30, 1959
. . . [The union] called a meeting with Personnel Director Mr. Spitz. Mr. Simon, International Representative for State X Civil Service Union Council, was present along with the officers of Local 1692. Mr. Spitz defended the failure to investigate the charges of discrimination because the information given by Mrs. Flagello to Mrs. Angell was given in confidence. The union representatives replied that this explanation was patently ridiculous. Mr. Spitz then telephoned Mr. Mayday, the Executive Director of the Employment Bureau. Mr. Spitz pointed out to Mr. Mayday over the phone that the union did have grounds for complaint and that the union's stand was not unreasonable. Mr. Spitz promised the delegation that an investigation would be made. The union pointed out to him that he need not have waited for the union to complain for this same information was already in the possession of the Division for a considerable period of time.

February 1959
During the middle of this month, an episode took place which seems to delineate the type of investigation which was taking place. Mrs. Angell was summoned to the office of Mr. Tank, Chief Counsel to the Employment Bureau. The Assistant Counsel, Mr. Thorne, and the Chief of Investigation, . . . and Mr. Olds were present. Mrs. Angell telephoned Mr. Glass and asked to have somebody from her union present; Mr. Glass offered to appear. When he arrived, Mr. Glass was told by Mr. Tank that he (Glass) had no right to be present. Mr. Tank stated, "We are here to investigate Mrs. Angell's charges against Mrs. Flagello." Mr. Glass protested that the actual purpose should be to determine from the facts whether or not charges should be brought against Mrs. Flagello and that Mrs. Angell had done her job well by reporting irregularities to her supervisor. Mr. Tank again insisted that Mrs. Angell be interrogated without Mr. Glass in the room. Mr. Glass then telephoned Mr. Spitz in protest. Mr. Spitz stated that he was unable to do anything about it. Mr. Tank stated that if Mr. Glass did not want Mrs. Angell to testify, "It's all right with me." There were forty minutes of questioning of Mrs. Angell after Mr. Glass had left. She testified as to what Mrs. Flagello had told her and of her

subsequent experiences for the remainder of the term. Mr. Tank showed no genuine interest in this probative evidence. He persistently questioned Mrs. Angell re possible bias or dislike of Mrs. Flagello. He asked why Mrs. Angell had not reprimanded Mrs. Flagello as soon as the latter had shown her the dotted cards. The investigators made disparaging remarks about Mrs. Angell's lack of exact and intricate statistical data. Finally, Mrs. Angell was instructed not to talk to her Union President concerning the interrogation.

Investigation

On February 3, 1959, the Union wrote to Mr. Spitz informing him that in order to make a complete, accurate and fair evaluation of the facts, all of the evidence should be secured. We indicated that, in addition to Agency Y, application cards were to be located in six other State X Employment Bureau Offices, two Industrial Offices, two Apparel Industry Offices [Agencies B and C] and two Service Offices. No attempt was made to locate application cards at any location except Agency Y. Dotted application cards are more likely to be found at the other six locations due to the nature of the jobs handled in those offices. Any fair investigation should insure that all of the evidence available be examined.

Summary

The record shows that there has been no effort on the part of high ranking Employment Bureau staff to correct discriminatory practices within its jurisdiction. This applies to . . . [the letter here repeats the names and positions of many of the upper-level officials mentioned above]. They have been negligent in the performance of their duties, to say the least.

State X Employment Bureau offices, as a result of this kind of administrative attitude and policy, are discouraged from reporting violations of hiring practices to the proper agency, [the] Anti-discrimination Commission; also it encourages employers to expect discriminatory preferences when placing orders with the State X Employment Bureau.

School children, not yet in the labor market have been victimized. The person who perpetrated the injury has been reinstated on the public payroll. The person who did her duty by reporting violations to her supervisor had been subjected to humiliating and insulting interrogation.

This is a most serious situation.

II. The first newspaper article on the subject of discrimination (March 17, 1959):

"GENTLEMEN'S AGREEMENT" BARED ON JOBS IN STATE

Dozens of . . . [City X] business firms have "gentlemen's agreements" with the State Labor Department's employment division under which the division's local offices discriminate against unemployed job applicants on the basis of race, the . . . [newspaper] learned today.

An inquiry has been started by the department on the basis of information turned over to it by the . . . [newspaper]. Preliminary checks of several cases showed "suspicious patterns," the department informed this newspaper.

"A thorough investigation will be made," a spokesman declared.

. . . [*Anti-discrimination Bureau*] *Promises Probe*

Commissioner . . . [chairman of the Anti-discrimination Commission], said his department will make an immediate investigation into the charges. This is being done, he said, with the knowledge and full approval of [the] Labor Commissioner. . . .

. . . [the anti-discrimination commissioner] said the allegations were surprising since the employment division has long had a "pronounced non-discriminatory" policy as well as a working agreement under which it reports any discriminatory job orders to . . . [the Anti-discrimination Commission].

This newspaper made a check with interviewers in the offices of the employment division and found at least five who seemed willing to supply job applicants on a racial basis.

Here are several examples of the "gentlemen's agreements" of which this newspaper learned:

A well known restaurant chain employs only whites in some of its food stores, only Negroes in others. The Employment Division Account interviewers who deal with this firm know from past experience what is wanted and make sure their referrals are of the correct race.

A large . . . farmers' association hires only Puerto Ricans as summer harvest workers. The Employment Division refers only Puerto Ricans to this outfit.

A big drug company prefers "whites only" for clerical jobs. Account interviewers handling this firm obligingly make only white referrals to the company's personnel office.

The "beauty" of the arrangement from the biased employer's point of view is that the Employment Division, a tax-supported public agency, performs the job of racial discrimination for him in advance. In this way he is protected from any possibility that a rejected applicant may complain to the . . . [Anti-discrimination Commission].

The unwanted applicants, Negro or white, never get past the desk of the account interviewer in the office of the Employment Division. They usually have no reason even to suspect they are being discriminated against.

The account interviewers who "co-operate" with the biased employer have equally simple motives, this reporter was repeatedly told. Their efficiency ratings are determined by the number of placements they make. Federal aid is also allocated to the division on this basis.

The persons giving information to this newspaper said they had not used official channels for their complaints because they feared retaliation from superiors. They insisted that any investigation by the Division into its own practices would result in a "whitewash."

To spot-check the stories told by the informants, this reporter posed as an employer and telephoned six account interviewers recently.

Only one interviewer flatly refused to take my order for two white clerical workers and heatedly informed me that my request was against the law.

After each call a second call was made cancelling the order so that job applicants would not be sent on wild goose chases.

III. The second newspaper article on the subject of discrimination (March 18, 1959):

BIAS COVERUP LAID TO STATE

Governor Sent Union Protest on Interviewer
Labor Department Probes "Gentlemen's Agreements" Charge

A detailed report charging that the state Labor Department's division of employment covered up for an interviewer accused of discriminating against Negro high school girls seeking jobs was sent to [the] Governor . . . today by a labor union.

. . . [the] assistant regional director of . . . [the Civil Service Employee's Union] also charged in a letter to [the] Governor . . . that the employment division "discouraged" employees from reporting bias cases to the . . . [Anti-discrimination Commission]. He asked for an investigation.

The union's action came after the . . . [newspaper] yesterday reported the existence of "gentlemen's agreements" between some business firms and the division under which the division referred only whites or only Negroes for certain positions.

Investigation Promised

A division spokesman said a thorough investigation of the complaints, originally reported to this newspaper by division employees would be made. The . . . [Anti-discrimination Commission] also promptly announced it would conduct a probe.

According to . . . [the assistant regional director of the union], the employment interviewer who discriminated against high school girls was assigned to two city high schools under the joint placement program sponsored by the state employment division and the Board of Education.

Early last year, . . . [the assistant regional director] said, the interviewer went on sick leave, instructing her replacement not to refer any Negro youngsters for Easter jobs. The replacement was told by the interviewer that "heavy ink dots" on the application cards indicated the applicant was a Negro, . . . [the director] said.

Reported to Superiors

The new interviewer reported the incident to superiors who ordered an investigation. The investigation disclosed, . . . [the assistant regional director] said, that the dots on the cards did indeed correspond to Negro applicants.

The investigation also showed that at least 13 placements recorded by the old interviewer were fraudulent, . . . [the assistant regional union director] continued. As of last month, he wrote, the interviewer had been reprimanded for the fraudulent placements but no bias charges had been placed against her.

"The record shows," . . . [the assistant regional director of the union] said, "that there has been no effort on the part of high-ranking members of the division of employment staff to correct discriminatory practices within its jurisdiction.

"The person who did her duty by reporting the above case of discrimination to her supervisor has been subjected to humiliating and insulting interrogation.

"The interviewer who committed the alleged discrimination was put on another division job when her sick leave ended," said . . . [the assistant regional director of the union].

INDEX

A

Adjustment of procedure
definition, 33
formal, 112-13, 113n
defined, 34n
of former employer procedure,
158-59
informal
defined, 34n
and local conditions, 35-36, 39, 113n
mentioned, 49
and unanticipated consequences,
36-47
various ramifications of, discussed,
33-47
Altman, Ralph, 240n
Altruism, 232, 235, 236, 237
difficulty in attaining, 238-39, 240n
Amplification
defined, 48
and discrimination, 197-98, 215
and further informal modification by
lower levels, 62
↓ and local conditions, 67-68, 69
and low morale, 117n
by management to refocus informally
modified procedures to original objectives, 68, 69
and occupational demand sheets, 61
and reappointment date procedure,
66-68
of reception procedure, 60
to determine placement quality, 98,
99
Annual ratings of personnel; see Personnel ratings
Antagonism between clients and staff,
86
Anti-discrimination Commission
findings of; see Discrimination
Anti-discrimination law and procedure
redefinition of, 184-200
Anti-discrimination policy, 167-68,
169, 170n, 178, 179, 182, 191-92,
198
Anti-discrimination procedure; see
Anti-discrimination law and procedure; Anti-discrimination policy
Application forms
inadvertent change of purpose,
39-40, 41, 45
and handicapped clients, 37-38,
40-46

mentioned, 36
procedure, 34, 35
and statistical records of production,
112-14
Aptitude testing procedure
and budgetary procedure, 124
discussed, 122-28
displacement of goals of, 123-28
and mistreatment of clients, 124-27,
161
as a pay-item, 124
purpose, 122
Argyris, Chris, 217n
Auditing procedure, 100-2
Autonomy, 233, 234-35, 237, 240,
241

B

Balzac, Honoré de, 9, 9n
Barnard, Chester I., 17, 17n, 217n
Baum, Bernard H., 179n, 180n
Becker, Howard S., 247n
Becker, Joseph M., 42n
Bendix, Reinhard, 13n
Bensman, Joseph, 6n, 7, 7n, 8n
Berliner, Joseph S., 134, 134n
Beveridge, Sir William, 241n
Bias
latent, 14, 208n
neutralization of, 208-13
unconscious, 208, 208n, 209, 216,
238
Bierstedt, Robert, 12n
Blau, Peter M., xn, 6, 7n, 9, 9n, 13,
13n, 14n, 15n, 17, 18, 18n, 19, 20,
20n, 21, 24, 24n, 25, 25n, 27, 28n,
33, 33n, 34, 34n, 35, 35n, 36, 36n,
37, 37n, 38, 39n, 42n, 46, 46n, 48,
48n, 49, 49n, 50, 50n, 51, 51n, 58,
58n, 59n, 60n, 62, 62n, 63, 63n,
64, 64n, 65n, 66, 66n, 67, 68, 69,
73, 74n, 75, 75n, 76, 76n, 77, 77n,
78, 78n, 79, 79n, 80, 80n, 81, 81n,
82n, 93, 93n, 94, 94n, 95, 95n, 96,
96n, 97, 97n, 98, 98n, 99, 109n,
144, 145, 145n, 146, 149, 152, 152n,
155, 155n, 167, 167n, 204, 204n,
205, 205n, 206, 207, 208, 208n,
209n, 210, 212, 213, 213n, 215,
216, 221, 222, 222n, 223, 238n, 245,
246, 247n, 248, 248n, 253, 254

compared to Blau's findings, 204-13
and amplification of procedure, 197-98, 215
bias coverup charge against agency, 180, 184, 193, 201, 201n, 262-63
and budgetary procedure, 186, 187, 206
as caused by employers, 236; *see also* Discrimination, and power structure
and checks and balances in bureaucracy, 237; *see also* Checks and balances
"dot" discriminatory coding of application cards, 169-78, 184, 185-86
how clients and power structure lead to, 225; *see also* Discrimination, and power structure
and letter to governor about scandal, 179, 256-60
moral dilemma and bureaucratic goals, 234
and newspaper articles about scandal, 180, 180n, 181, 188, 261-64
and personnel evaluation system, 186, 187, 188, 206
and power structure, 211-13, 216, 217, 225; *see also* Discrimination, as caused by employers; Discrimination, how clients and power structure lead to
Dismissal of officials
procedure involved, 106-7
Displacement of goals
and counseling procedure, 57
defined, 16-17, 88
discussed, 227-28
examples at agency studied, 227-28
and National Employ the Physically Handicapped Week, 46
of statistical records of production, 132, 161
of visits to employers, 46
Dixon, James P., Jr., 1
Due date procedure; *see* Reappointment date procedure
Durkheim, Emile, 31
Dynamics of bureaucracy; *see* Bureaucracy, as dynamic
Dysfunctional consequences
of application form procedure as used

at agency studied, 43; *see also* Application forms
of budgetary procedure, 152
of bureaucratic dynamism, 47, 143
and counseling procedure, 57
of detailed statistical records, 78-81, 83-88, 91-133, 160, 161-63
of early statistical records, 74
of former employer procedure, 152-58
of National Employ the Physically Handicapped Week, 43, 46; *see also* National Employ the Physically Handicapped Week
of performance measurements, 134n
of personnel evaluation system, 152
of time distribution records, 136, 137-43
Dysfunctions
criteria used in delineation of, 202
definition of, 22

E

Economic trends
influence of on bureaucracy studied, 21
Education
and control of "chiselers," 239n-40n
problems of, 240n
Employer
altruistic
need for, 236, 237
visits; *see* Visits to employers
Exposé of discriminatory practices at agency studied
documents about, 179, 180, 180n, 181, 188, 256-64

F

Fabrication of figures on statistical records; *see* Manipulation of figures on statistical records
Fabrication by bureaucrats
reason for, 227
Falsification of figures on statistical records; *see* Manipulation of figures on statistical records
Feelings of personnel
and effects on the organization, 68
F.E.'s; *see* Former employer clients; Former employer procedure

for, and neglect of possible real service, as rushed by officials, as useless

of promotional activity during National Employ the Physically Handicapped Week, 41

and statistical records of production, 131-33

by supervisors, 99

of procedures

conditions affecting, 28

of rules

and deviation from goals, 44

Morale of officials, 117, 117n, 237n

Mosher, William E., 241n

N

National Employ the Physically Handicapped Week

informal modification of procedure, 41, 45, 46

and malingering clients, 42, 43-44, 45

purpose, 40, 41, 42, 43, 45, 46

National Labor Relations Act, 174n

N.E.P.H. Week; *see* National Employ the Physically Handicapped Week

Neutralization of bias

steps to be taken for, 208-13

Newspaper articles on subject of discrimination, 180, 180n, 181, 188, 261-64

Note-taking, 250-52

O

Occupational coding procedure, 34, 35-36, 47

Occupational demand sheet procedure

and informal modification of, 69

lack of use by officials, 61-62

and reception counter procedure, 60

and restriction of output, 61

as used at agencies studied, 58-62, 62n

Occupations

bureaucratization of, 7

Organizational goals

of agency studied, 22

conflict in, 234

discussed, 33n

and loyalty of bureaucrat to, 232-35, 237

subversion of, 21

Organizational participants, 216, 216n-17n

Organizations

as an open system, 217n

Orwell, George, 71, 89, 89n

P

Parkinson, C. Northcote, 9, 10n, 158n

Participant-observation method of study

as used in this study, 24

problems, 246

Pay-items

and aptitude testing, 124

and the budgetary process, 102, 137

and counseling, 50, 50n, 53

defined, 137

and the former employer procedure, 146

and stress on placements, 102

Performance measurements, 134n; *see also* Statistical records of production

Personnel evaluation system

dysfunctional consequences of, 152

and emphasis on easier placements, 207

and emphasis on placement quantity, 103, 104, 106, 107, 186, 187, 188

and pressure on officials to "cut corners," 206

Personnel ratings, 56n, 79, 83, 100n, 105-6, 107

Placement figures

fabrication of, 170-73; *see also* Manipulation of figures on statistical records

Placement process, 34-35, 137

Placement production

Blau's findings compared to Agency C study, 93-98, 94n

broken needle, 91-93, 95, 96, 99, 105, 107, 108, 147n, 161

defined, 91-92

and budgetary appropriations, 93, 102-4; *see also* Budgetary procedure

credited on statistical records, 91-108

emphasis on to detriment of anti-

discrimination procedure, 170, 185, 186, 187-88, 205-6
quality of placements, 98-102, 103
Placements
former employer, 95; *see also* Former employer procedure
Placement service
defined, 50n
Plan of the book, 28-29
Plato, 235n
Post factum interpretations, 252-53, 254
Power structure
and discrimination, 211-13, 216, 217, 225
and dysfunctions, 217-18
and influence on modification of procedures, 211-13, 216, 217-18, 225, 226-27
internal and external to the bureaucracy and effects, 228
Pressure of "statistics"
and counseling of clients, 54, 55n
Problems of bureaucracy; *see* Bureaucracy, problems of
Procedures
bureaucratic defined, 33-34
generic and local, 34-36; *see also* under the exact title of procedure (e.g., Former employer procedure)
Procedures at agencies studied
and pressures toward dysfunctional ends, 163
Professions
bureaucratization of, 7
Promotion procedure, 105-6

Q

Quality of placements, 98-102, 103
Questionnaires as a study method
disadvantages, 247n

R

Reappointment date procedure
defined, 62
effects of local conditions on, 69
and modification, 69
various ramifications of, discussed, 62-68
Reappointment hours
and restriction of output, 129-30

Reception counter procedure
and amplification, 60
and occupational demand sheets, 60; *see also* Reception sifting procedure
Reception sifting procedure
discussed, 83-88
and dysfunctions, 83-88
redefinition of, 88
Redefinition
of anti-discrimination law and procedure, 184, 200
of counseling procedure discussed, 48-58
defined, 48
discussed, 68
formal, 51
informal, 51
and reappointment date procedure, 64
and reception sifting procedure, 88
and visits to employers, 116
Redfield, Robert, vii
Reference group, 109
Referral of clients to jobs
haphazard, 112, 161
selection of clients for, 37; *see also* Selection of clients
Referral of clients to tests
haphazard, 161
Referral procedure
and statistical records of production, 109-12
Renewal date procedure; *see* Reappointment date procedure
Replication, 20, 46, 223
Research methods used; *see* Methods used in this study
Responsiveness of bureaucrats to clients, dysfunctions of, 69
Restriction of output, 51n, 61, 86, 86n-87n, 88, 128-31, 133, 133n, 141, 162, 231, 232, 251, 252
Restriction of output reported on statistical records, 56
Ridgway, V. F., 134n
Riesman, David, 233, 233n
Rigidity
bureaucratic, 237
Roethlisberger, F. J., 133n
Rosenberg, Bernard, 6n, 7, 7n, 8n
Ross, Edward A., 165
Roy, Donald, 133n